(continued from front flap)

tulate, beyond Hebraism, a higher and fundamentally different world in which the creative, unifying power of art was prized above other forms of consciousness.

Although the aesthetic consciousness attained an extraordinary awareness of its prerogatives and powers with the early Romantics, it was obliged—as the century moved on and truth in other areas became more uncertain—to assume functions formerly borne by philosophy and religion. Arnold's attitude toward this change was characteristically open. He wanted to defend the aesthetic experience as the supreme achievement available to men in a civilization threatened by dehumanization, but he refused to allow poetry to be detached from other areas of knowledge. His lot as a poet and critic was to embody the pain of the struggle, to attempt to unify the baffling experience of life in the modern world. In his approach to the poetry and prose, Mr. Madden identifies the bearing of Arnold's work on this major issue of nineteenth-century European culture. In the process he adds to our understanding of a singularly contemporary figure whose relevance to twentieth-century literature is aptly noted by I. A. Richards: "We shall then be thrown back, as Matthew Arnold foresaw, upon poetry. It is capable of saving us; it is a perfectly possible means of overcoming chaos."

(from a photograph taken in 1886)

by William A. Madden

MATTHEW

A Study of the Aesthetic Temperament

ARNOLD

in Victorian England

INDIANA UNIVERSITY PRESS

BLOOMINGTON • LONDON   1967

PREFACE

The following chapters attempt to trace in Matthew Arnold's writings one phase of a process which influenced most of the literature of Europe in the nineteenth century: the emergence of the belief that the aesthetic consciousness was capable of organizing and transfiguring the whole of human experience.

The process by which this remarkable notion came to be accepted began in Germany towards the end of the eighteenth century when, in the words of one historian of philosophy, aesthetics seemed suddenly to open a new world into which philosophy "had hitherto had but occasional glimpses and of which she now took possession as of the Promised Land."[1] Looking back in 1827 upon the revolution which the discovery of this new world had effected in Western consciousness, Carlyle concluded that it was "a change originating not in individuals, but in universal circumstances, and belongs not to Germany, but to Europe." To English readers who wished to know more about the new "German Poetics" Carlyle was able to recommend the writings not only of "Kant, Schiller, Richter, and the Schlegels," but those of "their many copyists and expositors" in other countries as well.[2]

Despite a marked shift from idealist to empirical attitudes in philosophy generally, the tendency to endow poetry and art with an unprecedented power not only persisted but gained in clarity and precision as the nineteenth century progressed. This persistence can be seen in the similarity between the aesthetic treatises composed by

v

Schiller at the end of the eighteenth century and those composed by English aestheticians early in this century. Schiller, writing with the enthusiasm of a discoverer, had described the aesthetic impulse as going beyond the individual and as capable of binding the whole of society together in a new and higher form of culture. "Though [physical] need may drive Man into society," he wrote, "and Reason implant social principles in him, Beauty alone can confer on him a social character. Taste alone brings harmony into society, because it establishes harmony in the individual. All other forms of perception divide a man, because they are exclusively based on the sensuous or intellectual part of his being; only the perception of the Beautiful makes something whole of him because both his natures must accord with it."[3] A century later, writing under the influence of Ruskin, Arnold, Pater, and later German aestheticians, the English critic Edward Bullough accepted this view as axiomatic: "Only 'aesthetic culture' educates our whole being, enriches *all* our faculties and extends our total inward life beyond the small holding which in practical life is allotted to each of us."[4]

The central discovery behind the new attitude was described by the English poet Keats with characteristic precociousness: "Though a quarrel in the Streets is a thing to be hated," he wrote, "the energies displayed in it are fine; the commonest Man shows grace in his quarrels—By a superior being our reasonings may take the same tone—though erroneous they may be fine—This is the very thing in which consists Poetry."[5] Implicit in the remark was an assumption regarding the inescapable "subjectivity" of knowledge which was profoundly disturbing to Keats and which was to become more explicit as the century progressed. "When we call a thing aesthetic," Bullough observed, "the reason is to be sought as much, nay even more, in the subjective attitude of the recipient as in the objective features of the thing itself. Everything can, at least theoretically, become for me an aesthetic object, whether it be meant to affect me in his way or not."[6] For Keats, as for many later writers, the disturbing element in this view lay in the fact that while it was possible to regard a street quarrel either aesthetically or ethically, it was impossible to do so simultaneously, and this awareness inevitably gave rise to the question of which "subjective attitude," which mode of attention, was the most "human," the most "true."

The revolutionary significance of early Romanticism derived from its claims on behalf of the aesthetic mode as the one mode capable of reconciling alternative attitudes—ethical, scientific, philosophical, and religious—and thereby supplying an integrated and fully human response to experience. Wordsworth, for example, had spoken confidently of the poet as the one who "binds together by passion and knowledge the last empire of human society, as it is spread over the whole earth, and over all time,"[7] a position which was maintained throughout the century. There was, however, a significant difference between its initial formulation by the Romantics and its later formulations, which had to do with the altered context within which such statements were made rather than with the substance of the statements. During the century-long debate occasioned by the claims made on behalf of the poetic imagination, other kinds of awareness attracted equally eloquent advocates, and it became clear in the second half of the century that no decisive victory was possible. The result was a truce in the form of an agreement to disagree which in effect hypostasized the fragmentation of consciousness which the first generation of Romantics had hoped to escape. With the acceptance of epistimological pluralism, the confident, comprehensive faith of the early Romantics gradually contracted to a more exclusive, narrower aesthetic, characterized by "art for art's sake" attitudes late in the century.

The present study attempts to define Matthew Arnold's place in the debate which accompanied this historical process in England. It concentrates especially upon the life-long conflict which Arnold experienced between his innate sense of vocation as a poet, on the one hand, and, on the other hand, his ethical sense of duty as a Victorian citizen and his critical sense of duty as a member of the new "intelligentsia." As used here, the terms "vocation" and "duty" translate into a particular biographical and historical context the psychological distinction—made by William James—between the true self and other possible selves. The discrepancy between various potential selves (the discrepancy strongly felt by Keats[8]) produces, according to James, in all but heroically self-confident individuals a "conflict of different selves." James went on to describe how the conflict is resolved (if it is resolved) in the following words: "the seeker of his truest, strongest, deepest self must review the list of possible selves carefully, and pick out the one on which to stake his salvation. All other selves thereupon become unreal, but the fortunes of this self are real. . . . Our thought, incessantly deciding among many things of a kind, which ones for it shall be realities, here chooses one of the many selves or characters, and forthwith reckons it no shame to fail in any of those not adopted expressly as its own."[9]

In Arnold's case the operative discrepancy was between his image of himself as a poet—an image which he derived from his Romantic predecessors and which he felt to be representative of his truest, strongest, deepest self—and the image which his Victorian middle-class environment attempted to impose upon him as a member of the society which it dominated. The central thesis of this study is that Arnold's innate aesthetic temperament, exposed during his formative years to the powerful influence of earlier English and German Romantic poets and thinkers, resulted in a highly developed aesthetic consciousness with which he early and permanently identified his true self and his vocation, while his simultaneous exposure to the powerful countervailing ethical and intellectual currents of his generation inhibited the expression which he temperamentally craved. It was the inward crisis created by this predicament to which his poetry gave poignant expression and which his criticism was, in the main, an attempt to resolve. By approaching Arnold in this way, I have tried to identify more precisely the general bearing of Arnold's work on one of the major issues of nineteenth-century English and European culture, and, in the process, to add to our understanding of Arnold's poetry and criticism.

The present study, therefore, is not an exhaustive survey of Arnold's career and writings. "Dover Beach" is not discussed, for example, nor are the sonnets or later poems generally. The success of "Dover Beach"—Arnold's one tragic transcendence of his dilemma[10] —makes it something different in kind, I believe, from his other poems, while the sonnets and the later poems either fall outside of or, more often, repeat on a diminished level the characteristically Arnoldian "note" and pattern of the main body of his poetry discussed in Part Two. Part Three is similarly selective, though here again I hope not arbitrarily so, in presenting Arnold's prose. Several celebrated phrases and ideas do not appear—for example, Arnold's "touchstone" theory of criticism. My primary concern throughout has been to demonstrate the unifying theme that underlies and shapes the whole of Arnold's writings, and for this purpose relatively unfamiliar passages, especially those from Arnold's essays on religion, were often more relevant than better known remarks which have enjoyed wide currency.

The organization of the book was likewise determined by what I took to be the key to Arnold's life and work, his aesthetic temperament, and by a concern to elucidate the structure of thought and feeling which grew out of this temperament in an uncongenial environment. This structure of thought and feeling was fixed relatively early in Arnold's life, and the history of his writings is therefore less a history of conversion or change than a history of a sustained attempt to defend the poetic impulse, as Arnold understood it, against various alien encroachments. For this reason, the presentation of the poems and essays is not, strictly speaking, chronological; in referring to Arnold's "development" or "evolution," I have in mind his gradual discovery and remarkable extension of his innate temperament and its needs, rather than a consistent and conscious progression from one mode of thinking to another.

To interpret a man as complicated as Arnold, and especially to attempt to define something as elusive as his temperament, is obviously beset by perils. I can only hope that, in the result, the risk will seem to have been worth taking.

ACKNOWLEDGMENTS

A number of earlier studies of Arnold have explored, from other points of view, ground covered in the following chapters. The most recent of these studies, A. Dwight Culler's *Imaginative Reason: The Poetry of Matthew Arnold* (1966), appeared too late for me to make as much use of it as I would have liked in Part Two. I was, however, able to use an earlier essay ("Introduction," *The Poetry and Criticism of Matthew Arnold* [1961], ed. A. Dwight Culler, pp. ix–xx) which outlines the thesis which Professor Culler has now developed in his full-length exploration of Arnold's poetry, and I would like to acknowledge my indebtedness to this earlier essay and to recommend his book to readers who may be interested in a more detailed study of Arnold's poetry than they will find here. I am also indebted to Professor D. G. James, whose analysis of Arnold's temperament in *Matthew Arnold and the Decline of English Romanticism* (1961), is essentially the same as that offered in Part One; I was particularly glad to be able to refer to the supporting evidence which his study provides for my belief that Arnold's temperament was innately aesthetic. Professor James's diagnosis of Arnold's treatment of his temperament, however, differs radically from mine and leads him to a quite different interpretation of Arnold's place in English literary history. My debt to and difference with Professor William Robbins are of another kind. His account of the intellectual influences which helped to form the mature Arnold *(The Ethical Idealism of Matthew Arnold,* 1959) is, in my opinion, the best available. But whereas Professor Robbins sees Arnold as a moralist with a basically sound if somewhat unsystematic theology, my own view is that what gives to Arnold his characteristic bent and what makes his work of enduring interest are a function not of his theology or his ethics, but rather of his poetic gift and his life-long fidelity to that gift.

Of older books on Arnold I am conscious of having been greatly influenced at an early stage by Lionel Trilling's *Matthew Arnold* (1939) and by E. K. Brown's *Matthew Arnold: A Study in Conflict* (1947). Of other studies of the poetry, I found E. D. H. Johnson's chapter on Arnold in *The Alien Vision of Victorian Poetry* (1952) and Kenneth Allott's recent edition, *The Poetry of Matthew Arnold* (1965), especially helpful. I have also profited from the comments on Arnold's poetry in J. D. Jump's *Matthew Arnold* (1955), Paull F. Baum's *Ten Studies in the Poetry of Matthew Arnold* (1958), and W. Stacy Johnson's *The Voices of Matthew Arnold* (1961). Like all modern students of Arnold, I am greatly indebted to the editorial labors of Professors Tinker and Lowry on the poetry, and to those more recently of Professor R. H. Super on Arnold's prose.

My serious interest in Arnold began in graduate school over ten years ago under the guidance of Professor Warner G. Rice of the University of Michigan, and I should like to express here my gratitude to him for his kindness, help, and encouragement. I should also like to thank Professor Roy Battenhouse of Indiana University and Professor Margery Stricker of the University of Minnesota for reading drafts of the book.

To the Indiana University Graduate School, its former Dean, John W. Ashton, and the Research Committee of the University I am indebted for financial assistance on several occasions, and to Mrs. Valerie Gottesman and Mrs. Winifred Wertz for their prompt, meticulous, and cheerful typing assistance. To Walter Albee and Mrs. Patricia Thomas of the Indiana University Press go my special thanks for their careful reading of the text. For whatever errors of fact or flaws in style and judgment that remain I am, of course, fully responsible.

The dedication acknowledges help of another kind and my greatest obligation of all.

Bloomington, Indiana (1966)   W. M.

for Carol

CONTENTS

THE FORMATIVE YEARS:
SEEDS OF CONFLICT

INTRODUCTION

To no people, probably, does it so often happen to have to break in great measure with their vocation and with the Muses, as to the men of letters for whom you have summoned me to speak."[1] In these words Matthew Arnold, at the age of fifty-two, quietly summarized the central drama of his own life. Although spoken in the name of literature, the remark arose out of Arnold's conviction that he had himself been destined by temperament and talent to be a poet, and that circumstances had forced him "in large measure" to abandon his true vocation. Writing six years earlier on Sainte-Beuve, a man of letters whom he greatly admired and whose career had affinities with his own, Arnold had touched on the same theme: "Like so many who have tried their hand at *œuvres de poésie et d'art,* his preference, his dream, his ideal, was there; the rest was comparatively journeymen-work, to be done well and estimably . . . and with precious rewards of its own, besides, in exercising the faculties and in keeping off ennui; but still work of an inferior order."[2] The passage unquestionably described a preference which Arnold shared with the French critic, for still earlier he had confessed to his mother: "I sometimes grow impatient of getting old amidst a press of occupations and labour for which, after all, I was not born. Even my

3

lectures [as Professor of Poetry] are not work that I thoroughly like, and the work I do like is not very compatible with any other."[3] The letter goes on to add, characteristically, that "we are not here to have facilities found for us for doing work that we like, but to make them," but this conviction did not change Arnold's feeling about the obstacles which impeded his own special work. His sense of isolation, of having to work in an uncongenial, even hostile, environment appeared early and eventually became acute. "Reflect, too," he told his friend Arthur Hugh Clough, "as I cannot but do here more and more, in spite of all the nonsense some people talk, how deeply *unpoetical* the age and all one's surroundings are. Not unprofound, not ungrand, not unmoving:—but *unpoetical*."[4] It is not surprising that the frustration implied by this comment should have turned up in Arnold's poetry. "I go, fate drives me," a speaker laments in one early poem, "but I leave / Half of my life with you"; and in another poem it is almost as though, while still a young man, Arnold had read his doom in the face of a gipsy child:

> Ah! not the nectarous poppy lovers use,
> Not daily labour's dull, Lethaean spring,
> Oblivion in lost angels can infuse
> Of the soil'd glory, and the trailing wing.[5]

Despite the success and equanimity that marked his later years, Arnold never forgot the "glory" to which he had once aspired. He regarded himself in the latter half of his life as one who trailed the broken wing of a born poet who had been deflected from his true "line."

The consciousness of possessing with rare purity what he called "that desire for the truth and beauty of things which makes the Greek, the artist"[6] came to Arnold unusually early. He observed late in life that at the age of nine he had suddenly awakened to the beauty of Virgil's poetry, and all the biographical evidence indicates that from that point on the meaning of Arnold's life was inseparable from his desire to cultivate and express his poetic gift.[7] His brother has left an account of the intensity and steadiness with which Arnold nourished his powers of poetic expression, and of how, even in the midst of the political excitements of the late 1840's, "literature then and always" meant more to him than politics.[8] As an undergraduate at Oxford during John Henry Newman's last years there, he ignored the religious disputes which agitated the rest of the university, and Balliol in particular—his own college and the college of some of his father's best pupils. After competing for a first-year Hertford scholarship he seems even to have avoided, so far as he could, the conventional demands of academic life, to the chagrin of Clough, the family friend who felt most responsible for him.[9]

His attitude during the important Oxford years, an attitude which puzzled and occasionally angered his friends, Arnold later explained to Clough, who, like himself, had taken a second-class. When Clough complained that they probably did each other harm at Oxford, Arnold disagreed.

I do not think we did each other harm at Oxford. I look back to that time with pleasure. All activity to which the conscience does not give its consent is mere *philistercy*, and it is always a good thing to have been preserved from this. I catch myself desiring now at times a political life, and this and that; and I say to myself—you do not desire these things because you are really adapted to them, and therefore the desire for them is merely contemptible—and it is so. I am nothing and very probably never shall be anything— but there are characters which are truest to themselves by never being anything, when circumstances do not suit.[10]

While at Oxford Arnold had managed to pursue his poetic vocation to the exclusion of other interests, turning to books, to poetic composition, to the theater, and to the Oxford countryside in order to avoid uncongenial distractions and to allow his inward poetic life to develop. When the pressure of circumstances after he had left Oxford made escape from his environment impossible, he preferred silence and the decent obscurity of a school inspector's difficult life, in short, to be "nothing," rather than pervert his gift in the "philistercy" of a more ambitious career.[11]

The question of why Arnold "broke" with his vocation and with the Muses probably has no certain answer.[12] Some have seen his passage from poetry to prose as a natural and not uncommon one; others have argued that it was rooted in some inner defeat, either self-inflicted or brought on by external pressures. Arnold's own explanations belong, in the main, in the latter category; a quatrain which appeared as the epigraph to his last volume of poems indicated that his break with poetry was as desolating as it was involuntary.

> Though the Muse be gone away,
> Though she move not earth to-day,
> Souls, erewhile who caught her word,
> Ah! still harp on what they heard.[13]

Not only was Arnold conscious that his Muse had "gone away," but he was convinced that something accidental and peculiar— though here he was less clear—had been responsible. He tried often, notably in one of his essays, "The Function of Criticism at the Present Time," to explain the event to himself; indeed, the explanations began before his career as a poet had ended. For the most part, he placed the blame on his environment; there was not only the barrenness, aridity, "multitudinousness," and unpoeticalness of the age, but also the special pressure of feeling that he was an unpopular poet, that he had no audience.[14] Yet he also blamed himself, tracing his failure both to a natural want of "robustness" and to his mistaken treatment of his talent.

These explanations touch on two elements in Arnold's formative experience which no study of his career can ignore. One was the concept of the poetic office which he had acquired from his readings; the other was the alien influence of his immediate environment and more particularly of that created by his father, Dr. Thomas Arnold of Rugby. To understand the central drama of Arnold's life it is necessary, first, to reconstruct what he conceived the function of the poet to be, for it is clear from his withdrawal in 1853 of his major poem, "Empedocles on Etna," that his concept of poetry and of the poetic office was in some way at odds with the kind of poetry he could best write. Secondly, it is necessary to explore, so far as possible, Arnold's relationship to his father, whose influence was both powerful and ambiguous. The purpose of the two chapters which follow is to suggest how these two factors, working on a temperament innately poetic, created for the young Arnold the situation which gave rise to his remark in 1875 on the difficulty of following a literary vocation in Victorian England.

CHAPTER ONE

The Poetic Office

Arnold's view of the poetic office, from his first mention of it in the early letters to Clough until the appearance of his last essays in criticism, had as its base the views of the previous generation of Continental and English writers who gave expression to the new aesthetic consciousness which had emerged at the beginning of the century. In his correspondence with Clough he consistently employed an aesthetic idiom congenial to that consciousness.[15] His position was most succinctly stated when he told Clough in 1852 that "modern poetry can only subsist by its *contents*: by becoming a complete magister vitae as the poetry of the ancients did; by including, as theirs did, religion with poetry, instead of existing as poetry only, and leaving religious wants to be supplied by the Christian religion."[16] Arnold had thus committed himself to the view that as a "magister vitae" poetry was a power by which other spheres of human interest, other modes of awareness, could be reconciled and made subservient to man's quest for happiness and perfection.

The evidence that has survived is too scant to establish with any exactness the influence of individual writers in Arnold's working out of this position. His discovery of Virgil at the age of nine has been mentioned, and his acquaintance with Words-

worth and Byron likewise began very early. He continued to
build upon this mixed base throughout his formative years by
drawing upon a variety of writers both within and outside the
Rugby and Oxford curricula. A list of the authors he is known
to have read during the impressionable years of early maturity
is sufficient to indicate the extent of his exposure to what he
called "modern thought" and "modern feeling." From Germany
there were Lessing, Kant, Herder, Goethe, Schiller, Schelling,
Humboldt, and Heine; from France there were Chateaubriand,
Sénancour, Lamartine, Cousin, Vigny, and George Sand. It
seems reasonably certain that these Continental writers, along
with the great English Romantics, Carlyle, and, from America,
Emerson, played a decisive role in Arnold's aesthetic education.[17] Arnold had taken on a considerable measure of classical
ballast during his early years at Rugby, and he continued to
read the Latin and Greek classics throughout his life, but his
response to Antiquity was deeply influenced by the Romantic
aesthetic and sensibility which he had assimilated from his
readings in the literature of the previous generation.

The impact of these readings upon Arnold relative to his
early family and school environment at Fox How and Rugby
was later described by a niece, Mrs. Humphry Ward. In the
early 1840's, according to Mrs. Ward, Arnold, his brother Tom,
and a small circle of friends at Oxford, "discovered George
Sand, Emerson and Carlyle, and orthodox Christianity no
longer seemed to them the sure refuge it had always been to
the strong teacher who trained them as boys. . . . [George
Sand's] *Consuelo,* in particular, was a revelation to the two
young men brought up under the 'earnest' influence of Rugby.
It seemed to open to them a world of artistic beauty and joy
of which they had never dreamed; and to loosen the bonds of
an austere conception of life, which began to appear to them
too narrow for the facts of life."[18] Arnold was likewise reading
Goethe and Schiller in these same years, the former through

Carlyle's and the latter through both Carlyle's and Bulwer-Lytton's translations, and it was Goethe and Schiller who, according to Arnold's own recollection, opened to the young poet that larger, liberal world of Continental thought to which he was later to defer so often in his criticism.[19] His indebtedness to Goethe Arnold always freely acknowledged; his acquaintance with Schiller has received less attention, even though in the 1830's Schiller, perhaps even more than Goethe, represented for English writers like Carlyle and Bulwer-Lytton the new movement of thought and feeling which looked to poetry for a cure for the ailments of society.[20]

It is likely that Schiller's ideas first became known to Arnold through Carlyle's essays, in which the *Letters on Aesthetic Culture* (Carlyle's translation of the German title) are described as one of the deepest, most compact pieces of reasoning Carlyle had ever read. Moreover, Carlyle fully recognized that Schiller's solution for contemporary intellectual and social problems was pre-eminently that of the aesthetic man. He presented, with surprising sympathy, Schiller's view of poetry as the supreme human achievement, including in itself, Carlyle said, "the essence of philosophy, religion, art."[21] In his review of the Goethe-Schiller correspondence, Carlyle had noted that Schiller's life was "emphatically a literary one, that of a man existing only for Contemplation; guided forward by the pursuit of ideal things," and that this pursuit explained Schiller's hostility toward the middle-class society then emerging: his "remoteness from whatever is called business," his "aversion to the tumults of business, and indifference to its prizes."[22] Goethe's influence upon Schiller was stressed, perhaps overstressed, by Carlyle: "if Schiller was a Priest," he wrote, "then was Goethe the Bishop from whom he first acquired clear spiritual light, by whose hands he was ordained to the priesthood."[23]

The implications of the new movement were therefore clear

to Carlyle, and in those of his early writings which had deeply
impressed young readers like Arnold, Carlyle had welcomed
the new movement almost without reservation. Referring to
Schiller's view of Christianity as a true "aesthetic religion," he
translated part of an important letter in which Schiller commented on the "aesthetic direction" of Wilhelm Meister's education in Goethe's famous novel, a passage which may be
taken as one of the central statements of the new aesthetic
philosophy: "Within the aesthetic temper," Schiller wrote,
"there arises no want of those grounds of comfort which are
to be drawn from speculation: such a temper has a self-sub-
sistence, has infinitude within itself: only when the Sensual and
the Moral in man strive hostilely together, need help be sought
of pure Reason. A healthy poetic nature wants, as you yourself say, no Moral Law, no Rights of Man, no Political Metaphysics. You might have added as well it wants no Duty, no
Immortality, to stay and uphold itself withal."[24] Although
Carlyle judged the last point "singular," his portrait is on the
whole warmly appreciative, Schiller's aesthetic view seeming
to him as much superior to those of the eighteenth-century
English school of "taste" as his moral treatises were to those
of the English Utilitarians.[25]

Arnold's knowledge of Schiller was not confined, however,
to what Carlyle had said about him. In 1868, writing to Bulwer-
Lytton to thank him for a copy of the latter's newly collected
Miscellaneous Prose Works, Arnold revealed another early
contact with what Carlyle called "German Poetics." Much in
the three volumes, Arnold told Bulwer, would be new to him
since most of the work had originally appeared anonymously
in periodicals and he had not read it all; but, he adds, "Other
parts of it, well-known and familiar to me, carry me back to
the happiest time of my life—*The Student, The Life of Schiller,* came into my hands just at the moment I wanted something of the kind. I shall never forget what they then gave to

me—the sense of a wider horizon, the anticipation of Germany, the opening into the great world."²⁶ The interest of Bulwer's sketch of Schiller in the present context is its probable impact upon Arnold at an important time in his life and its emphasis upon Schiller's quasi-religious view of poetry and drama, a view which Arnold presumably associated with his discovery of the "great world," and of Germany in particular.

Bulwer remarks in his *Life* that the journal founded by Schiller, entitled *Die Horen,* to which Goethe, Herder, and Hölderlin also contributed, was dedicated to "that aesthetical cultivation—that development of beauty" which Schiller regarded as "the flower and apex of human accomplishment."²⁷ Having surveyed Schiller's life and works, ending with the later dramas—the "magnificent" *Bride of Messina* is described as "unequalled as lyrical tragedy"²⁸—Bulwer concluded his long sketch with a panegyric that was well calculated to appeal to the young Arnold.

. . . his object was not that of severe and logical reasoning; it was to exalt the art to which most of his essays were devoted; to make the great and pure popular; to educate the populace up to purity and greatness. The ideal philosophy, as professed by Schiller, was, in fact, a kind of mental as well as moral Christianity, which was to penetrate the mind as well as the soul—extend to the acts of man as well as his creeds: to make all nature a temple—all artists priests: Christianity in spirit and in effect it was—for its main purpose was that of the Gospel faith, viz., to draw men out of this life into a purer and higher air of being . . . to make enjoyment consist in something beyond the senses. What holy meditation was to the saints of old, the ideal of Aesthetic art was to the creed of Schiller.²⁹

As a practising poet, Arnold, like Goethe and Schiller, was to find the metaphysics of German Idealism uncongenial, but the idea of harmonizing and ennobling human experience through poetry, if we may judge by Arnold's concept of the poetic office as described in the letter to Clough, had an enormous appeal. It affected not only his idea of poetry in general, but his judgment of his own poems, his response to his environment, and inevitably, therefore, his eventual decision to turn to criticism.

The nature and importance of the German influence can be seen in Arnold's use of Goethe and Schiller in his 1853 *Preface*, his first published piece of prose criticism. The opening and briefer section of the *Preface* is given over to Arnold's reasons for withdrawing "Empedocles on Etna," the title poem of a volume of poetry which he had published the year before.[30] This poem, Arnold said, had been intended to portray one of the last Greek religious philosophers, whose situation was of interest because it was similar to the situation of the modern poet in that "the calm, the cheerfulness, the disinterested objectivity" of the classical Greek period were gone, and the doubts and discouragements of Hamlet and Faust were growing. Arnold argued that a poem on such a subject, so far as it offered an accurate representation of the central character, might provide some pleasure, because, as Aristotle had said, all knowledge is pleasurable. But, he goes on to say, citing Schiller as an authority, to be *poetical* a poem must provide the pleasure proper to poetry: "it is not enough that the poet should add to the knowledge of men, it is required of him also that he should add to their happiness. 'All art,' says Schiller, 'is dedicated to Joy, and there is no higher and no more serious problem, than how to make men happy. The right art is that alone, which creates the highest enjoyment.' "[31] The description which then follows of the sources of joy in "the great primary human affections" is more reminiscent of Wordsworth than of Schiller, but for Arnold's purposes Schiller and Wordsworth represent essentially the same thing: a point of view that exalts poetic vision above other human activities. Schiller's statement that poetry must make men happy was not perhaps, by itself, very illuminating, but Arnold's use of it to go beyond Aristotle and establish his own critical position (and thus prepare the reader for the arguments which were to follow) reveals how profoundly Arnold was attracted to the "Hellenism" of his German predecessors.

The specific requirements of poetry as set down in the remainder of the *Preface* Arnold derived from Goethe rather than Schiller: the need for a suitable "action," the need for *Architectonicè* (Arnold at this point mentions Goethe by name), the pre-eminence of Greek tragedies as models—these ideas were scattered throughout Goethe's *Werke*, which Arnold had purchased in 1847. "Few Germans, perhaps few men of any modern nation," says Serlo, Wilhelm Meister's co-worker in the effort to reform the German theater, "have a proper sense of the aesthetic whole: they praise and blame by passages; they are charmed by passages."[32] "We have poems," Arnold wrote, "which seem to exist merely for the sake of single lines and passages; not for the sake of producing any total impression."[33] The need for a "total impression" explained the all-importance of "a great action," a point which Goethe had vigorously advanced, as Arnold knew and recorded in his notebooks. "*Was ist wichtiger als die Gegenstände, und was ist die ganze Kunstlehre ohne sie? Alles Talent ist verschwendet, wenn der Gegenständ nichts taugt.*"[34] These ideas—of the "aesthetic whole," of a "total impression," of a "great action"—were related to that admiration for Greek art which was to remain one of the fundamental passions of Arnold's life and for which he found the highest sanction in both Goethe and Schiller. In concluding the *Preface,* Arnold returned to his opening theme, declaring that the business of artists "is not to praise their age, but to afford to the men who live in it the highest pleasure which they are capable of feeling"; and this they can do, he said, only by combining (and Arnold again cites Goethe) mastery of technique with "soul and matter."[35]

Whereas Schiller and Wordsworth may be seen as providing

the basic aesthetic principle on which the general argument of
the 1853 *Preface* turns—that poetry must give joy—Goethe
may be said to have provided the technical arguments which
enabled Arnold, while withdrawing his own "Empedocles on
Etna," to defend the use of ancient actions in modern poetry,
to argue the indispensability of aesthetic form, and to advance
what was, in Lionel Trilling's phrase, a religious theory of
poetry.[36] Although other important influences went into the
making of this early essay,[37] the spirit that informs it is the
spirit of Weimar classicism, with its ideal of educating and
liberating humanity through art. Schiller had been quick to
point out that Goethe presented the new aesthetic ideal with
great imaginative power in *Wilhelm Meister,* which Arnold
had read in Carlyle's translation while he was still an undergraduate at Oxford, and Arnold's first work of criticism was
a response to the same "caprice," the same want of principle
and high taste in contemporary English poetry and criticism,
that *Wilhelm Meister* had been intended to overcome in German audiences. Meister had objected to Serlo's opportunism as
a theater manager—"It is a false compliance with the multitude to raise in them emotions which they *wish,* when these
are not emotions which they *ought,* to feel"[38]—and Arnold was
similarly opposed to the tendency of contemporary English
poetry to cater to the existing tastes of English readers. The
morality of what people *ought* to feel, as Carlyle's summary of
Schiller indicates, was linked to the new ideal of a completely
perfected harmony, not to the prevailing ethical attitudes of
the Philistines.

In the brief supplementary "Advertisement" written in the
following year, Arnold showed that the relevance of art to
nonliterary aspects of Victorian culture was already present in
his mind when he composed his *Preface;* the virtues of great
poetry, he wrote in 1854, could cure England's "incredible
vagaries" not only in literature and in art, but in religion and

morals as well.[39] The moral aspects of the new gospel in art were defined by Carlyle in his comment on the ethos behind the *Letters on Aesthetic Culture*. Schiller, he wrote, had traced out "a system of morality, in which the sublimest feelings of the Stoic and the Christian are represented but as stages in our progress to the pinnacle of true human grandeur; and man . . . is confidently called upon to rise into a calm cloudless height of internal activity and peace, and *be*, what he has fondly named himself, the god of this lower world."[40] In calling attention to the "profound moral impression" and the joy which accompany great art, Arnold's 1853 *Preface* was in effect offering the first of what was to be a series of his own essays on the aesthetic education of man, the point of view that informed his criticism being the one that Goethe had formulated: Whoever has art, has religion. This "aesthetical form of religion," according to Bulwer, had saved "many who would otherwise have been lost in the pathless wilds of infidelity,"[41] and it is hardly an exaggeration to claim that it performed a similar function for Arnold, who sought in the creative activity of poetic composition, and later in the reading and criticizing of poetry, the consolation and hope of which his break with the religious faith of his father had deprived him. Because the environment which Arnold held responsible for his separation from his Muse was, in some respects, the environment represented by his father, the latter's role in Arnold's formative years requires examination.

CHAPTER TWO

The Unpoetic Environment

The extent to which Arnold's sense of vocation as a poet determined his early responses to his environment can be seen
in his correspondence with Clough. The letters show him
resisting at times the commercial, utilitarian ethos of his own
middle class, at other times the moral strictures of his immediate circle, and at still other times the general confusion
of thought arising from the claims and counterclaims of contemporary European philosophy and theology. "My dearest
Clough," he wrote in 1849, "these are damned times—everything is against one—the height to which knowledge is come,
the spread of luxury, our physical enervation, the absence of
great *natures,* the unavoidable contact with millions of small
ones, newspapers, cities, light profligate friends, moral des-
perados like Carlyle, our own selves. . . ."[42] "I am sure," he
wrote again in 1852, "that in the air of the present times *il
nous manque d'aliment,* and that we deteriorate in spite of our
struggles—like a gifted Roman falling on the uninvigorating
atmosphere of the decline of the Empire."[43] "There is a power
of truth in your letter," he wrote the next year; "yes—*con-
gestion of the brain* is what we suffer from—I always feel it
and say it—and cry for air like my own Empedocles."[44] The
epithets which Arnold applied to his environment in these

18

years varied, but they were consistently pejorative—"unpoetic,"
"arid," "barren," "multitudinous," and so forth. It was not,
however, until 1849, when his first volume of poems appeared
and was all but ignored by the public, that the inner struggle
which had been slowly gathering strength came to a crisis.

Arnold's sense of poetic vocation, which evolved gradually
in his own mind during the forties as he attempted to work
out some viable relationship with his environment, was increasingly permeated by the concept of poetry which he was
absorbing from his readings. His sympathy with the new aesthetics expressed itself at first in his conviction regarding the
primacy of form in poetry and in his belief that the purpose
of poetry is pleasure. The desire to "keep pure our Aesthetics"[45]
appeared especially in his defense of "the *beautiful*" as "alone
being properly *poetical* as distinguished from rhetorical, devotional or metaphysical."[46] The latter terms were more than
casual ones; Arnold saw the incompatibility between a poetic
life and the spirit of the age as the inescapable result of particular elements in the life around him to which these terms
had reference. He detected a "rhetorical" bias in the literature
and lives of the practical, narrow, Evangelical middle class,
in the "hideosities," "Solecisms," "crudities," and "affectations"
of the "Trimmer-X-Hannah-More-typed spirit" to be found
among "the born-to-be-tight-laced of my friends and acquaintance." To be praised by such people was a danger to the poet,
Arnold warned Clough, because it was capable of leading even
the strong-minded writer to "talk of his usefulness and imagine
himself a Reformer, instead of an Exhibition."[47] Closely related to the practical "rhetorical" view of life, but elevated by
a nobler concern, was the "devotional" bias of the religious.
Arnold told Clough that he, Clough, succeeded in "the hymn,
where man, his deepest personal feelings being in play, finds
poetical expression as *man* only, not as artist:—but consider,"
Arnold adds, "whether you attain the *beautiful,* and whether

your product gives PLEASURE, not excites curiosity and re-
flexion."[48] Finally, from an entirely different direction but
equally fatal to the poet, there were the claims of the intellect
and of modern thought, what Arnold referred to as the merely
"metaphysical." Against Clough's "depth-hunting" in poetry he
once again opposed the all-importance of form "as the sole
necessary of Poetry as such: whereas the greatest wealth and
depth of matter is merely a superfluity in the Poet *as such*."[49]
Clough's depth-hunting, Arnold argued, had led his friend
into allegory and unnecessary preoccupation with ideas; "to
solve the Universe as you try to do," he complained, was "irritating."[50] Arnold felt, as Goethe and Schiller had before him,
that the born poet's "gift of poetical expression" was in danger
of being "overlaid and crushed" by thought, rendering his
poetical gift "of no use to him to help him express himself."[51]

The chronology of events is far from certain, but it is clear
that what Arnold felt to be an alien environment had driven
him back in upon himself and upon the talent and activity in
which he felt himself most competent and at ease. Unlike the
earlier Romantics, however, Arnold was troubled not only by
what he called the barrenness of the age, but by misgivings
about his own "robustness" and by disturbing religious doubts.
The attempt to organize his experience poetically thus came
to have more than a merely professional interest for Arnold;
it involved him in a struggle to preserve his identity against
both the age and his inner confusion. It was in part because
of the enormous burden which he thus came to place upon
poetry and upon his own creative talent that he was threatened
for a time with a psychological paralysis from which he could
finally escape only at the sacrifice of what he believed to be
his true vocation. Moreover, in this struggle his friend Clough
sometimes seemed to Arnold to side with the enemy, and
much of what Arnold saw in Clough had been learned by the
latter from Arnold's father. To this extent, as several critics

have remarked, Arnold's debate with Clough, carried on in their correspondence, was an extension of Arnold's prior debate with his father. It was, indeed, a continuation of his earlier revolt against certain values which his father represented and an anticipation of his later attacks on Victorian society in general.

While it would be possible to overemphasize the differences between Arnold and his father, since they had much in common, it would be a more serious mistake to underestimate them. A father-son relationship involving the very positive personality of Dr. Arnold was bound to be an important factor in the life of the son, and the clue to the relationship in this case was the aesthetic son's reaction to the exceptional intellectual and moral energy of his father. Arnold's brother Tom remarks in his brief autobiographical sketch that his father recognized Matthew's exceptional gifts early, and that he "never thought of prescribing to him in any way either the field within which or the aims toward which, he should set his genius to work."[52] Yet, at least on one occasion, the father did prescribe the field and aims toward which his son's talents should *not* go when he ruled out Law—his own suggestion was Medicine—as a suitable profession for his son to pursue at Oxford. More importantly, he seems never to have taken an interest in his son's poetic ambitions. "Matt does not know what it is to work," the father complained in 1840, "because he so little knows what it is to think. But I am hopeful about him more than I was . . . . Alas! that we should have to talk of prospects only, and of no performance as yet which deserves the name 'earnest reading.' "[53] Dr. Arnold was particularly worried, according to one of Arnold's grandchildren, by what he interpreted as "the lack of moral thoughtfulness in his son Matthew," and for a time he separated the youthful Matthew from his other children.[54]

It seems likely that what led to Dr. Arnold's uneasiness, an uneasiness later shared by other members of the family, were simply manifestations of the eldest son's peculiar temperament and a penchant for poetry which in the Arnold household might easily have been mistaken for fecklessness of character. In his biography of the father, Arthur Stanley observed of Dr. Arnold's attitude during his later years as Headmaster at Rugby that, "although his practical turn of mind was modified, he remained eminently practical to the end of his life."

"I always think," he used to say, "of that magnificent sentence of Bacon, 'In this world, God only and the angels may be spectators.'" "Stand still, and see the salvation of God," he observed in allusion to Dr. Pusey's celebrated sermon on that passage, "was not the advice which is needed in ordinary circumstances; it would have been false advice when they were to conquer Canaan." "I cannot," he said, "enter fully into these lines of Wordsworth—

> To me the meanest flower that blows can give,
> Thoughts that do often lie too deep for tears

There is to me something in them of a morbid feeling—life is not long enough to take such intense interest in objects themselves so little."[55]

For a sensitive son who later identified poetry and all high intellectual activity with the detachment of one who *is* a spectator of life, and the poet as one who "flees the common life of men," such a temperament and attitude might well have seemed an implicit condemnation of himself. That the atmosphere of "industrious peace" created by Dr. Arnold was hardly congenial to poetic activity is suggested by the surprise of Wordsworth's son-in-law, Edward Quillinan, an intimate of the Arnold family, when he discovered that "there was any *poetry* in the family," a discovery that also puzzled another observer, Crabb Robinson.[56] The temperamental incompatibility of father and son was genially but none the less accur-

ately summed up in the observations which each made of the
other. "Matt flits from flower to flower," Dr. Arnold confided
to a friend. "Ah, my poor father," said the son, "he had many
excellencies, but he was not a poet."[57]

The general tone created by Dr. Arnold at Fox How and
Rugby may be inferred from the younger Thomas's statement
that "for us [Matthew and Thomas], and for all of his children,
the precept flowed steadily from his life still more than from
his lips, 'Work.' Not, work at this or that—but, Work."[58] Comments by those who knew him indicate that Dr. Arnold communicated this intense practicality as much by the manner and
force of his personality as by specific prescriptions. James Martineau noticed a characteristic "force" and "movement" which,
as much as anything Dr. Arnold said, impressed those who
came into contact with him,[59] and Clough later commented on
the activist bias in his revered teacher: "There are men—such
was Arnold—too intensely, fervidly practical to be literally,
accurately, consistently theoretical . . . ; born to do, they know
not what they do."[60] This was the defect which Arnold was
to attribute to the Victorian age generally, and to this extent
at least his hostility to an excessive activism and practicality
first found expression in his instinctive rebellion against the
influence of his father. That the spirit of Rugby, which gave
institutional expression to Dr. Arnold's bias, was not altogether congenial to Arnold is clear from Justice Coleridge's
comment that no one could have been less like the typical
Rugby boy than Matthew when he went up to Oxford in
1841.[61] Arnold's notorious dandyism as an undergraduate, his
cultivation of Béranger,[62] his seeming indifference to religious
disputes and academic pursuits, his "coldness" towards friends,
his visits to hear Newman in St. Mary's chapel, all expressed a
resistance to the anti-Tractarianism and strong ethical tone
of "earnestness" which at that time characterized the Rugby

circle. Not that Arnold dismissed what his father and his fellow-Rugbeans represented; it was simply that, as he told Clough in 1845, "I have other ways to go."[63]

In this context, Arnold's overt comments on his father, made relatively late in life, are of particular interest. First of all, they derived from two distinct points of view: one personal, which he communicated privately to his mother, and the other the popular view, widely shared by those who had known Dr. Arnold, which the son expressed in his public tribute, "Rugby Chapel." This famous elegy, with its portrait of a dedicated, energetic, forceful leader carrying others along with him by the strength of his convictions and his sympathetic interest in their welfare, belongs with Dean Stanley's *Life* and Thomas Hughes' *Tom Brown's School Days* to the literature of the legendary "Arnold of Rugby," who embodied as perhaps no other public figure of the time the moral earnestness and energy of the mid-Victorian ethos. This public image of his father Matthew Arnold, in one part of himself, certainly respected and even admired, but it was not the image of a man with whom he felt a strong personal rapport. "Rugby Chapel" itself is an impersonal, public tribute to a well-known religious leader in which the speaker of the poem makes allusions to religious beliefs which Arnold himself did not hold. Arnold's own view of his father, as he explained to his mother, was rather that of an intellectual liberator who had represented at its best what the son called the "historical sense," for Arnold was especially impressed by the intellectual curiosity and the open-mindedness towards modern ideas which accompanied his father's moral earnestness. From Arnold's point of view as a mature critic, his father was not primarily a devout Christian leader but a courageous teacher of modern ideas, and it was this side of his father's work that he saw himself carrying on in his own criticism.[64]

There was, however, a third Dr. Arnold who, whether as an

ethical force ɵr as an intellectual teacher with a strong historical sense, represented for Arnold as a young poet something quite different, something alien and threatening which Arnold also detected in his father's favorite pupil, Clough. The editor of the Clough correspondence has observed that Arnold's letters present the curious spectacle of the son of Dr. Arnold attempting to remedy in Clough the effects of the father's teaching.[65] While there was much in Clough, as in his father, to attract Arnold, and both men exercised considerable influence on the young poet in the late 1830's and early 1840's, there was one important difference; for Clough, as for Dr. Arnold, poetry tended too much towards mere ornament and dilettantism and "pococurantism" to be taken wholly seriously.[66] Although Clough, like Arnold, was capable of using persiflage to conceal his inner life from his friends, the inner life which he concealed concentrated itself, after the manner of his teacher, around moral and intellectual problems almost to the complete exclusion of aesthetic concerns. The arguments in his poem called "The Poet," which would have gratified Dr. Arnold, could not but have struck a raw nerve in the young Arnold to whom it may have been addressed:

> And can it be, you ask me, that a man
> With the strong arm, the cunning faculties,
> And keenest forethought gifted, and, within,
> Longings unspeakable, the lingering echoes
> Responsive to the still-still-calling voice
> Of God Most High,—should disregard all these,
> And half-employ all those for such an aim
> As the light sympathy of successful wit,
> Vain titillation of a moment's praise?

And again:

> No, nor on thee be wasted,
> *Thou trifler, Poesy!*

Heaven grant the manlier heart, that timely, ere
Youth fly, with life's real tempest would be coping;
    The fruit of dreamy hoping
    Is, waking, blank despair.[67]

There was enough of the father in Arnold's own make-up to make Clough's "apostrophes to duty" attractive as well as irritating, and the correspondence reflects Arnold's instinctively felt need to keep the spiritual son of his father at a distance. As Lionel Trilling remarks, the letters to Clough show Arnold "fighting for his life as a poet and possibly for something more than that, and it is not extravagant to say that his dispute with Clough was in effect his dispute with his father. He was not dealing with ideas merely, but with his very heart."[68]

The opposition between the father's ethical and the son's aesthetic interests is apparent in their respective responses to contemporary literature. Dr. Arnold's theory of poetry was close to that of John Keble, an early friend and spiritual adviser who was also Matthew Arnold's godfather. "Poetical feelings," Dr. Arnold wrote in his one brief essay on literary theory, "are merely . . . all the brightest and purest feelings of our nature"; anything that put men above themselves, that awakened "devotion," "admiration," or "love," or "any danger to call forth courage, any distress to awaken our pity," belonged to the *poetical temper,* and *poetical feelings*; for the very essence of poetry is, that it exalts and ennobles us."[69] With this moral theory of poetry, as theory, the son would perhaps have had no quarrel, provided it were rightly interpreted, but the tastes of Arnold *père* reveal an insensibility in applications of the theory which characterizes a kind of temperament quite different from that of his son. Keble's *Christian Year* Dr. Arnold described as "without equal, the Bible excepted, in the English language,"[70] thus expressing the

Rugby tendency to look to literature for edification and to ignore or disparage poets whose "morality" was unclear or dubious. Even under the careful editing of Stanley, the literary judgments recorded in the biography of Arnold's father reveal a figure almost completely devoid of aesthetic interest as Arnold understood it. Having looked at *Don Juan,* the Doctor was "determined not to read it," for he was annoyed by what he saw "in glancing over the leaves."[71] Byron's *Cain* seemed "almost awful" in that "such a man" should have succeeded in uttering some truths.[72] Of Goethe's *Faust* he believed that Margaret's speech at the end saved the poem from being "a piece of Devilry," but he could not "get over" the blasphemous Prologue.[73] Among modern English writers, Dr. Arnold thought of Coleridge as a theologian rather than as a poet; and while Wordsworth was a close friend and family hero, portions of the Immortality Ode, as noted earlier, struck him as morbid. Addison and Pope are mentioned, but Shelley and Keats are not. But perhaps the most revealing touchstone was Dr. Arnold's admiration for Macaulay and Carlyle. For a son to whom in his later years both Carlyle and Macaulay were, for different reasons, profoundly distasteful, there was likely to be little encouragement or sympathy from a father with Dr. Arnold's temperament and tastes.

Arnold's deepest response to his father's personality was too obscure, instinctive, and unsettling, and too mixed up with filial love and respect, to permit explicit formulation beyond apologetic and evasive remarks in letters to his mother, but it did find oblique expression, on one occasion at least, in his poetry.[74] In "Sohrab and Rustum" the threatening forces which Arnold was indirectly resisting in the letters to Clough found successful embodiment in the figure of Rustum; like all viable poetic personae, the figures of both Sohrab and Rustum had their roots beyond the reaches of the poet's discursive awareness in his most deeply felt experience, and this gives to the poem a pathos and power notably absent from "Rugby Chapel." Although the father-son motif occurs elsewhere in Arnold's poetry—in "Balder Dead," *Merope*, "Fragment of an 'Antigone'," and "A Picture at Newstead," for example—and although in every case a conflict is involved, "Sohrab and Rustum" is the only poem in which such a conflict occupies the center of interest.[75] It was unique in other ways as well, for Arnold was "surprised by the suddenness with which his creative power was awakened and by the slightness of the materials out of which it had been kindled." He was in some anxiety to complete the poem "at one heat," and when it was finished he commented, "I have had the greatest pleasure in composing it—a rare thing with me."[76]

The strong appeal of the materials upon which the poem is based was reflected in part in Arnold's instinctive feeling about the "rightness" of the story, which he described, without elaborating, as "a very noble and excellent one." We can only speculate in such matters, but it seems probable that the tragedy in which an unrecognized son is unwittingly killed by a famous father found a responsive chord in the lonely poet-son of the famous "Arnold of Rugby." But there was another element in the materials which also appealed to Arnold, and this was the Oriental setting, which, as he told Clough, he made a deliberate effort to bring out in his similes.[77] The Oriental setting enabled Arnold to "distance" a theme that might have proved too intimately personal to allow direct treatment and at the same time provided a plot and imagery appropriate to the ethical-aesthetic tension which underlies the "action" of the poem. The aesthetic element in the Oriental sources is suggested in Arnold's account of his enthusiastic response to the *Bhagavad Gita,* a work which he recommended to Clough as a corrective for the preoccupation with action and moral scrupulosity which he detected in his friend.[78] In defending poetry and his way of life against Clough's "apos-

trophes to duty," Arnold was not so much attacking moral
seriousness as expressing an instinctive antipathy towards the
self-conscious, *voulu,* duty-ridden type of spirituality which
Clough seemed to him to represent: "I find that with me a
clear almost palpable intuition (damn the logical senses of the
word) is necessary before I get into prayer," he objected to
Clough, "unlike many people who set to work at their duty
self-denial etc." He added that his "one natural craving is not
for profound thoughts, mighty spiritual workings etc. etc. but
a distinct seeing of my way as far as my own nature is concerned: which I believe to be the reason why the mathematics
[at Oxford] were ever foolishness to me."[79] In thus formulat-
ing his "natural" need by opposing an intuitive apprehension
of spiritual realities both to energetic asceticism and to abstract speculation, Arnold touched on the central difference
in temperament which set him apart both from Clough and
from his father, for Clough did not like the *Gita.*

The appeal of "the Oriental Poem" for Arnold went beyond
the setting, and even beyond the "style and feeling," which he
singled out for praise in writing to Clough, and included the
doctrine as well. Like other poets before and after him, Arnold
found the Hindu doctrine peculiarly congenial. Its similarity
to the aesthetic mode of experience in general has been frequently pointed out.[80] The "palpable intuition" which Arnold's
temperament required could be got only from the kind of
sustained meditation, through inward recollection, which he
found recommended in the *Gita.* "The Indians distinguish between meditation or absorption—and knowledge," he explained to Clough, "and between abandoning practice, and
abandoning the fruits of action and all respect thereto. This
last is a supreme step, and dilated on throughout the Poem."[81]
The likenesses between the Hindu method of meditating upon
the object to be known and Arnold's concept of the poet's
disinterested relation to his world, their common insistence

on the need to lose the self in the object contemplated instead of asserting it in activity, explains the profound attraction of the *Gita* for Arnold, and accounts for his sudden creative response to the Oriental story.

Both the action and the imagery of "Sohrab and Rustum" lend support to the conclusion that the legend of a father-son conflict, dressed in the trappings of the remote and contemplative East, provided appropriate materials for the successful objectification of Arnold's instinctive sense of the opposition between his own aesthetic temperament and the powerful ethical bias of his father, of Clough, and of the age. The poem opens with the young Sohrab, restless and alone, waiting for morning to break over the hostile Persian and Tartar camps on the banks of the Oxus. The young "Tartar," we learn, has been obsessed by a concern which has made his life until now an unhappy one:

> I seek one man, one man, and one alone—
> Rustum, my father; who I hoped should greet,
> Should one day greet, upon some well-fought field,
> His not unworthy, not inglorious son.[82]

The father-image provokes in Sohrab's mind an instinctive defensiveness—he is *not* unworthy, *not* inglorious. The long-sought father—though Sohrab does not yet know this—is now in the opposing Persian camp, weary, sullen, and aloof. Rustum is introduced through a speech in which he laments his not having a son, instead of "that one slight helpless girl I have," as he has long believed. More particularly, he wants a son whom he could "send to war" (ll. 230–231)—a son, he says, like the young Sohrab whose challenge to the Persians he has just learned of and been asked to accept. Ignorant of Sohrab's identity, Rustum agrees to the challenge of single combat, and when father and son finally confront each other on the plain, Rustum has pity on the "slender," "softly rear'd" boy (l. 318), while Sohrab in turn, feeling a strange affinity with the aged warrior, impulsively embraces Rustum's knees and asks his name. Suspicious lest the youthful challenger take fright at learning his true identity and somehow do harm to his reputation as a warrior, Rustum tells the youth to carry out his challenge, taunting him with the insinuation that perhaps he is afraid. The son replies, "I am no girl, to be made pale by words" (l. 381), and the battle begins.

Sohrab gains an early advantage, but instead of killing his father he spares him out of some unexplainable feeling, proposing a truce and friendship. In fury, the father rises:

> "Girl! nimble with thy feet, not with thy hands!
> Curl'd minion, dancer, coiner of sweet words!

> ❋   ❋   ❋

> ". . . thou hast sham'd me before both the hosts
> With thy light skipping tricks, and thy girl's wiles."
>   [ll. 457–458, 468–469]

The "unnatural conflict" (l. 481) is renewed, and eventually Rustum fatally wounds the boy, whom he now rebukes bitterly for his foolish search for fame. Sohrab, dying, replies that it was his own "filial heart" and something strange in his opponent that unnerved his arm (ll. 543–547). Incredulous at the hint that the youth may be his son, the older man declares that "the mighty Rustum never had a son" (l. 578). Sohrab answers: "Ah yes, he had! and that lost son am I" (l. 580), revealing the mark of Rustum's seal upon his arm as proof. Rustum, at last acknowledging Sohrab as his son, yields to uncontrollable grief, at which Sohrab consoles the father by asserting that this tragic end was foreordained:

> "Surely my heart cried out that it was thou,
> When first I saw thee; and thy heart spoke too,
> I know it! but fate trod those promptings down

Under its iron heel; fate, fate engaged
The strife, and hurl'd me on my father's spear."

[ll. 711–715]

"Some are born," Sohrab concludes, "to do great deeds," as
Rustum has done, just as some are born, like himself, "to be
obscured, and die" (ll. 773–774). He asks as an epitaph for
his tomb the words:

> Sohrab, the mighty Rustum's son, lies there,
> Whom his great father did in ignorance kill!

[ll. 792–793]

The poem closes with the famous passage in which the Oxus
River, a "foil'd circuitous wanderer," at last finds its tranquil
goal in the "luminous home of waters."

It seems clear enough that the poem gives symbolic statement to Arnold's feeling as a poet toward his father and,
beyond this, to his sense of his predicament in an uncongenial
age. Energetic, successful, and famous though he is, Rustum
is devoid of precisely those qualities that Arnold saw as characteristic of the poetic temperament and which he embodies in
the gentle Sohrab. It is not too much to say that in the poem
Arnold portrays his father as unwittingly instrumental in his
own "death" as a poet. The mockery of "girl," "dancer," "coiner
of sweet words" strikes home on the one side, as does the
epitaph chosen by the son on the other side, and together they
contribute to the sense of fatality in which the tragedy is
resolved, beautifully rendered in the concluding coda which
sets the personal tragedy in the larger perspective of the tragic
movement of life and history as Arnold had come to accept
it. But there is more. The poem not only depicts the death of
Sohrab, "the coiner of sweet words"; it also portrays Sohrab's
disproof of his father's taunting charges of effeminacy. According to the poem, Sohrab, had he wished, might have slain his

father with the father's own weapons of war, but restrained himself out of filial piety.

It is appropriate, therefore, that the 1853 volume, in which Arnold gave "Sohrab and Rustum" the place of honor as the lead-poem, also contained his first piece of critical prose. If the poem was a symbolic statement of Arnold's belief that, as a poet, he was born to be "obscured, and die," the 1853 *Preface* announced the critic who "was born to do great deeds." As a critic, Arnold, bearing his father's seal upon his arm, emerged to fulfill his father's wish for a son to carry on his fight. Although he carried on the fight with a difference that would have distressed Dr. Arnold had he lived, there was more than a little of his father's thought in Arnold's critical effort. In this respect "Sohrab and Rustum" did full justice to Arnold's ambiguous relationship with his father. When Dr. Arnold died unexpectedly in 1842, at the age of forty-seven, Arnold's first response indicated the nature of the role which his father had played in his life up to that time: "The first thing which struck him when he saw the body was the thought that their sole source of *information* was gone, that all that they had ever known was contained in that lifeless head."[83] Absorbed in the cultivation of his poetic gifts, Arnold had been content to rely upon his father for intellectual guidance in the great social and theological issues of the time. In later assessing his friendship with Clough, which he associated with his own "period of development" and which was perhaps closest at the time of Dr. Arnold's death, Arnold saw their principal tie in their common "intellectual bonds—the strongest of all."[84] These bonds had been forged at Rugby according to Dr. Arnold's intellectual conviction that his basic task was to give his Rugby students a "notion of criticism, not to swallow things whole, as the scholars of an earlier period did."[85] The relation of this "notion of criticism" to Dr. Arnold's views of contemporary

English society as it had developed by 1840, and to his son's similar views of that society in 1860, is suggested by a remark in one of Dr. Arnold's letters: "My fondness for Greek and German literature has made me very keenly alive to the mental defects of the Dissenters as a body; the characteristic faults of the English mind,—the narrowness of view, and a want of learning and a sound critical spirit,—being exhibited to my mind in the Dissenters almost in caricature."[86]

The words might have been written by Arnold himself, if Dr. Arnold's mention of "Greek and German literature" were understood to mean Sophocles and Goethe rather than Thucydides and Niebuhr. That it referred to the historians rather than the poets explains why the intellectual influence of Dr. Arnold's "critical spirit" was not without its ironic consequences. The psychological effect of the sudden loss of his father's intellectual guidance upon Arnold was similar to that described by a biographer of Clough: "The breaking of the chain did not so much set Clough free to go his own way, as enforced on him the necessity of finding a way that could be his own."[87] Conscious of his want of intellectual robustness, Arnold adopted several of his father's basic commitments— his "historical sense," his concept of the relationship between church and state, and his pragmatic criterion of viability rather than of logical consistency in applying principles to settle disputes.[88] But when Arnold applied the "critical spirit" to his father's religious faith, the core of Dr. Arnold's intellectual and moral program at Rugby, he found that faith impossible. For those of Dr. Arnold's students, and notably for Clough and Arnold himself, who were unable to lay their religious doubts as Dr. Arnold had done, the search for truth took precedence over action, and as a result, after Dr. Arnold's death, they were set "wandering" in search of some light by which to guide their actions.[89] This intellectual restlessness not only provided the ground-note of melancholy which characterizes Arnold's poetry but, in his literary as well as his nonliterary criticism, gave an importance to his aesthetic bias which explains the difference that he felt distinguished his own critical effort from his father's.[90] The critical spirit of which his father was the most outspoken Victorian representative thus had its effect upon the inner life of the poet. This effect can be traced both in the subject matter and tone of Arnold's poetry. More generally, his writings as a whole bear witness to the difference between a temperament that instinctively expressed itself in poetry and literary criticism and one like his father's, which expressed itself in sermons, political pamphlets, and lectures on history.[91]

For all his indebtedness to and respect for his father, Arnold's mature position was removed by a generation from that of his father; more importantly, it was given consistency and point by a fundamentally different kind of personality. Whereas his father was a moralist and man of action anxious to convey his broad interpretation of Christianity to an endangered society, Matthew Arnold was a poet anxious to move beyond what seemed to him discredited religious dogmas to some new vision. The fundamental inspiration, the integrating principle, of Arnold's mature work was not a desire to reform contemporary society in the light of an unsophisticated Broad-Church Christianity, nor even his father's almost religious devotion to history; it was, rather, his own religious devotion to poetry, which reached out toward a vision of society that he formulated according to an ideal of poetry which he had learned from sources other than his father. The process by which Arnold made the passage from nostalgia for the lost world of childhood to full acceptance of the quite different world of his maturity is the story of his career as a poet; and his subsequent extension of his mature point of view into various areas of contemporary life and thought is the story of his criticism.

POETRY: THE AESTHETIC
CONSCIOUSNESS AT BAY

INTRODUCTION

SOME REMARKS in the late essay on "The Study of Poetry," in which he distinguished between a "real," a "personal," and an "historical" estimate of a poet's work, provide a convenient point of departure for the study of Arnold's poetry, since these distinctions can be applied to the judgments which Arnold passed at various times on his own poems.[1] "Viewed *absolutely*," he told Clough on one occasion, "[my poems] are certainly little or nothing."[2] This was a "real" estimate, an evaluation of his poetry by the standard of "what is truly excellent." The other two estimates were closely related to the first. The "personal" estimate appeared in Arnold's various remarks on the failure of his poetry to "animate," its tendency rather to appeal to readers by adding "zest to their melancholy or grace to their dreams,"[3] instead of rejoicing its readers, as great poetry should. Finally, his description of his completed work, in a late letter, as a record of "the main movement of mind of the last quarter of a century"[4] provided the "historical" estimate, an appeal to standards that, by Arnold's own admission, lay outside the province of literature proper but which might nevertheless be invoked to help to explain and assess a poet's work.

Here, as in other matters, Arnold remains one of his own

best critics, for the "personal" and the "historical" judgments contain valuable clues for the study of his poems. The "personal" estimate calls attention to the pervasive melancholy which he saw as the characteristic "note" of his own nature as well as of his poetry, a feeling which embodied his deepest response to his inner history and to the spirit of the age with which that history was connected. The "historical" estimate, on the other hand, provides a framework for studying individual poems as moments in the general expansion of Arnold's consciousness during his creative years and for judging his poetry as a coherent body of work in which individual poems appear as subordinate figures in a larger pattern.[5] The chapter which follows attempts to suggest the connection between the formative experience outlined in Chapters One and Two and the "personal" melancholy which attended Arnold's Muse throughout his poetic career; Chapter Four explores at some length the nature of the "movement of mind" reflected in the poetry as a whole; and Chapter Five treats two special groups of poems, one expressing Arnold's optimism and the other his deep faith in poetry, both of which indicate an essential continuity between the poetry and his prose.

CHAPTER THREE

The Note of Melancholy

When Clough complained in the early 1850's of the treatment he had received from Arnold in years past, Arnold replied by referring with rare frankness to his state of mind in the late forties, more particularly to the *sang-froid* in his make-up which he felt had probably been responsible for the irritation that he had caused Clough and his other friends. This essay in self-analysis proved to be painful in the extreme and in concluding it Arnold wrote, "I am past thirty, and three parts iced over—and my pen, it seems to me is even stiffer and more cramped than my feeling."[6] The "cramped" feeling was one symptom of a natural "coldness and want of intellectual robustness" to which he referred in the course of the letter; Arnold had discovered in himself, he believed, "not want of faith exactly—but invincible languor of spirit."[7] The discovery must have been fairly recent. Just five years before, he had told Clough that necessity, not inclination, kept him aloof from his friends. Their intellectual probings into controversies of the day, Arnold thought, were only too congenial to him; he resisted being drawn into their introspective circle on the ground that their endless self-questioning would infect his own spontaneity. By 1853, however, he had come to the conclusion that this early concern to maintain "intellectual seclusion," to bar

41

out "all influences that I felt troubled without advancing me," had been needless because his innate lassitude and want of intellectual power were in themselves a sufficient bar.[8] This shortcoming in himself, as Arnold now saw it, a profound spiritual languor combined with a constitutional incapacity to reason his way out of it, convinced him that he could never be the kind of poet he wanted to be.

The relation between the "languor of spirit" and his "personal" estimate of his poetry is suggested by a remark which Arnold made in the last year of his life in a letter to Sidney Colvin. In his "English Men of Letters" monograph on Keats, Colvin had discussed at some length Spenser's influence upon Keats, citing the testimony of one of Keats's friends that the reading of the *Faerie Queene* at the age of fifteen had awakened Keats's genius. "How true it is," Arnold wrote to Colvin by way of comment on the passage, "that one's first master, or the first work of him one apprehends, strikes the note for us; I feel this of the 4th Eclogue of Virgil, which I took into my system at 9 years old, having been flogged through the preceding Eclogues and learnt nothing from them; but 'Ultimae Cumaei,' etc. has been a strong influence with me ever since."[9] In an address to the Wordsworth Society delivered several years before he wrote this letter to Colvin, Arnold had spoken of "the ineffable, the dissolving melancholy of [Virgil's] lovely lines" concerning the inevitability of disease, sorrow, and death.[10] Similar references to the Roman poet's "sweet and touching sadness" occur elsewhere in the writings, and on the occasion of giving the lecture "On the Modern Element in Literature" with which he inaugurated his Professorship of Poetry at Oxford in 1857, he commented at some length on the source of Virgil's melancholy. In the light of the late letter to Colvin, Arnold's analysis of the poetry of his "first master" has unusual interest.

Having postulated in the opening part of the lecture the

"adequacy" of Pindar, Aeschylus, and Sophocles as interpreters of Greek culture, Arnold went on to consider the poets of Rome who had flourished in the time of Cicero and Augustus, an epoch even "fuller" and "richer," he said, than the age of Periclean Greece. After dismissing Lucretius as too "over-strained, gloom-weighted, morbid" to be an adequate inter-preter of this age, Arnold turned to Virgil. A subtle alteration of tone and heightening of style immediately appears with the mere mention of Virgil's name—the "poetical name which of all poetical names," Arnold wrote, "has perhaps had the most prodigious fortune." Referring to his "almost affectionate ven-eration" for the Roman poet, Arnold discussed the central ques-tion of the "adequacy" of Virgil's poetry, and then concluded with a moving tribute to a poet whom he described as "the most beautiful, the most attractive figure in literary history."[11] Between the opening and closing encomiums, however, Ar-nold had found the work of his own master wanting as a poetic interpretation of the grand epoch of imperial Rome. Over the whole *Aeneid* "there rests an ineffable melancholy: not a rigid, a moody gloom, like the melancholy of Lucretius; no, a sweet, a touching sadness, but still a sadness; a melancholy which is at once a source of charm in the poem, and a testimony to its incompleteness." Although he was "a man of the most delicate genius, the most rich learning, . . . the most sensitive nature," Virgil lived "in a great and overwhelming world," and he was "conscious, at heart, of his inadequacy for a thorough spiritual mastery of [his] world."[12]

The unmistakable echoes in this important passage of Ar-nold's earlier allusions, in the letters to Clough, to his own want of an idea by which to master the world and to the sad charm of his poetry suggest that Arnold felt his own melan-choly to be related to a similar want of "spiritual mastery." It is as though Arnold saw himself as a minor nineteenth-century Virgil writing in the great and overwhelming world

of the Victorian Pax Britannica.[13] "The poet's matter," he told
Clough in the late forties, "being *the hitherto experience of
the world, and his own,* increases with every century," hence
the difficulties confronting the modern poet were enormous;
as for himself, "you may often hear my sinews cracking under
the effort to unite matter."[14] That nothing in a complex society
could finally be "solved" weighed him down, he wrote again,[15]
and he bitterly scored Keats and Browning for striving for
"movement and fulness" without understanding "that they must
begin with an Idea of the world in order not to be prevailed
over by the world's multitudinousness."[16] Arnold's bitterness
was tinged perhaps with frustration. If, as he claimed, "modern poetry can only subsist by its *contents,*"[17] and if the contents required some comprehensive, ordering Idea, his own
poetry manifestly failed in a way that the poetry of Keats,
whatever its flaws, had not failed. "Fret not yourself to make
my poems square in all their parts, but like what you can," he
told his sister in 1853. "The true reason why parts suit you
while others do not is that my poems are fragments—*i.e.,* that
I am fragments."[18] This sense of fragmentariness, of a want
of intellectual robustness and a consequent inability to order
experience, was not the least of the causes behind the Arnoldian melancholy.

Both Arnold's want of an Idea and his sense of fragmentariness related to two particular influences in his early experience.
One was the poetic vision—powerfully expressed in Wordsworth's poetry—of man and nature as mutually adapted to
one another. The other was the still older tradition of Christianity represented by his father. Each had given to Arnold's
early life a direction and "warmth" which he was later deeply
conscious of having lost and the memory of which cast a long,
diminishing shadow over his later life. As a result of their
early association in his experience, it seems likely that the two
elements were bound together in Arnold's emotional life. After

he had broken with the theological commitments of his father—belief in the divinity of Christ and in a personal God—
he found himself unable to derive the joy from natural beauty
which Wordsworth had felt on grounds that may be described
as religious if not Christian. The connection between the
Christian and the Wordsworthian elements is made by Arnold himself in a letter to Clough in 1853: "If one loved what
was beautiful and interesting in itself *passionately* enough, one
would produce what was excellent without troubling oneself
with religious dogmas at all. As it is, we are *warm* only when
dealing with these last—and what is frigid is always bad."[19]
Arnold could for this reason praise the work of an obscure poet
named Skeffington, whom he described as a "rapturous Christian," simply for the "fire" which his poetry, with all its faults,
conveyed, in contrast to the debilitating melancholy of the
"unintoxicated honest" like himself.[20]

An entry in the Yale Manuscript dating from the critical
years following his father's death reveals Arnold's awareness
of the effect which his religious disillusionment had upon his
inner life: "I cannot conceal from myself the objection which
really wounds & perplexes me from the religious side is that
the service of reason is freezing to feeling, chilling to the religious moods & feeling & the religious mood are eternally the
deepest being of man, the ground of all joy & greatness for
him."[21] There is no conclusive evidence that Arnold ever held
the particular religious beliefs to which his father subscribed;
it is virtually certain that he did not hold them for very long
as a young man. But it is a reasonable inference that the son
of Dr. Arnold shared his father's basic religious commitments
during his early youth, if only as the unquestioned and reas-
suring background to his own more immediate interest in
literature.[22] As "the ground of all joy and greatness in man,"
religion could not but have a general bearing on Arnold's view
of literature, and in fact its relevance to the poet and to the

life of the imagination in particular was for Arnold quite direct and explicit. Citing Shakespeare to the effect that "if imagination would apprehend some joy it comprehends some bringer of that joy,"[23] Arnold believed that the imagination of a Dante or a Shakespeare could readily conceive such "bringers" as would have been effectively intelligible to readers who shared their religious beliefs. With the general decline of Christian belief among the educated, these once powerfully effective images—whether of character, event, or symbol—were no longer available to the modern poet. As Arnold was to put it in a late poem, through the representative voice of Sénancour:

> "While we believed, on earth he went,
> And open stood his grave.
> Men call'd from chamber, church, and tent;
> And Christ was by to save.

> "Now he is dead! Far hence he lies
> In the lorn Syrian town;
> And on his grave, with shining eyes,
> The Syrian stars look down."
>   ["Obermann Once More," ll. 169–176]

The tension implicit in these lines and in the cryptic statement of the Yale Manuscript explain the melancholy of Arnold's poems. Whatever inherent penchant for melancholy or want of robustness Arnold may have had in his nature, his drift into religious agnosticism developed that original tendency far beyond what it would have been under less unsettling circumstances. Because the Christian story could no longer be accepted as true, it could at best merely remind the "unintoxicated honest" poet of what had been lost and indicate the kind of equivalent inspiration and language that was needed by genuinely modern poetry.

The effect of Arnold's early religious denudation, as often

with richly endowed natures, extended itself into his intellectual and emotional life generally. It probably played a
part in the unhappy affair with "Marguerite," a young French
girl around whom Arnold's inner crisis focused itself in the
late forties in an episode which gave a fresh poignancy to his
sense of disillusionment. Although theoretically it should have
been possible, independently of any particular religious or romantic commitments, still to love the true and the beautiful,
Arnold discovered that his own emotional life was too intimately and too early associated with particular beliefs and
aspirations for him to be able to discard them and to transfer
his emotions to some more acceptable explanation of life, as
his critical intellect demanded, without great pain. This feeling of distress found expression in the poems, which record
the process of the transfer.

When he read Arnold's prose, Henry James was quick to
recognize that Arnold's intellectual confusion and emotional
frustrations had induced a peculiarly "modern" self-consciousness and sadness. In a review of *Essays in Criticism,* written
before he could have had any knowledge of Arnold's comments
on Virgil in the inaugural lecture, James singled out the melancholy "note" in Arnold's writings in terms remarkably similar to those which Arnold had used in describing Virgil's
poetry: "That Mr. Arnold thoroughly understands his time we
do not mean to say, for this is the privilege of a very select
few; but he is, at any rate, profoundly conscious of his time.
This fact was clearly apparent in his poems, and it is even
more apparent in these Essays. It gives them a peculiar character of melancholy—that melancholy which arises from the
spectacle of the old-fashioned instinct of enthusiasm in conflict (or at all events in contact) with the modern desire to be
fair,—the melancholy of an age which not only has lost its
naiveté, but which knows it has lost it."[24] James's distinction
between the "old-fashioned" and the "modern" consciousness,

separated by the great psychological divide created by the loss
of naiveté, was very close to the distinction which Schiller
had made at the beginning of the century between "naive"
and "sentimental" poetry. Schiller, like Arnold, believed that
the heavy readings in philosophy which he had undertaken in
the hope of healing the inner division of head and heart had
permanently impaired his creative power by making it impossible for his imagination to function spontaneously as it had
earlier. Having steeped himself in Kant, Schiller found that
the old "living glow" was gone. "I now *see* myself *create* and
form," he wrote. "I watch the play of inspiration; and my
fancy, knowing she is not without witnesses of her movements,
no longer moves with equal freedom."[25] This experience lay
at the root of Schiller's distinction between the spontaneous
art of the Ancients and the self-conscious art of the modern
world, a distinction felt, if less clearly articulated, by the English Romantics as well. In Arnold the conflict became overt
and conscious very early and gave rise to the melancholy that
forms the general emotional atmosphere within which the
"main movement of mind" recorded in his poetry takes place.
An understanding of the drift of that movement not only takes
us near to the center of a common mid-Victorian experience,
but, as we consider Arnold's response to it, helps to explain
his break with poetry and throws light on the motive underlying the criticism which first attended and eventually replaced
the poetry.

CHAPTER FOUR

The Main Movement of Mind

As a record of Arnold's inner evolution, his poems may be divided, for analytical purposes, into three major categories. Each category represents a distinct phase in that evolution and each phase displays itself in a peculiar structure of feeling employing a correspondingly appropriate poetic imagery. In the first category belong the poems of nostalgia, in which the loss of naiveté and spontaneity is still fresh and in which, as yet, no alternative possibility for attaining wholeness is contemplated. In the second category belong the poems of dialogue, in which the loss of naiveté has been accepted and the dialogue of the mind with itself is confronted, but with the issue held in suspense while the persona explores alternatives. In the third category are the poems in which both the nostalgia and the dialogue have been conquered and the persona speaks out of stoic resignation to a life of drastically curtailed hopes and ambitions. These last may for convenience be called poems of morality. Finally, standing apart from the poems which constitute the main body of Arnold's poetry and requiring separate discussion are several poems in which a note of hope, a sense of recovery, struggles for expression. These poems, as we shall see, not only anticipate the optimism of the criticism but announce its basic theme as well.

In his most productive decade, between 1842 and 1852, Arnold was in fact composing all three types of poems, the various moods which the poems express obviously having occurred alternately rather than consecutively. The stoic note is present, for example, in some of the early poems, while the nostalgic note can still be heard in relatively late ones, and occasionally two different moods appear side by side in a single work. Yet Arnold described his poems not only as "fragments," but as the record of a "movement of mind," and there is evidence to indicate that the three "phases" are valid as historical as well as analytical categories. The successive volumes of poetry published between 1849 and 1867 betray a general shift in the "idea" that orders the antagonistic impulses out of which a majority of the poems in each volume arose, and the direction of the movement is that suggested by the chronological pattern just described. An analysis of the poems within this framework has the advantage of using Arnold's own judgments of his poetry as a guide in exploring his evolution as a poet, judgments which explain both the persistence of the note of melancholy in his poetry and the changes in the quality of that melancholy as the "movement of mind" carried the poet into new areas of experience.

POEMS OF NOSTALGIA

In what one critic has called the myth of "loss, endurance, and recovery" which governs Arnold's poetry as a whole,[26] the poems of nostalgia represent the initial desolating phase of loss and dislocation during which the dominant emotional impulse is retrospective. As the name implies, the poems of nostalgia give voice to a poetry of memory; looking back to a time of prelapsarian innocence and order, they are haunted by the pathos of innocence and order lost. Arnold's poems in this genre differ from earlier poems dealing with this traditional theme mainly in the intensity and the peculiar quality of their pathos; as a result of the earliness, suddenness, and finality of the loss, they strike a desperate, almost hopeless note. The loss of naiveté which separates the present from the past has entailed intellectual dislocation and a consequent loss of a capacity to focus—in Carlyle's word, to "vent"—emotions on appropriate objects, actions, or values. Arnold's nostalgia arises in his reaction to, and recoil from, the dilemma posed by the discovery that without order the feelings tend to become random and objectless, while without feeling any attainable order becomes mechanical and stultifying. Indeed, it may be doubted that Arnold experienced for very long a world in which joy and order were harmonized, a world of intellectual naiveté and emotional spontaneity, since even in the earliest poems the persona speaks not of the possession, but of the memory of such a world.[27]

The imagery by which Arnold renders his nostalgia is drawn from three main sources: from memories of his own childhood, from nature, and from the historical past. These vehicles, with their corresponding cluster of subordinate images—though Arnold's repertoire of imagery is not a large one—evoke an imaginative world in which the speaker finds temporary refuge from the confusions and fevers of the present. The persona either judges the present by alluding to a happier past, near or remote, or focuses upon a present world of natural beauty from which he feels himself alienated. Thus the nostalgia is rendered in both temporal and spatial terms. On the one hand, there is the poetic landscape, most frequently the "mild pastoral slope" of "The Scholar-Gipsy," which is an unpopulated terrain that stands opposite the speaker, reminding him of a spontaneous life of unselfconscious integrity which he himself lacks. On the other hand, there is an imaginative evocation of the historical past, which extends the childhood motif into history and enables the speaker to generalize his sense of loss and alienation in an aimless, hectic present which includes the whole of modern society.

An early prize poem, "Cromwell," is of interest mainly for the way in which it employs the theme of childhood, in Wordsworthian fashion, as the formative period in a childhood-youth-manhood pattern of personal development.[28] Approximately 130 lines, a little less than half of the poem, are given over to the youthful Cromwell, whose childhood dreams are described as not being "idle" since the "man / Still toils to perfect what the child began" (ll. 45–46). After the "first sorrow, which is childhood's grave" (l. 82) has awakened the ambiguous passions of Youth, still—in a variation of the Wordsworthian concept of the child as father to the man—

> . . . Memory's glance the while
> Fell on the cherish'd past with tearful smile;
> And peaceful joys and gentler thoughts swept by,
> Like summer lightnings o'er a darken'd sky.
> The peace of childhood, and the thoughts that roam,
> Like loving shadows, round that childhood's home.
>
> [ll. 69–74]

Peace, joy, gentleness, and innocence, all attach themselves to the memory of childhood, in opposition to the "unrestful lot" (l. 86), the "follies" (l. 79), the "strife" (l. 102) of youthful passions and ambitions. Significantly, however, the mature hero's sense of "the calm, sweet peace—the rest of home" (l. 113) is, in fact, deeper "than childhood ever knew" (l. 116),

> Green happy places—like a flowery lea
> Between the barren mountains and the stormy sea,
>
> [ll. 117–118]

a country of the mind, therefore, in which the "fleeting thoughts" of the once "heedless child" (ll. 51–52) ripen, after childhood has departed:

With common cares unmingling, and apart,
Haunting the shrouded chambers of his heart.

[ll. 57–58]

Thus the dreams of childhood preserved in the heart long after childhood has been left behind take on a significance which they could not have had during childhood itself; the landscape of childhood is the adult speaker's symbolic projection of the "green happy places" which haunt his heart.

In this early poem Arnold has difficulty reconciling a personally appealing theme with his assigned subject, an ambitious and successful man of the world. Except for the obviously derivative Wordsworthian echoes and occasional near-bathos ("tearful smile"), the long passages on childhood in the first part have an authority of felt experience that is notably lacking in the latter half of the poem, which is devoted to Cromwell's final years and death.

Within the pattern established by "Cromwell," with its emphasis upon the decisive importance of childhood in forming the man, the treatment of childhood in "Stanzas in Memory of the Author of 'Obermann'" illuminates in a particularly useful way Arnold's own childhood experience and the impact of that experience upon his personal development. The poem derives directly from the encounter with that sorrow that is childhood's grave, mentioned in "Cromwell," but the Obermann stanzas lead to a quite different kind of maturity from that which Arnold imagined for the Puritan hero. Comparing his lot with the lives of three poets of the previous generation who had "attain'd . . . to see their way" (ll. 47–48)—Goethe, Wordsworth, and Sénancour—the speaker in this poem identifies himself with the last, on the grounds that Sénancour's clear head, chilled feeling, and icy despair represent the *maladie* peculiar to a generation which, unlike Wordsworth, cannot avert its eyes "from half of human fate" and, unlike Goethe,

was born too late to find a clear course through the mists and
storms of a post-Revolutionary age. The speaker attributes
this inability to attain either "Wordsworth's sweet calm" or
"Goethe's wide / And luminous view" to the special circumstances of his generation's childhood:

> But we, brought forth and rear'd in hours
> Of change, alarm, surprise—
> What shelter to grow ripe is ours?
> What leisure to grow wise?
>
> Like children bathing on the shore,
> Buried a wave beneath,
> The second wave succeeds, before
> We have had time to breathe.
>
> [ll. 69–76]

The absence of a leisure in which to "ripen" accounts for the
stifled atmosphere, the sense of feeble struggle against overwhelming odds, which characterizes the Arnoldian nostalgia
in its more desperate moments. Like Empedocles in a later
poem, the persona of the Obermann stanzas cries for air, but
he can only pledge himself to preserve the spiritual childhood
of those Children of the Second Birth (l. 144) who, like Sénancour (and unlike Cromwell, whose childhood dreams bear
ambiguous fruit in mature action), have kept themselves unspotted from the world.

The fruits of worldly success had been contemplated in another early prize-poem, "Alaric at Rome," in which the actions
of maturity are associated, as in "Cromwell," with childhood
dreams. Alaric gazes down from a hill overlooking Rome, reflecting upon the great victory he has just won:

> Perchance his wandering heart was far away,
> Lost in dim memories of his early home,
> And his young dreams of conquest.
>
> [ll. 169–171]

Similarly, Rustum, at the close of his battle with the young Sohrab, "remember'd his own early youth, / And all its bounding rapture" (ll. 619–620), recalling with particular joy his early life with his parents:

> . . . all the pleasant life they led,
> They three, in that long-distant summer-time—
> The castle, and the dewy woods, and hunt
> And hound, and morn on those delightful hills
> In Ader-baijan.
>
> ["Sohrab and Rustum," ll. 627–631]

In a late poem Arnold envisions Heine, too, though engaged in a different kind of warfare, as longing, in the midst of the brilliance of "hot Paris drawing rooms," to remove his spirit

> out of the din,
> Back to the tranquil, the cool
> Far German home of his youth!
> ["Heine's Grave," ll. 149–151]

There is this difference, however, between the childhood of an Alaric or Rustum or Cromwell (significantly, two of these men of action are the subjects of early poems and Rustum, a later creation, is disillusioned with action) and that of modern spirits like Heine and Arnold himself: the former saw their childhood dreams bear fruit in active lives of heroic scope; the latter look back to childhood as a "sheltered time" uncorrupted by and superior to the feverish, unsatisfactory life of maturity. Arnold consistently employs childhood to evoke an air of innocence, joy, and peace by way of defining the strife, unhappiness, and unrest of an abortive and aimless maturity. Even in the two early poems, the "dreams of wide dominion" attributed to the heroes of the past are haunted by a "Whispering from all around, 'All earthly things must die.'" ("Alaric at Rome," ll. 175–180)

The theme of childhood is seldom far removed in Arnold's poetry from a feeling for nature which is reminiscent of Wordsworth, although as a reflection of his own sensibility Arnold's treatment may best be described as post-Wordsworthian.[29] The memory of the Wordsworthian harmony of man and nature remained one of Arnold's touchstones of joy and wholeness all his life, but it was a memory, a sense of wholeness irrecoverably lost rather than preserved and transmuted in the exalted philosophic mood of Wordsworth's mature Philosopher. The natural landscape which objectifies Arnold's feeling is therefore correspondingly different. In "Memorial Verses" the conjunction of childhood, an instinctive harmony with nature, and a spontaneous happiness serves as the poem's central theme. The speaker feels that the "titanic" force of a Byron and the wisdom of a Goethe may again find worthy spokesmen, but where, he asks, "will Europe's latter hour / Again find Wordsworth's healing power?"

> He too upon a wintry clime
> Had fallen—on this iron time
> Of doubts, disputes, distractions, fears.
> He found us when the age had bound
> Our souls in its benumbing round;
> He spoke, and loosed our hearts in tears.
> He laid us as we lay at birth
> On the cool flowery lap of earth,
> Smiles broke from us and we had ease;
> The hills were round us, and the breeze
> Went o'er the sun-lit fields again;
> Our foreheads felt the wind and rain.
> Our youth return'd; for there was shed
> On spirits that had long been dead,
> Spirits dried up and closely furl'd,
> The freshness of the early world.

[ll. 42–57]

Arnold composed "Memorial Verses" as a formal "dirge," and the point of view of the poem, which gives an account of Wordsworth's liberation of English consciousness from the debilitating grip of skepticism, doubt, and social and political unrest, is deliberately historical. The poem is successful, however, because Arnold's own sensibility is in control. The "early world" suggested by the phrase "cool flowery lap" reflects a landscape symbolic of a consciousness premodern in its spontaneity, premoral in its cool unawareness of passion, and presocial in its sheltered seclusion. Here, as elsewhere in Arnold's poetry, a quiet contemplativeness is suggested by the use of flowers to create a world of frail, innocent, and transient beauty characteristic of childhood itself. It is because this state of "naive" consciousness, of spontaneous simplicity, is consistently portrayed as something to be recovered, something apart and past which can be only temporarily revived by the experience of Wordsworth's poetry and wistfully desired by a generation that has lost the "freshness of the early world," that Arnold's poetic use of nature may be described as post-Wordsworthian. In "The Buried Life" Arnold's conversion of Wordsworth's poetic idiom to his own purposes is even more evident:

> But often, in the world's most crowded streets,
> But often, in the din of strife,
> There rises

—not, as for Wordsworth, the transfixing memory of lovely natural objects and sounds, but rather—

> an unspeakable desire
> After the knowledge of our buried life;
> A thirst to spend our fire and restless force
> In tracking out our true, original course.

[ll. 45-50]

Wordsworth's confident, tranquil recollection and renewal of his early experience is replaced by a debilitating doubt and introspection.

The difference in sensibility which separates the two poets as observers of nature is equally apparent in "Lines Written in Kensington Gardens," "The Youth of Nature," and "The Youth of Man." The first of these poems arises from an occasion very similar to that which inspired Wordsworth's "Tintern Abbey," and it evolves by exploiting the same dialectic between the peace and loveliness of nature and the "hum" and "jar" of the crowded city. But the ground-note of "Lines Written in Kensington Gardens" is plaintive rather than joyful, the voice is that of one earnestly seeking, rather than confidently possessing, spiritual union with the Soul of all things. Upon returning to the scenes of his youth after the feverish excitement of the French Revolution, Wordsworth had explored an undiminished love of "beauteous forms," the memory of which had consoled him during his five-year absence:

> These beauteous forms,
> Through a long absence, have not been to me
> As is a landscape to a blind man's eye:
> But oft in lonely rooms, and 'mid the din
> Of towns and cities, I have owed to them
> In hours of weariness, sensations sweet,
> Felt in the blood and felt along the heart.[30]

The spell of natural forms is as powerful as ever; the joy of their presence remains as fresh as upon the first encounter. Arnold, on the other hand, portrays a speaker almost apologetic in his yearning to escape the "girdling city's hum," and secondly, someone who is conscious, as Wordsworth seldom is, of other lives, other responses, other modes of existence.

> In the huge world, which roars hard by,
> Be others happy if they can!

> But in my helpless cradle I
> Was breathed on by the rural Pan.
>
> [ll. 21–24]

The feeling for nature is correspondingly tentative; nature's serenity is not in harmony with the speaker's inner existence but is the measure of what he lacks.

> I, on men's impious uproar hurl'd,
> Think often, as I hear them rave,
> That peace has left the upper world
> And now keeps only in the grave.
> Yet here is peace forever new!
>
> [ll. 25–29]

The discrepancy between the speaker's troubled introspective consciousness and the peace of nature is evident.

> The will to neither strive nor cry,
> The power to feel with others give!
> Calm, calm me more! nor let me die
> Before I have begun to live.
>
> [ll. 41–44]

While the prayer to the "calm soul of all things" with which the poem concludes recalls Wordsworth's faith in nature's power to beneficently shape the moral conduct of man—"His little, nameless, unremembered acts / Of kindness and of love"—the note of desperation in the prayer in Arnold's poem, especially in the phrase "helpless cradle," is utterly un-Wordsworthian. A devouring self-consciousness has distanced nature; Arnold's description of the landscape merely contributes to the overall impression of alienation.

"The Youth of Nature" opens with yet another elegiac tribute to Wordsworth, uttered this time against the background of the Lake Country:

> The gleam of The Evening Star
> Twinkles on Grasmere no more,

> But ruin'd and solemn and grey
> The sheepfold of Michael survives;
> And, far to the south, the heath
> Still blows in the Quantock coombs,
> By the favourite waters of Ruth.
>
> [ll. 18–24]

As in "Memorial Verses," the passing of the Romantic age and especially of the Wordsworthian sensibility is recorded:

> He grew old in an age he condemn'd.
> He look'd on the rushing decay
> Of the times which had shelter'd his youth:
> Felt the dissolving throes
> Of a social order he loved;
> Outlived his brethren, his peers,
> And, like the Theban seer,
> Died in his enemies' day.
>
> [ll. 28–35]

The central theme of "The Youth of Nature" calls to mind Wordsworth's famous remarks regarding the likeness of "emotion recollected in tranquility" to real emotion, but a characteristically Arnoldian pathos appears in the emphasis placed upon the inadequacy of poetry for expressing the deepest feelings:

> Cold the elation of joy
> In his gladdest, airiest song,
> To that which of old in his youth
> Fill'd him and made him divine.
>
> [ll. 95–98]

Recollected emotion is no longer what it had been for Wordsworth, "an emotion, kindred to that which was before the subject of contemplation," but rather a pale memento of an experience which the poet is unable to recapture.[31] Nature Herself speaks to the point:

"Weak is the tremor of pain
That thrills in his mournfullest chord
To that which once ran through his soul."

[ll. 92–94]

The controlling emotion of "The Youth of Nature" is not simply nostalgia for the Wordsworthian world, but the oppressive experience of man's transiency set against the calm, inscrutable, perennial beauty of the natural world. The effect is close to the Virgilian *lacrimae rerum.*

The pantheistic note faintly struck in "The Youth of Nature"—the poet's song is seen as a reflex of those cosmic forces of life at work in "the unlit gulph" of the poet—is more explicit in the companion piece, "The Youth of Man." Here, too, the contrast with Wordsworth is notable. As in "Lines Written in Kensington Gardens," the speaker prays for the restoration of joy and beauty rather than rejoicing in a Presence whose light is the light of setting suns.

Murmur of living,
Stir of existence,
Soul of the world!
Make, oh, make yourselves felt
To the dying spirit of youth!

[ll. 51–55]

The aging couple's memory of the past as interpreted by the narrator is dominated by the recollection of a childhood spent in the sheltered seclusion of a rural retreat.

. . . the castled house, with its woods,
Which shelter'd their childhood—the sun
On its ivied windows; a scent
From the grey-wall'd gardens, a breath
Of the fragrant stock and the pink,
Perfumes the evening air.
Their children play on the lawns.

They stand and listen; they hear
The children's shouts, and at times,
Faintly, the bark of a dog
From a distant farm in the hills.
Nothing besides!

[ll. 64–75]

The bitter-sweet pain of the occasion is elevated, in the conclusion, to the level of a universal nostalgia which includes
the speaker:

Well I know what they feel!
They gaze, and the evening wind
Plays on their faces; they gaze—
Airs from the Eden of youth
Awake and stir in their soul;
The past returns—they feel
What they are, alas! what they were.

[ll. 88–94]

In "The Future" the memory of the freshness of an early
world and of oneness with nature, associated with Wordsworth
in the poems just discussed, is related more generally to a
"primitive" age of man, to the "childhood" of the race:

Who can see the green earth any more
As she was by the sources of Time?
Who imagines her fields as they lay
In the sunshine, unworn by the plough?
Who thinks as they thought,
The tribes who then roam'd on her breast,
Her vigorous, primitive sons?

[ll. 27–33]

Closer to the "snowy mountainous pass" which cradles "the
new-born clear-flowing stream" (ll. 9–12), primitive man—
the poem here refers specifically to the biblical characters Re-
bekah and Moses (ll. 36, 45)—could better guard the inner

"spring of feeling," could more easily attain the vision "Of God, of the world, of the soul" which flashed on Moses "when he lay in the night by his flock" (ll. 39–46). Wordsworth's achievement, in Arnold's view, lay in his ability to restore through his poetry the fresh and vital spontaneity and therefore the joy of this early world which the moderns had lost. "The Future" attempts to sound a note of hope, but like Arnold's other poems, it is most effective in recording the consequences of the disappearance of this early world.

Arnold's projection of the values associated with childhood into an historical past may be seen in three other, quite different, poems, two of them among his major achievements. "Bacchanalia: or, The New Age" transposes the contrast between the individual's memory of a sheltered childhood and his sense of the inadequacy of the present—as treated, for example, in "The Youth of Man"—into a contrast between Wordsworth's generation and his own. The structure of the poem is organized around an analogy between the quiet nature of Rural Pan (Arnold's own natal deity, Dr. Arnold notwithstanding) and the world of the Past, on the one hand, and between the violent nature of Bacchus and the world of the Present on the other hand. The imaginative landscape of Rural Pan reflects the innocent, premoral, spontaneous existence of quiet contemplation.

> The business of the day is done,
> The last belated gleaner gone.
> And from the thyme upon the height,
> And from the elder-blossom white
> And pale dog-roses in the hedge,
> And from the mint-plant in the sedge,
> In puffs of balm the night-air blows
> The perfume which the day forgoes.
> And on the pure horizon far,
> See, pulsing with the first-born star,

> The liquid sky above the hill!
> The evening comes, the fields are still.
>
> [I, 8–19]

Suddenly, "the wild Maenads" break into the calm "Youth and Iacchus / Maddening their blood":

> Loitering and leaping,
> With saunter, with bounds—
> Flickering and circling
>
> ❀   ❀   ❀
>
> Loose o'er their shoulders white
> Showering their hair.
>
> [I, 20–22, 26–27]

Part Two of the poem pursues the analogous contrast between the speaker's memory of the previous generation, with its "now silent warfare" out of which have risen "one of two immortal lights" (II, 20–24)

> up into the sky
> To shine there everlastingly,
> Like stars over the bounding hill.
> The epoch ends, the world is still
>
> [II, 25–28]

and the turmoil of the present upon which the "stars" gaze down in detachment:

> Thundering and bursting
> In torrents, in waves—
> Carolling and shouting
> Over tombs, amid graves—
> See, on the cumber'd plain
> Clearing a stage,
> Scattering the past about,
> Comes the new age.
>
> [II, 29–36]

The poem expresses a preference for the past not simply because it was better but primarily because it is past, fixed and orderly in its stillness and unable, like the disorder and action of the Bacchanalian present, to stir and distract the soul.

By combining and organizing these various images of nostalgia in an appropriate myth, Arnold produced in "The Scholar-Gipsy" a poem in which innocence, pastoral contemplativeness, and the simple hope of a golden past amplify one another in an imaginative world of perpetual childhood, against which is set "the sick fatigue, the languid doubt" of the present. Inspired by a reading of Glanvil's *The Vanity of Dogmatizing* (and by Keats's stanzaic form) and even more by Arnold's memory of his own Oxford days, the poem succeeds in creating a symbolic figure adequate to the burden of an immense nostalgia.[32] The centrality of the nostalgic impulse is reflected both in the poem's basis in Glanvil and seventeenth-century Oxford, to which Arnold's prefatory note to the poem calls attention, and also in the reference in the opening stanza to "the quest" which the poem itself is about to enact. Moved by the story of the "Oxford scholar poor" who, endowed with "pregnant parts and quick inventive brain," had "tired of knocking at preferment's door" and had abandoned his studies for life among the gipsies (ll. 31–40), the poet-narrator's own inventive brain begins to reconstruct the Gipsy Scholar's new life and in the process creates a figure, landscape, and action that embody the values from which the narrator feels himself being cut off and for which he yearns.

The distinctive mark of the poem's hero is his success in preserving a childlike innocence, the freshness of an early world. He is, above all, a "truant boy" (l. 218).

> For early didst thou leave the world, with powers
>   Fresh, undiverted to the world without,
>   Firm to their mark, not spent on other things;
>   Free from the sick fatigue, the languid doubt,

Which much to have tried, in much been baffled, brings,
O life unlike to ours!

[ll. 161–166]

The inborn powers and the preserved innocence are traced to
the Scholar-Gipsy's fortunate birth,

O born in days when wits were fresh and clear,
  And life ran gaily as the sparkling Thames;
    Before this strange disease of modern life,
  With its sick hurry, its divided aims,
    Its heads o'ertax'd, its palsied hearts, was rife

[ll. 201–205]

and to the protagonist's cultivation of his true self in a free,
spontaneous, contemplative contact with nature:

Trailing in the cool stream thy fingers wet,
  As the slow punt swings round:
And leaning backward in a pensive dream,
  And fostering in thy lap a heap of flowers

[ll. 75–78]

    Oft thou hast given them store
  Of flowers—the frail-leaf'd, white anemony,
Dark bluebells drench'd with dews of summer eves,
And purple orchises with spotted leaves—.

[ll. 86–89]

The Scholar-Gipsy thus inhabits the typical pastoral-childhood
landscape of nostalgia in the Arnoldian myth, "watching, all
an April day, / The springing pastures and the feeding kine"
(ll. 107–108), while the narrator of the poem identifies himself with those who from a distance watch the protagonist
"when the stars come out and shine, / Through the long dewy
grass move slow away" (ll. 109–110).

In addition to the pleasures of nature enjoyed in studied
leisure, the Scholar-Gipsy's existence possesses for the nar-

rator another element, the vital spiritual dimension of hope. "Rapt, twirling in [his] hand a wither'd spray, / And waiting for the spark from heaven to fall" (ll. 119–120), he is set apart not only from his more active seventeenth-century contemporaries but, especially, from the narrator and modern men generally, "Who wait like thee, but not, like thee, in hope" (l. 170). An explicitly religious note appears in the contrast between the Scholar-Gipsy and modern "Vague half-believers of our casual creeds, / Who never deeply felt, nor clearly will'd" (ll. 172–173), among whom the narrator numbers himself. In a passage which reflects Arnold's own inner tensions and his sense of defeat, the speaker in the poem warns the Scholar-Gipsy that he must "fly our paths, our feverish contact fly," lest he too grow distracted "And then thy glad perennial youth would fade / . . . and die like ours" (ll. 222–230). In the concluding tableau, which portrays a "grave Tyrian trader" fleeing the competitive, bustling world of the "merry" and "light-hearted" Greeks and escaping to the simpler life of the "shy traffickers" (ll. 232–250) on the Iberian peninsula, the poem presents an archetype, from an even remoter age, of the uncorrupted, ancient, primeval life of self-dependence, innocence, and hope represented in the poem as a whole by the Scholar-Gipsy himself.[33]

The situations of the Scholar-Gipsy and of the narrator of the poem are thus parallel but distinct. The Scholar-Gipsy flees the life of conventional study and social conformity to a more primitive life among the gipsies in order to await the "spark" that will provide him with insight into the life of men and, according to the poem, give him the power which that insight has to loose the tongue (ll. 45–50). Correspondingly, the narrator escapes to the earlier age—earlier both historically and psychologically—of the Scholar-Gipsy in order to contemplate a way of life free from those "repeated shocks" of the modern world that "Exhaust the energy of strongest souls / And numb the elastic powers" (ll. 144–146). Although it is unnecessary and would be dangerous to press too closely the significance of the "spark from Heaven," it clearly is meant to include a spiritual insight into life as well as artistic skill in utterance. It is significant, on both counts, that although he nurses his "*one* aim, *one* business, *one* desire" (l. 152) with "unclouded joy" (l. 199), the Scholar-Gipsy does not in fact encounter the "spark" without which his life must remain a perpetual quest; he is left, rather, to continue his wanderings "pensive and tongue-tied" (l. 54). Thus there is implicit in "The Scholar-Gipsy" a dual sense of longing and frustration. One feels both in the Scholar-Gipsy and in the poet-narrator a frustrated desire to penetrate the ultimate and unattainable meaning of life and to discover the means of expressing it. Unlike his protagonist, however, the speaker has abandoned hope, classing himself with those who "waive all claim to bliss, and try to bear" life in a "close-lipp'd patience" that is "near neighbour to despair" (ll. 191–196). Though muted by the hopeful expectancy, the unclouded joy, of the "truant boy" who occupies the foreground of the poem, the narrator's nostalgia, centering in the loss of that expectancy and joy, extends to a desire for the peace of death: "we others pine, / And wish the long unhappy dream would end" (ll. 191–192). It is the ultimate nostalgia, a longing to return to unconsciousness.

Glanvil's anecdote and the figure of the Scholar-Gipsy provided a spark which loosed Arnold's tongue, enabling him to create a world in which he contemplates, in a language intelligible to his generation, his own and their dilemma. Like the Scholar-Gipsy, Arnold had haunted the Oxford countryside in a lonely quest for the "heaven-sent" skill of the poet—the power to "bind" the minds of other men by skill in language and a special insight into the "workings of men's brains" (l. 46). But for Arnold, as for the Scholar-Gipsy, the spark does not descend, or at least the spark that did descend was not of the kind which the Scholar-Gipsy seems to anticipate. For Arnold the modern poet's intuition and skill bear precisely on the paradoxical discovery that the spark does not fall: that the modern Scholar-Gipsy waits in vain. The current of modern life has so altered, faith has become so attenuated, that as a poet, Arnold can only record the discrepancy between the charm of the early hope and the ennui of the later despair, measuring the one by the other. The persona of the poem identifies himself both with the Scholar-Gipsy and with modern man: he has experienced both the hope of the one and the lassitude of the other. And like the Tyrian trader, he carries his memory of the better world with him to a new country, there undoing the corded bales of his vision for the benefit of those sensitive and innocent enough to recognize the worth of the content. But as Arnold discovered, the Philistine public of Victorian England was not very interested in the goods of the modern counterpart of the earnest Tyrian who confronted "the shy traffickers" on the Iberian peninsula.

Although "The Scholar-Gipsy" is greater—because it is more coherent—than "Stanzas from the Grande Chartreuse," the latter holds the greatest biographical interest of all of Arnold's poems of nostalgia. This poem not only includes the themes of "The Scholar-Gipsy" but goes beyond them by bringing into the foreground the predicament of the narrator of the earlier poem as he directly confronts the ultimate spiritual origins of the "sick fatigue" and "languid doubts" of the modern world. The difference between the two poems is most evident in the submersion of the pastoral landscape which occupies such a large place in "The Scholar-Gipsy" and dominates the other poems of nostalgia. The consolations of "rural Pan" have been unable to compensate for the poet's deepest loss, at the hands of "rigorous teachers," of his youthful "faith" and "fire." In "Stanzas from the Grande Chartreuse" the peculiar Arnoldian feeling for the "mild pastoral slope"—for moonlight, the "pale blue convolvulus," the "warm green-muffled Cumner hills," the "long dewy grass,"—appears very briefly and then only incidentally. Amidst the starkness of the mountain landscape and the general oppressiveness of the monastery, the speaker notices a

> garden, overgrown yet mild,
> See, fragrant herbs are flowering there!
> Strong children of the Alpine wild
> Whose culture is the brethren's care;
> Of human tasks their only one,
> And cheerful works beneath the sun.
>
> [ll. 55–60]

As "children of the Alpine wild," the garden flowers suggest the theme of childhood explored elsewhere in the poem, but the "pastoral" associations with which this theme properly belongs are overlaid and all but obliterated by the speaker's deep religious melancholy. The disappearance of the pastoral landscape, frequently associated in Arnold's poems with the name of Wordsworth, suggests the connection in Arnold's experience between his feeling for nature and his religious history. Both Wordsworth and Christianity had been powerful elements in his formative experience; with his disavowal of the latter as he had been taught it in his youth, the former became, at best, only partially relevant. During Arnold's undergraduate years the most influential English representative of the precarious alliance of Romanticism and Christianity had been John Henry Newman, but already as an undergraduate Arnold had found Newman's solution impossible; he was already composing poetry in which his post-Wordsworthian sensibility was evident. He was never entirely to escape the memory of either Wordsworth or Newman, and "Stanzas from the Grande Chartreuse" indicates the deep and important connection between Romanticism and Christianity in Arnold's experience, but it also represents a turning point in Arnold's career, portraying the dire consequences entailed if he should continue to indulge his nostalgia and refuse to confront the world of the present in which he found himself.

The imagery and the action with which the poem opens—as the band of pilgrims ascends

> Through Alpine meadows soft-suffused
> With rain, where thick the crocus blows,
> Past the dark forges long disused,
>
>   *❖   ❖   ❖*
>
> Through forest up the mountain-side
>
>   [ll. 1–3, 6]

marks the psychological shift from the benign and gentle pastoral world of "The Scholar-Gipsy" to a more severe mountain country which is described in images almost Dantesque:

> The autumnal evening darkens round,
>
>   *❖   ❖   ❖*
>
> While hark! far down, with strangled sound
> Doth the Dead Guier's stream complain,
> Where that wet smoke, among the woods,
> Over his boiling cauldron broods
>
>   [ll. 7, 9–12]

The "spectral vapours white" which soon appear amid the "limestone scars" and "ragged pines" (ll. 13–14), as the pilgrims continue to mount "the stony forest-way" (l. 20), prepare the reader for the "cowl'd forms" that "brush by in gleaming white" (l. 36) in the monastery now in view. Once inside the monastery gate, in the realm of "death in life" (l. 54), the speaker begins his reflections on the central question of the poem, "what am I, that I am here?" (l. 66). The speaker's faith, we learn, has been "prun'd" and his "fire" "quench'd" by stern "masters of the mind" who have shown him "the high white star of Truth" (ll. 67–75).[34] The truth he was urged to seek evidently involves, as a condition for its pursuit, the relinquishing of early hopes and desires which the speaker has found it difficult to abandon, although he can no longer entertain them seriously. The emotional impulse of the poem derives from the speaker's consciousness of having "so much unlearnt, so much resign'd" (l. 75). What he experiences is not the excitement of aspiration but a feeling of loss and desolation, and this feeling controls the imagery and argument alike. While the speaker recognizes his predicament as a personal matter to be solved by himself as best he can, he asks his teachers to recognize that for one with his background to have undergone enlightenment at their hands was bound to be painful. His presence among the monks is not, he argues, a result of emotional capitulation to superstition, but of his failure to find in the austere vision of "Truth" the warmth and fire which will satisfy his ineradicable longings.

The dilemma posed in the juxtaposing of an inescapable but joyless truth and a joyful but "exploded" illusion (l. 98) is evident in the various sets of antithetical images which objectify the tensions in the poem: childhood and maturity, past and present, solitude and society, desire and reason, hope and despair. In this case childhood operates, both literally and symbolically, in opposition to the aridity of maturity which serves as the point of departure for the speaker's reflections. It functions literally—and historically—in the speaker's identification of himself with those "whose bent was taken long ago" (l. 198):

> We are like children rear'd in shade
> Beneath some old-world abbey wall
> Forgotten in a forest-glade,
> And secret from the eyes of all.
>
> [ll. 169–172]

Symbolically childhood embodies a nucleus of values—peace, solitude, innocence, naiveté, happiness—which the "foreign air" of the modern world has destroyed. Moreover, as projected into the past, "childhood" includes the historical world of "our fathers" and beyond them of the "old-world abbey," the Gothic "pointed roofs," and the world of medieval faith generally—the "childhood" of the modern world—symbolized by the Grande Chartreuse. Thus the personal disenchantment of the speaker takes on a larger dimension as representative of a cultural revolution that has overtaken Europe, and beyond this of a cosmic alienation which Arnold refers to when in another poem he speaks of "something that infects the world" ("Resignation," l. 278).

The speaker's account of Carthusian life, however, reveals a new complexity in the persona's feelings toward his childhood and the historical past. On the one hand, the attraction of the cloistered life, the fundamental sympathy which binds those Christians who believe with those Romantics who grieve in joint opposition to the modern world, is conveyed in references to the "shade," the "secluded dells," the "forest-glade," the yellow tapers which shine as "emblems of hope," and the sound of organ music at the end; all these represent one side of the speaker's feeling for the place and for the religious and poetic memories of his youth. On the other hand, and much more impressively, the cloistered life is rendered in images of death—"ghostlike," darkness, coffins, blood, the white forms that "brush by," "white uplifted faces," silence, and quite specifically "death in life." The force of the latter imagery is heightened, moreover, by contrast with a third cluster of images of life in the world: the "passing troops in the sun's beam— / Pennon, and plume, and flashing lance!" whose active life leads men "to life, to cities, and to war" and to the social life of pleasure of the "gay dames" in "sylvan green," whose laughter and cries make the "blood dance" as the "bugle-music

on the breeze / arrests with a charm'd surprise" (ll. 188–190).
Judged both from the intellectual point of view of his masters
and by the instinctive desires of youthful worldly ambitions, the
speaker's return to the cloister is a longing for death. Moreover,
by juxtaposing the wan and feeble light of the tapers to the
flash and color of life outside the cloister, Arnold presents a
structure of feeling of greater complexity than the simple opposition of head and heart, present and past, childhood and
maturity which characterizes most of the poems of nostalgia.
The speaker in the Grande Chartreuse stanzas is caught between three rather than two worlds: the memory of childhood
and the past, with their religious "emblems of hope"; a youthful life of pleasure and action in the world; and the lonely,
austere ideal of the "high white star of Truth." A paralysis of
indecision lies at the center of the poem; the narrator is no
longer able to entertain the fruitless dream of Romantic aspiration—"What helps it now that Byron bore," "What boots it
Shelley"—which he associates with the past, nor to enter the
world and undertake a life of action, nor yet to follow the
painful dialogue of the mind with itself which is the way to
Truth.

The poem's emotional impulse is therefore not primarily
nostalgia for religious faith or romantic inspiration—choice
here has in any case been taken out of his hands by his
"rigorous teachers"—but a longing for freedom from the intolerable pressure of inner tensions; and since this cannot be
secured through choice, the speaker turns instinctively to the
peace to be found in death.

> . . . if you cannot give us ease—
> Last of the race of them who grieve
> Here leave us to die out with these
> Last of the people who believe!
>
> [ll. 109–112]

Like the ancient Greek who on some northern strand, "thinking of his own [dead] Gods,"

> In pity and mournful awe might stand
> Before some fallen Runic stone

[ll. 82–83]

the modern man of intellect, standing in the Grande Chartreuse, has no gods of his own to think upon as he contemplates
the passing both of Romanticism and of Christianity; he has
only the distant, cold star of "Truth." A residual, hopeless desire for *something* has led the narrator to the "living tomb"
of the cloister, not in renewed faith but in the vague expectation that in this "desert" of the past he will find the peace that
comes with the death of desire.[35]

In rendering the *ne plus ultra* of Arnold's nostalgia, "Stanzas
from the Grande Chartreuse" leads naturally to a consideration
of the poems of dialogue, for once the consolations of the
memory of early joys, the peace of nature, or the charm of a
lost past were seen as intellectually dishonest as well as harmful to activity, the only alternative was to confront the modern
self-consciousness created by the dialogue of the mind with
itself. The emotional aridity and general depression which
attended this decision is suggested by Arnold's poetic handling
of the subtle attractions of death in the "Stanzas from the
Grande Chartreuse." In an early poem, "The New Sirens," he
indicates that he had for a time given, or tried to give, himself to the Romantic muse (ll. 226–232), but with disillusioning results: the emotional and intellectual fluctuations which
this pursuit entailed had produced only exhaustion (ll. 195–
202). The speaker at one point calls for a return of the sirens
(ll. 171–176), but he is already aware that the "slow tide"
had set "one way" (l. 220), and he asks to be set free.

> The eye wanders, faith is failing—
> O, loose hands, and let it be!

Proudly, like a king bewailing,
O, let fall one tear, and set us free!
[ll. 223–226]

Having made his choice, Arnold resolved to work within the
limits imposed by the modern consciousness—the abandonment of the illusions of Christianity and Romanticism. Thus,
although the poems mentioned thus far have been classified as
poems of nostalgia, there is "movement" within the type; as the
past, real or imagined, seems less and less recoverable, the
persona comes more and more to confront the fact of a blank
and joyless present. "Stanzas from the Grande Chartreuse," in
particular, records the moment of transition between the two
phases in which the speaker returns, one last time, to a past
that is acknowledged to be dead. Even before the memory
of the past spent itself in the creative effort of the Grande
Chartreuse stanzas Arnold had begun searching for a new
"idea," a new ground for joy, a new religion. The beginnings
and results of the search are evident in the dialogue poems,
some of which were composed and published side by side with
the poems of nostalgia in his first volume of poetry.

DIALOGUE POEMS

Like the poems of nostalgia, Arnold's dialogue poems employ
a fairly consistent set of images to embody a characteristic
structure of feeling. The focus shifts from the "earlier" images
of childhood, pastoral upland slopes, and the historical past,
to the intermediate period of Youth, to a nature alternately of
the plains and of the cosmos, and to the world of the present.
The unifying impulse behind the imagery is no longer nostalgia
for a "primitive," given integrity and simple spontaneity but
rather the search for a new-earned wholeness based on intellectual and moral mastery of the complex "modern" conscious-

ness. The various mechanisms of retreat which trigger the poems of nostalgia—the flight to nature as in "Lines Written in Kensington Gardens," or retreat into childhood and the past as in the Grande Chartreuse stanzas, or both as in "The Scholar-Gipsy"—are suspended. Instead, the speaker "fronts" the modern world and follows out to its logical and psychological end the dialogue that attends Youth. As in the Wordsworthian pattern of the three ages, Youth in Arnold's poetic myth constitutes a distinct epoch in the life of the individual, the transitional phase between the spontaneous innocence of childhood and the complex world of maturity. The epithet most frequently applied to this period is "wandering," the sense of between-ness that is merely latent in the poems of nostalgia becoming explicit. Preoccupation with the lovely but vanished world of the past gives way in the dialogue poems to preoccupation with a present which is severed from the "dead" past and struggling to deliver a future as yet "powerless to be born." Finally, the conscious "thought" of the personae becomes an important element in the accumulated residual emotion which the poems attempt to express, and as a result the melancholy is in a way less personal and, at times, even more desiccating than in the poems of nostalgia; it arises not from an instinctive up-welling of the heart's regrets for a lost wholeness but in the intellectual and emotional effects of the baffling complexity of the present.

Arnold's fondness for the epithet "wandering" in rendering the phase of Youth is readily explained. On the one side there are the hopes associated with the new world that opens up with the arrival of Youth: dreams of happiness, infinite longings of vague passions to be realized, stirrings of ambition. In the Arnoldian pattern these longings are related especially to the yearning for fulfillment in action and pleasure, to life as lived in a modern city set in a "plain," between the secluded country of childhood and the distant sea of maturity and the future. The early frustration of youthful ambitions, on the other hand, the felt discrepancy between ideals which seem to the young actually attainable and the exigencies of a real world which impose themselves with increasing authority, sets the reflective intellect in motion. The world of Youth is therefore a world of thought as well as of passion, of the dialogue of the mind with itself as well as of emotional fluctuations between joy and despair; the speaker's paramount concern is, in Arnold's words to Clough, to see his own way clearly. The persona "wanders" in an intellectual and emotional search for some identity in a strange, bewildering landscape.

As Arnold experienced it, the absence of a central idea especially distinguished the modern epoch. The world of thought is associated in the dialogue poems with the pure, dry, clear, but somewhat chilling air of mountains and stellar spaces. The serene but lonely and somewhat dizzying altitudes of the intellectual quest in turn drive the youthful speaker back into the "plain" world of activity, pleasure, and the "worldly" life of society, and, since he is attempting both to master the world and to penetrate the "far regions of eternal change," the landscape of the dialogue poems alternates between the two worlds represented in "Stanzas from the Grande Chartreuse"—in the imagery of pennon and lance and song, on the one hand, and of the "high white star of Truth," on the other. Mountain and plain thus objectify the poles of the modern dialogue, which arises in a conflict between the desire for solitude and the desire for society, between a life of contemplation and thought and a life of passion and action, while the melancholy which attends the dialogue expresses the speaker's sense that the conflict is insoluble, that indeed the peculiar mark of modernity is this insolubility. More particularly, the poems explore the meaning of modernity in terms of the hopes and frustrations that attend the search for love and/or knowledge which characterizes the period of Youth. The quality of

modern life is emotionally apprehended and expressed through
the symbolic landscapes in which the youthful persona con-
ducts his pursuit of self-discovery and also through the explicit
arguments that intervene in the process.

The "wandering" of youth, once it has commenced with
"the first sorrow which is childhood's grave" ("Cromwell," l.
82), is marked by an increasing restlessness:

> . . . still, in spite of truth,
> In spite of hopes entomb'd,
> That longing of our youth
> Burns ever unconsum'd,
> Still hungrier for delight as delights grow more rare.
>
> ["Empedocles," I, ii, 367–371]

In "Youth and Calm," a poetic fragment which Arnold composed in 1851 as part of a longer poem and eventually published separately in 1867, the basic question raised by the
conflict between "truth" and "longing" is clearly formulated.
The speaker, contemplating the "limpid brow" of a dead youth,
reflects on the difference between the calm that comes with
death and the "more grateful" calm (l. 21) which youth anticipates, the calm of satisfied desire. The former is not "life's
crown":

> 'Tis all perhaps which man acquires,
> But 'tis not what our youth desires.
>
> [ll. 24–25]

The calm of the dead youth's "marble sleep" (l. 21) has its
own peculiar attractiveness and beauty, but it is in fact a
mockery of "the bliss youth dreams," with its yearning "For
daylight, for the cheerful sun, / For feeling nerves and living
breath" in life "on this side [of] death" (ll. 16–19). The alternative to death's calm, a life of harmonious fulfillment which
is the "joy our youth forebodes" ("Empedocles," I, ii, 375),

Arnold elsewhere associates with insight and with love; it is
the failure to attain either that gives to the modern dialogue
moral and intellectual dimensions which are mutually rein-
forcing.

The progress of the dialogue as frustrations accumulate is
complex, but it is possible to infer from Arnold's poetry a
fairly clear pattern. The crucial experience is the discovery
that union with another through love, or knowledge, is rare
if not impossible. This discovery serves as the theme, para-
doxically, of Arnold's "love poems." The dialogue is then complicated by the recognition, after the speaker has been thrown
back upon himself, that it is scarcely possible even to know
oneself, that only a joyful love, not intellectual analysis, can
"fill up the void which in our breasts we bear" ("Empedocles,"
I, ii, 376), and yet love itself proves too transient to provide
a permanent basis for life. This is the theme of "The Buried
Life." Finally, the question of how to live out existence in such
a universe reinforces the intellectual quest for an explanation
adequate to both experience and reason. The finding of such
an explanation of life, upon which man's future depends, is
the theme of "Empedocles on Etna."

Although the "Marguerite" with whom Arnold identified
his crucial experience in love remains shadowy,[36] the experience itself is vividly realized in the "Switzerland" series and
several other poems. In these poems Arnold's subject is the
persona's sense of his relationship to Marguerite, rather than
Marguerite herself; the poems depict an intensely self-conscious speaker in the grip of love but hampered, to adopt
Schiller's phrase, by love's consciousness of having witnesses.
The "witnesses" are various. There are, apparently, moral res-
ervations—

> Again I spring to make my choice,
> Again in tones of ire

I hear a God's tremendous voice:
"Be counsell'd, and retire."

["Meeting," ll. 9–12]

But the restraints of conscience or of social decorum are only
a part of the pervasive self-consciousness which prompts the
lover constantly to examine his motives and responses. The
very diversity of the causes given to explain the unhappy outcome of the affair—the "God's tremendous voice" already
cited, the speaker's lack of "trenchant force" ("A Farewell,"
l. 33), the lovers' different backgrounds ("Parting," l. 66), the
idiosyncrasies of "guiding Powers" ("Meeting," l. 13), the
lovers' late meeting ("Too Late," ll. 5–8), Marguerite's fickleness ("Isolation. To Marguerite," ll. 10–12)—betrays rather
a self-reflective uncertainty that has infected the very seat of
consciousness, undermining the speaker's confidence in his own
reasoning as well as all spontaneity of emotional movement;
sensitively alert to these inner misgivings and unsure of what is
outside him, the speaker is unable to forget himself in the
object of his love; he is unable to move beyond the analysis
of his own inner movements.

The impulse to surrender to love is genuine but never very
strong in the Marguerite poems, since it is haunted from the
beginning and is finally checked and dissipated by the speaker's pervasive sense of transiency and flux. The titles which Arnold attached to the poems—"Parting," "A Memory-Picture,"
"A Farewell," "Too Late," "Separation," "The Terrace at Berne
(Composed Ten Years After the Preceding)," "Faded Leaves"
—themselves reflect the overwhelming pressure of the intuition
that "Time's current strong / Leaves us fixt to nothing long"
("A Memory-Picture," ll. 57–58). In this respect the poems
reflect an experience which has to do with the poet's relationship to the "general Life" as Arnold described it in "Resignation" and again in the late "Epilogue to Lessing's Laocoön."

His eye must travel down, at full,
The long, unpausing spectacle;
With faithful unrelaxing force
Attend it from its primal source,
From change to change and year to year
Attend it of its mid career,
Attend it to the last repose
And solemn silence of its close.

> ["Epilogue to Lessing's
> Laocoön," ll. 145–152]

Love, as part of a universal, irreversible movement which sweeps man onward, is powerless to fulfill man's dreams or even to delay for long their inevitable dissipation in the weariness and despair of isolation. The corollary sense of man's solitude, his essential loneliness, arises from this consciousness of perpetual movement:

> thou hast long had place to prove
> This truth—to prove, and make thine own:
> 'Thou hast been, shalt be, art, alone.'
>
> ["Isolation. To Marguerite," ll. 28–30]

The dialogue in the love poems moves between transiency and fixity (that "true sign of Law" as Arnold called it in his inaugural lecture), and between isolation and communion. Marguerite's fickleness, for example, is a function of the speaker's sense of the inevitable ephemeralness of human emotion: "Self-swayed our feelings ebb and swell— / Thou lov'st no more;—Farewell! Farewell!" ("Isolation. To Marguerite," ll. 11–12). All experience escapes backward into the dim region of lost memories.

> Once I said: 'A face is gone
> If too hotly mused upon;
> And our best impressions are

Those that do themselves repair.'
Many a face I so let flee,
Ah! is faded utterly.

["A Memory-Picture," ll. 9–14]

The pervasive effect of this time-ridden consciousness[37] on Arnold's general outlook is suggested in "The Buried Life," a poem which explores the nature of love as an apparently contradictory example of man's general alienation from himself, his fellowman, and the universe.

When our world-deafen'd ear
Is by the tones of a loved voice caress'd—
A bolt is shot back somewhere in our breast,
And a lost pulse of feeling stirs again.

[ll. 82–85]

Yet the pulse of feeling awakened by the "loved voice" is not directed toward the beloved, but spends itself within the speaker's heart in a vague and melancholy yearning of which the beloved is the occasion rather than the object:

The eye sinks inward, and the heart lies plain,
And what we mean, we say, and what we would, we know.
A man becomes aware of his life's flow. . . .

[ll. 86–88]

A sense of affirmation is felt, but it is difficult to know what precisely is being affirmed since the nature of the "hidden self" (l. 65) as well as its destiny are left obscure. Does the speaker read "in another's eyes" his own heart or the other's, or their mutual plight? The eye sinks *inward* and "man" becomes aware of *his* life's flow, so that

he thinks he knows
The hills where his life rose,
And the sea where it goes.

[ll. 96–98]

Much depends on whether the emphasis in these concluding lines falls on "thinks" or on "knows."[38] Even if they are read as offering the lovers' mutual discovery of themselves in the moment of love, what they discover about themselves, what they mean and say and know, is left ambiguous. There is a suggestion of possible union in a platonic universe ruled by love, of harmony with "the stir of the forces/Whence issued the world" ("Parting," ll. 89–90) for which the speaker longs in another Marguerite poem; but these forces are discernible not in fixity, but in the movement, the flow, of life, and this time-consciousness inevitably suggests death. In the Arnoldian landscape, at any rate, hills represent birth and the sea death, and between them runs the River of Life. What the persona discovers, it seems, is that larger impersonal movement which encompasses both lovers and carries all men to the sea.

In 1848, at the end of the Marguerite episode in his life, Arnold wrote to Clough with some bitterness, dismissing the experience as a necessary phase in a young man's education and, like his simultaneous discovery of the limitations of one of his favorite poets, Béranger, as "one link in an immense series of cognoscenda et indagenda" now happily "despatched." "We know beforehand all [women] can teach us: yet we are obliged to learn it directly from them," Arnold wrote, and cited some lines from one of his poetic fragments which asked why man should fix his "fruitless gaze" upon his mistress's "little moment life of loveliness/Betwixt blank nothing and abhorred decay" rather than on the mystery of birth and death which "preface and post-scribe" her beauty.[39] For Arnold, the discovery of passionate love is both simultaneous with and inseparable from the discovery of love's limitations;[40] love reflects but it does not dispel the mystery of life itself, nor can it compensate for the weight which the insolubility of the mystery thrusts upon the thinker-lover. The momentary illumination granted by love occurs within a context of "nameless sadness" ("The Buried Life," l. 3) and simply offers "a lull in the hot race" (l. 91) rather than the attainment of the goal.

That lover and beloved participate in a universal alienation Arnold makes clear in one of the finest of the Switzerland poems:

> Yes! in the sea of life enisled,
> With echoing straits between us thrown,
> Dotting the shoreless watery wild,
> We mortal millions live *alone*.
>
> ❀   ❀   ❀
>
> Who order'd, that their longing's fire
> Should be, as soon as kindled, cool'd?
> Who renders vain their deep desire?—
> A God, a God their severance rul'd!
> And bade betwixt their shores to be
> The unplum'd, salt, estranging sea.
>
> ["To Marguerite—Con-
> tinued," ll. 1-4, 19-24]

The love poems, like the letters to Clough, thus reveal a consciousness exploring itself in the presence of another rather than in communion with the other. The love experience gives rise to rhetorical questions—"Alas, is even Love too weak/ To unlock the heart, and let it speak?" ("The Buried Life," ll. 12–18)—which are echoed in the letters to Clough—"But have I been inside you, or Shakspeare? Never."[41] Just as he admired but did not share the "fire" of the Christian poet Skeffington, so Arnold could both envy and mock, but not attain, the state of these "happier men" who

> Have *dream'd* two human hearts might blend
> In one, and were through faith released
> From isolation without end

Prolong'd; nor knew, although not less
Alone than thou, their loneliness.

["Isolation. To Mar-
guerite," ll. 38–42]

The poems dealing with love are thus pervaded by the pathos
of a disabused love analogous to the melancholy of the Grande
Chartreuse stanzas associated with the exploded dream of
Christianity: both romantic love and Christian faith were joy-
bringing, but both are illusory. The New Sirens of romantic
aspiration, with their claims to be able to satisfy the spirit,
are exposed as "Sirens" by the "unlovely dawning" of the critical mind in which they stand "loveless, rayless, joyless."

So far as they record a past experience that once promised
joy and fulfillment, the love poems might be classified with the
poems of nostalgia; there is this essential difference, however:
the "modern" consciousness which occupies the foreground in
the poems is prior to the experience of love and, in effect, has
disabled spontaneity of feeling from the outset. Both religious
faith and oneness with the pastoral nature of Rural Pan had
once been known and felt; it was the memory of this lost
childhood faith and feeling for nature which had inspired the
poems of nostalgia. In the poems of dialogue not only have
these been lost, but their loss has infected the capacity to
feel in the present. Although the seclusion, joy, and innocence
of the past are sought in love, the "love" experience objectified
in the poems is dominated by doubt and confusion, wandering
and restlessness, and the melancholy of the earlier nostalgia
is given a new quality by the failure of this hope.

The connection between the dialogue initiated by the disillusioning experience with love and the intellectual search
for the meaning of life in which the dialogue culminates appears in "Mycerinus," a poem that tacitly questions the existence of justice or of meaning of any kind in life. The "Pow-

ers of Destiny" (l. 6) arbitrarily pass sentence of early death
on Mycerinus, who "rapt in reverential awe" had

> sate obedient, in the fiery prime
> Of youth, self-govern'd, at the feet of Law;
> Ennobling this dull pomp, the life of kings,
> By contemplation of divine things.
>
> [ll. 9-12]

Unlike his father, who had "lov'd injustice, and liv'd long"
(l. 13), Mycerinus had ordered his life on the premise that

> Man's justice from the all-just Gods was given:
> A light that from some upper fount did beam,
> Some better archetype, whose seat was heaven,
>
> [ll. 20-22]

only to have "heaven" crown his life with this "unjust close"
(l. 30). Rebelling out of cynical disillusion, Mycerinus turns
to an abandoned life of the senses, to which the Powers seem
equally indifferent: "not less his brow was smooth,/And his
clear laugh fled ringing through the gloom" (ll. 112–113) as
his people watch and wait and wonder. The detached, noncommittal weighing of moral alternatives in "Mycerinus" is
repeated in the intellectual order in "In Utrumque Paratus,"
which sets Neoplatonic and "absurd" cosmologies side by side,
without argument. This is as far as the speaker's intellectual
quest can take him: juxtaposed ideas of the universe as an
extension in time and space of the divine Idea, and, on the
other hand, as the solipsistic dream of a mind which is itself
a dream.

This moral and intellectual dialogue continues in "A Question," "Youth's Agitations," and "Self-Deception." "A Question:
To Fausta," which reminded Swinburne of Shelley, opens with
the statement of fact:

Joy comes and goes, hope ebbs and flows
    Like the wave;
Change doth unknit the tranquil strength of men

[ll. 1–3]

and ends with the question: "Do we go hence and find that
they [these dreams of ours] are dead?" (l. 17). The dialogue
is here still regarded with relative detachment, although the
speaker addresses his question to "Fausta" in terms that might
well prejudice the case. "Youth's Agitations" carries the argument a step further, portraying discontent as the one thing
common to youth and age, and refraining from any mention
of the possibility of fulfillment in another life. The poem is of
particular interest for the way in which it suggests that Arnold's youth, like his childhood, was cut prematurely short and
ended almost before it had begun. "Self-Deception," finally,
projects the discontent of "Youth's Agitations" into a state of
pre-existence in which the soul wanders, as tremulous, as
eager, and as frustrated as in its present life; there, too, "We
but dream we have our wish'd-for powers." The question with
which the poem ends suggests the broken utterance of a poet
reduced to a prose of desperation:

Ah! *some* power exists there, which is ours?
Some end is there, we indeed may gain?

[ll. 27–28]

With "Growing Old" and "The Progress of Poesy" the
rhythm of disillusionment, the movement from hope, through
search, to despair, is complete. First published in 1867, "Growing Old" answers its own question "What is it to grow old?"
It is to be

frozen up within, and quite
The phantom of ourselves,

To hear the world applaud the hollow ghost
Which blamed the living man.

[ll. 32–35]

The logical and psychological end of the dialogue of Youth
is revealed in "The Progress of Poesy"; as a terse expression of
the hopelessness of the youth's search for joy, which had begun
in earnest for Arnold with the Marguerite experience, the poem
elaborates with bitter irony the subtitle, "A Variation," and
briefly disposes of the once hopeful aspiration toward insight,
communion, and order. Here the dialogue—elsewhere precar-
iously and momentarily balanced in detached contemplation
—has settled into despondency; the intellectual search, ending
in no certain answer, has succeeded only in killing "the
princely heart" ("The New Sirens," l. 78).

The most comprehensive and compelling of the dialogue
poems is "Empedocles on Etna."[42] Like "Stanzas from the
Grande Chartreuse," "Empedocles" marks both the culmination
of a type of poem and a turning point in Arnold's experience.
Just as "Stanzas from the Grande Chartreuse" combines the
several themes treated separately in other poems of nostalgia
and in its tacit acceptance of the doctrine of the "rigorous
teachers" marked the end of nostalgia, so "Empedocles on
Etna" rehearses at length the moral and intellectual debate
treated fragmentarily in the shorter dialogue poems, and, by its
condemnation both of intellectual aspirations to some form of
final insight and of moral rebellion against the Powers of Destiny, marks the end of the struggles of youth and the acceptance of the stoic resignation of manhood. The moral and
intellectual tensions which had induced Arnold's ennui and
despondency are embodied in the relationships between Empedocles, Pausanias, and Callicles; in these relationships, and
in the action which ends in Empedocles' death, the antagon-
isms of Arnold's own inner drama are objectified. The poem is

both a triumph of Arnold's poetic power over his mind's dialogue with itself and an elegy on his own death as a poet.

Act I of the poem consists largely of Empedocles' advice to his disciple Pausanias on how to live in the world and concludes with his sending Pausanias back to society. The substance of Empedocles' argument, which presents what amounts to Arnold's mature creed for those who wish to live in the modern world, is a mixture of the stoicism of Epictetus, the work-ethos of Carlyle, and the philosophical monism of Lucretius. Lucretius sets the ground for the argument.

> All things the world which fill
> Of but one stuff are spun,
> [And] we who rail are still,
> With what we rail at, one.
>
> [I, ii, 287–290]

Man, like the material universe, is one, that is, with the finite, benevolent, "o'er labour'd Power" that "Fain would do all things well, but sometimes fails in strength" (I, ii, 291, 295). Empedocles therefore condemns alike the "children of a weak age" who invent gods whom they can blame for their own weakness (I, ii, 301–305), those who invent gods to fulfill hereafter desires which are frustrated now (I, ii, 312–316), and thinkers who conceive of an all-wise god to invest with the knowledge that they themselves cannot attain (I, ii, 339–346). He warns his disciple that man's fundamental error is to think that he has a *right* to bliss, instead of conforming himself to the necessities imposed by the nature of things, by what *is*.

> The world's course proves the terms
> On which man wins content;
> Reason the proof confirms.
>
> [I, ii, 222–224]

Within the limitations imposed by reason there is discernible to man some scope still for human effort (I, ii, 423): Man must "work as best he can/And win what's won by strife" (I, ii, 269–270). He must not "fly to dreams, but moderate desire" (I, ii, 386) and accept "the joys there are" (I, ii, 421). He must be neither cynical and (like Mycerinus) turn in despair to a brutal life of the senses, nor be superstitious and (like the Romantic rebel) forsake society for an illusory private dream. Asked by Pausanias at the end of his discourse whether he will revisit the city of Catana, Empedocles replies that, "a wanderer from of old," he will return "to-morrow or some other day,/In the sure revolutions of the world" (I, ii, 471–472), and dismisses his disciple.

As Act II opens it is evening, and Empedocles is alone at the summit of Etna meditating on his personal predicament. This portion of the poem is given over to a series of monologues in which the protagonist rehearses his past history and analyzes his present state of mind. The monologues are interpersed with and related to the songs from the harp-player Callicles, a friend of Pausanias and Empedocles whom Pausanias has entreated to follow the protagonist, at a distance, that he might comfort him by his music.

It is obvious at the opening of Act II that Empedocles is unable to follow the advice he had given a few hours earlier to his disciple, who now has "his lesson" and as a

> good, learned, friendly, quiet man,
> May bravelier front his life, and in himself
> Find henceforth energy and heart.

> [II, 8–10]

"No energy can reach" Empedocles' own weariness, his "hurt" no courage can cure (II, 13–14); the meditated suicide which has brought him to the summit of Etna is announced:

No, thou art come too late, Empedocles!
And the world hath the day, and must break thee,
Not thou the world. With men thou canst not live,
Their thoughts, their ways, their wishes, are not thine;
And being lonely thou art miserable,
For something has impair'd thy spirit's strength,
And dried its self-sufficing fount of joy.
Thou canst not live with men nor with thyself—
O sage! O sage!—Take then the one way left;
And turn thee to the elements, thy friends,
Thy well-tried friends, thy willing ministers,
And say: Ye helpers, hear Empedocles,
Who asks this final service at your hands!
Before the sophist-brood hath overlaid
The last spark of man's consciousness with words—
Ere quite the being of man, ere quite the world
Be disarray'd of their divinity—
Before the soul lose all her solemn joys,
And awe be dead, and hope impossible,
And the soul's deep eternal night come on—
Receive me, hide me, quench me, take me home!

[II, 16–36]

These reflections are interrupted by Callicles' account of the
myth of Typho, the Titan who has been buried under Etna
in punishment for his rebellion against Zeus. Typo is portrayed
as a type of the Byronic figure, a "Titan king" who as a "self-
helping son of earth" is

Rail'd and hunted from the world,
Because [his] simplicity rebukes
The envious, miserable age!

[II, 105–107]

As head of the Olympian gods Zeus symbolizes for Empedocles both intellect and society, which conspire to crush the
simple, passionate, lonely rebel under their tyrannic rule.

Callicles, he says, "fables, yet speaks truth" (II, 89), for, according to Empedocles, the song gives mythic expression to the universal triumph of mind and "cunning" over passion and simplicity, and he is "weary of it" (II, 108). To escape both mind and the "littleness united" of the present age, Empedocles has decided to abandon his former role. He lays aside the circlet and robe, the ensigns of the kingly office.

A second song immediately follows, in which Callicles recounts the tale (with obvious analogues to the previous story) of Apollo's triumph over and brutal slaying of Marsyas in the mythical competition for supremacy in music. Olympus, a friend whom Marsyas had taught to sing, stands aloof and watches the contest. But when it is over, he covers his eyes and laments the death of the simple Phrygian faun, who is defeated by Apollo's cleverness and is flayed alive by the latter for punishment. "Ah, poor Faun, poor Faun! ah, poor Faun!" (II, 190). Empedocles responds to this second song by laying aside the ensign of his poetic office as votary of Apollo. The service of Apollo has been too solitary, isolating him from the "jars of men," perhaps, but unable to "fence him from himself" and the sound of "the beating of his own heart" (II, 205–214). Empedocles recalls the joys of early days when, in the primitive life represented by Marsyas, "neither thought/Nor outward things were clos'd and dead to us," when—in the Wordsworthian mode—

> we receiv'd the shock of mighty thoughts
> On simple minds with a pure natural joy.
>
> [II, 242–243]

But those days are gone, and for those like himself "whose youth fell on a different world" and "whose mind was fed on other food" (II, 262–265), the austere service of Apollo has become unbearably painful and life itself has come to seem intolerable;

Who [now] has no friend, no fellow left, not one;
Who has no minute's breathing space allow'd
To nurse his dwindling faculty of joy—
Joy and the outward world must die to him,
As they are dead to me!

[II, 271–275]

What then is left?

Where shall thy votary fly then? back to men?—
But they will gladly welcome him once more,
And help him to unbend his too tense thought,
And rid him of the presence of himself,
And keep their friendly chatter at his ear,
And haunt him, till the absence from himself,
That other torment, grow unbearable;
And he will fly to solitude again,
And he will find its air too keen for him,
And so change back; and many thousand times
Be miserably bandied to and fro
Like a sea-wave, betwixt the world and thee,
Thou young, implacable God! and only death
Can cut his oscillations short, and so
Bring him to poise. There is no other way.

[II, 220–234]

He is thus unable to find the true "poise" and self-identity
which he describes later, "Being one with which we are one
with the whole world" (II, 369–372).

Callicles' stories illustrate Empedocles' assertion that there
is something as inhuman in the Apollonian service as in the
tyranny of Zeus, requiring a "detachment from pity and fear
alike" that isolates the poet from the human condition. Contemplating his predicament as one who has survived the
"older world, peopled by Gods" (II, 285) into the "younger,
ignoble world" (II, 292) of the present, Empedocles wonders
if nature herself is not weary with his weariness, but concludes

that the "mild and luminous floor of waters" still lives and that only he has lost hope and spirit (II, 315 ff.). He envisions being driven, even after death, as he has been during life, in a homeless journey "Over the unallied unopening earth,/Over the unrecognising sea" (II, 360–361); mind and thought

> will be our lords, as they are now;
> And keep us prisoners of our consciousness,
> And never let us clasp and feel the All
> But through their forms, and modes, and stifling veils.
>
> [II, 351–354]

So driven, and eventually returning once again, in the revolution of time, "to this meadow of calamity" (II, 365), he will only repeat his previous life of struggle, fleeing once again "for refuge to past times," to the "soul of unworn youth," only to have reality once again "pluck us back,/Knead us in its hot hand, and change our nature" (II, 382–386). Feeling the "numbing cloud" momentarily lift, and hopeful that he therefore is not completely dead, Empedocles leaps into the "sea of fire," calling on the elements to save him. The poem concludes with Callicles' stately, noncommittal hymn to Apollo.

As a projection of his own central experience, "Empedocles on Etna" is Arnold's greatest achievement. The various impulses at war within himself are successfully objectified in the three *dramatis personae,* each of whom has a poetic life of his own within the "action" of the poem. Empedocles, the "last of the Greek religious philosophers," embodies the nostalgia and dialogue that arise from his situation, a situation which Arnold described in the 1853 *Preface* as much like that in the middle of the nineteenth century. Pausanias, the disciple, who is younger, more practical (he is a physician), and less obsessed by memories of past joys, embodies the cheerful stoicism by which intelligent men can alone survive in the world. Finally, Callicles—also young, a poet, and the friend of both

men through completely unlike either—embodies the aesthetic
consciousness which records the movement of life with detachment and serenity, moving in the social world of the city,
the mythic world of the past, and the lovely world of nature
with ease and self-assurance.

The relationship between Empedocles and Pausanias and
the actions of each suggest two further comments about Arnold's personal history. First, despite Arnold's later demurrer,
Empedocles' ethical creed as presented in Act I is—as an
ethical creed—one that is meant to be lived by, one in fact by
which Pausanias managed to live; secondly, Empedocles' state
of feeling, despite his creed, is not one in which anyone could
survive for long. The protagonist cannot accept the creed
which he affirms for Pausanias' benefit because that creed is
tolerable only to younger men brought up on the lesser hopes
and narrower ambitions of an "ignobler" world. The poem
thus deals with the death of the earlier and better world into
which Empedocles, like Arnold, had been born, and with the
consequences of its passage: Empedocles'—and Arnold's—
decision to lay aside the poet's robe because the "veils" of
modern doubt and introspection had destroyed the naive spontaneity of that earlier, happier life without providing any
equivalent joy or inspiration.

> We shut our eyes, and muse
> How our own minds are made,
> What springs of thought they use,
> How righten'd, how betray'd—
> And spend our wit to name what most employ unnamed.
>   [I, ii, 327–331]

The desire for escape from such a world, implicit in the
nostalgia of the narrators in "The Scholar-Gipsy" and "Stanzas
from the Grande Chartreuse," is fulfilled in Empedocles' sui-
cidal leap:

> ... and only death
> Can cut his oscillations short, and so
> Bring him to poise. There is no other way.
>
> [II, 232–234]

The simple, spontaneous Phrygian strains of Marsyas, the Byronic rebellion of Typho, and Empedocles' quest for love and fulfillment are each baffled and defeated in turn. To escape the hopeless nostalgia and the intellectual dialogue which make the modern world intolerable, the only alternative to self-destruction is the stoic doctrine, adopted by Pausanias, of self-knowledge and self-realization within the limits set by the narrower world of the present.

At the end of "Stanzas from the Grande Chartreuse" the speaker of that poem was confronted by the choice between death, a life of worldly action, and the lonely search for truth, whereas at the end of "Empedocles on Etna" the decision has been made: for Pausanias, a life of action in the world within the framework of a stoic morality grounded in resignation; for Empedocles, death. The prison of self-consciousness created by the "cunning" of the mind is in both cases escaped. When Empedocles told his disciple in the opening discourse in Act I that "mind is the spell which governs earth and heaven," Pausanias had replied in a statement whose truth is born out later by Empedocles' own arguments and action: "Mind is the light which the Gods mock us with,/To lead those false who trust it." Raised in a later world, Pausanias has no illusions and finds Empedocles' advice to "nurse no extravagant hope" acceptable. The true function of mind in the modern world, Arnold makes clear, is that assigned to it in the Pausanian view: not to penetrate the mystery of life but to see the limitations of the human condition and to compel the will to accept them as a basis for useful activity. The intellectual quest, as Empedocles discovered, leads only to a paralysis of indecision and the death of the heart; the will must therefore intervene either to send men back to the world of action, or, as in the case of Empedocles, to precipitate self-destruction.

But there is still Callicles, through whom Arnold objectifies the aesthetic consciousness itself. It is Callicles whose words open and close the poem, and who, in the myths of Cadmus-Harmonia, Zeus-Typho, and Apollo-Marsyas and again in the concluding lines implicitly identifies the poet's role with that of the bringer of joy, the artist who transmutes disaster into lovely music by the power of his lyre. Prior to Empedocles' appearance, Callicles had charged that the hero was "half mad," "too scornful, too high-wrought, too bitter"; he thereby prepares the reader for and helps to interpret the denouement:

> 'Tis not the times, 'tis not the sophists vex him;
> There is some root of suffering in himself,
> Some secret and unfollow'd vein of woe,
> Which makes the time look black and sad to him.
>
> [I, i, 150–153]

Although in the opening scene Pausanias patronizes Callicles, comparing him to the "new dancing-girl" whom the guests at the feast from which they have come were spoiling (I, 35), and later calling him "a boy whose tongue outruns his knowledge" (I, 161), it is the young poet who, throughout the poem, proves himself master of experience through the power of his art:

> The lyre's voice is lovely everywhere;
> In the court of Gods, in the city of men,
> And in the lonely rock-strewn mountain-glen,
> In the still mountain air.
>
> [II, 37–40]

Callicles thus represents the triumph of the poetic power over the inner world of human pain and suffering and the outer world of nature, converting both into beautiful things by the gift of his art. Only to Typho, the rebel against life, does the lyre sound hatefully (II, 41), his groans of rebellion "almost drown[ing]/The sweet notes whose lulling spell/Gods and the race of mortals love so well" (II, 64–66). Empedocles, in identifying with Typho in his rebellion against "the subtle, contriving head," likewise rejects the charm of the lyre and decides upon death.

In the light of what has already been said about Arnold's personal history and his other poems, "Empedocles on Etna" emerges as his most ambitious work, written in order to exorcise the Romantic demon which, with the passionate, unattainable, "youthful" longings that it awakened and that lay at the root of Arnold's restlessness and melancholy, possessed his muse. In the death of Empedocles, Arnold brings an end to these longings and to his intellectual search, and at the same time announces the creed of his own maturity:

> To see if we will poise our life at last,
> To see if we will not at last be true
> To our own only true, deep-buried selves
> Being one with which we are one with the world.
>
> [II, 369–372]

Arnold in the role of Empedocles obviously sees no hope of finding such poise in the stoic message that is passed on to Pausanias; the stoicism is a strategy that Arnold-Empedocles recommends for those who can accept it. Forced to choose between a stoic life of resignation and suicide, Arnold in real life chose resignation; Empedocles' suicide, as he later remarked, was not a course of action literally recommended in the poem. But there is another sense in which Arnold did not accept the Pausanian creed. Empedocles' suicide is symbolic of something which had happened to Arnold himself: he had buried his Romantic aspiration and with it his hope of attaining happiness in "a world he loves not" and in which he "must subsist in ceaseless opposition" (II, 267–268). Because his own emotional life was so deeply rooted in the earlier happy world of Typho, Marsyas, and the youthful Empedocles, his accept-ance of its passing compromised his effectiveness as a poet; henceforth, his aesthetic consciousness would express itself in Pausanian poems of morality or in criticism.[43]

Callicles—representing Arnold's aesthetic consciousness—witnesses this self-mutilating action on the lower slopes of Mount Etna, and by his songs attempts to incorporate Em-pedocles' suicide into the larger framework of the universal movement of life. But at the end of the poem he withdraws from the scene:

> Not here, O Apollo!
> Are haunts meet for thee.
> But, where Helicon breaks down
> In cliff to the sea.
>
> [II, 421–424]

Arnold's self-awareness and fidelity to his inner experience is remarkable; for Arnold the poet the lines are a courageous statement of defeat. To the Apollo described by Callicles, with his cruel, superhuman, Olympian superiority, just as to the Arnold who wrote the poem, such haunts of tragedy *are* meet. Just as Apollo had flayed poor Marsyas while Olympus stood by and wept, so Arnold the poet had disinterestedly converted the agony of Arnold the man into poetry. It is Callicles, not Apollo, who finds the Etna summit unfit for habitation. His attempt to console Empedocles is unsuccessful. The ending of the poem thus objectifies Arnold's aesthetic consciousness as it turns away from the intolerable burden of attempting to portray the agony of experience in the modern world and anticipates Arnold's own rejection of the poem. Although Callicles can enter into the life of nature and the world of ancient myth, he is unable to bring joy to Empedocles; he can neither relieve nor transmute his suffering. Thus the poem itself affirms what Arnold was later to say in his *Preface*: that the state of Empedocles is beyond poetic redemption, is inherently "unpoetical," and therefore is not a fit subject for poetry. In effect, Arnold the Romantic poet has dissociated Arnold the Romantic (Empedocles) from Arnold the poet (Callicles), and both of these from Arnold the moralist (Pausanias). Arnold is indeed "fragments."

When Apollo and his choir of Nine appear in the concluding tableau, Callicles reports what he hears:

> Whose praise do they mention?
> Of what is it told?—
> What will be forever;
> What was from of old.

> [II, 457–460]

Callicles thus "frames" the tragedy in poetry, but he does not enter into it. "Empedocles on Etna" embodies a paradox: it represents the momentary triumph of Arnold's poetic power over his modern self-consciousness in poetry which tells the story of the triumph of that self-consciousness over his muse. At the conclusion of the poem each of the three elements of Arnold's inner life has found its proper end: Empedocles—the symbol of his aspiring Romantic impulse—is "buried"; Pausanias—the kindly, practical stoic—goes into the city; Callicles —the aesthetic consciousness—remains apart, turning away at the end from the human tragedy to listen to the stories of the divine Apollo and the Graces. Arnold's aesthetic consciousness can no longer enter into the pain of Arnold the man, but it will at least honor the severe and god-like detachment of those artists who in the past had been able to make music out of their pain.

POEMS OF MORALITY

The third category of Arnold's poems, the poems of morality, consists for the most part of simple variations on the Pausanian morality presented in Act I of "Empedocles on Etna." In variety and scope they are the least impressive of the three categories into which Arnold's poetic "fragments" fall. The creed of stoic resignation proposed by Empedocles was not a creed to inspire poetry, but a stern ethical doctrine by which practical men could live in the kind of world which Empedocles finds unendurable. The structure of feeling characteristic of the poems of morality reflects the resignation, simple melancholy, and force of will implicit in such a position. Not only are nostalgia and the desire to escape absent, but the dialogue of the mind with itself has been brought to an end by acceptance of the conclusion that final insight into the meaning of life is beyond human powers. As a record of the third phase of Arnold's inner evolution, the poems of morality measure the extent of Arnold's loss and constitute a poetic commentary on the reply which he made in middle-age to a well-wisher who had complimented him on his youthful appearance: "I am all gray hairs within."[44]

His letters indicate that in the early fifties, convinced that the mind mocks man, that in intellect no final resting place could be found, on the contrary that the intellect discovers merely the perpetual flux of time and mirrors this flux in its own eternal restlessness, Arnold deliberately turned to character, to the "fixity" of the inward spiritual self. In an important letter to his sister "K," written in January, 1851, he describes his feelings toward this change in his outlook.

[It is] as if we could only acquire any solidity of shape and power of acting by narrowing and narrowing our sphere, and diminishing

the number of affections and interests which continually distract
us while young, and hold us unfixed and without energy to mark
our place in the world; which we thus succeed in marking only by
making it a very confined and joyless one. The aimless and unset-
tled, but also open and liberal state of our youth we *must* perhaps
all leave and take refuge in our morality and character; but with
most of us it is a melancholy passage from which we emerge shorn
of so many beams that we are almost tempted to quarrel with
the law of nature which imposes it on us. I feel this in my own
case. . . .[45]

The letter captures the tone as well as the substance of the
poems of morality as expressions of the terminal stage in Arnold's "melancholy passage" from the remembered joys of innocent childhood, through the excitements and hopes of youth
and its intellectual dialogue, to the cool and detached but narrow, joyless, and uninspiring stability of the mature man. In
their dull intensity, monotony, and narrowness of emotional
range, the poems which objectify this last stage approximate
to the more despondent dialogue poems, but they are qualified
by a force of will which distinguishes them from the latter.
At the end of the letter to his sister in which he laments the
passage of youth, Arnold recalls Thomas à Kempis' advice:
frequenter tibi ipsi violentiam fac; "so I intend not to give myself the rein in the following any natural tendency, but to make
war against it." The poems of morality have the authority of
this resolution, an authority painfully earned and sustained,
but they also reflect the bleakness of a moral experience which
lacked the faith to lighten the burden of the "unnatural" asceticism which it demanded.

The stark effect of the poems is due in part to Arnold's inability to invent an appropriate poetic landscape equivalent to
the pastoral slope of the nostalgia poems or to the burning
plain or stellar spaces of the dialogue poems; in general, the
"thought" of the poems unfolds either in the timeless and

spaceless center of the inner world of the will, or in historical
settings, as in "The Sick King in Bokhara," which have no
essential relation to the moral themes. But there is one persistent image in these poems, that of the moon-drenched scene
which serves as a psychological landscape in a way suggested
in a passage by Sainte-Beuve: "Being as I now am a purely
critical intelligence, I can stand by and sadly watch the death
of the heart. I judge myself and remain calm, cold, indifferent,
I am dead . . . what the world commonly calls the heart is
dead in me. Intelligence shines on this cemetery like a dead
moon."[46] In Arnold's poetry there is one important difference:
the moon is not a cold critical intelligence, but a palely warm
poetic imagination; and it shines not on a dead heart but, alternatively, on a heart "tossed" by passion or on a buried soul in
a state of passionless repose.

"Palladium" effectively exploits the burial image, in conjunction with the Troy-myth, to describe the psychological
state of mind of a speaker who has taken "refuge in morality
and character." Just as the Palladium, "high 'mid rock and
wood,"

> stood, and sun and moonshine rain'd their light
> On the pure columns of its glen-built hall
>
> [ll. 5–6]

while battle raged on the plain below

> So, in its lovely moonlight, lives the soul.
> Mountains surround it, and sweet virgin air;
> Cold plashing, past it, crystal waters roll;
> We visit it by moments, ah, too rare!
>
> [ll. 9–12]

The image that emerges is that of a mausoleum in a moon-lit
landscape, the "buried" soul dwelling in peace under the pale
light and the cool stone. The contrast between the moon-lit

world on mountain slopes and the hot noon of strife on the plain is repeated, in a slightly altered context, in "A Summer Night," which also records Arnold's movement from inner fluctuations to at least a tentative moral resolve. Walking in a "deserted, moon-blanch'd street," the speaker is reminded of another, similar night, one that was "far more fair," when

> the same restless pacings to and fro,
> And the same vainly throbbing heart was there,
> And the same bright, calm moon
> And the calm moonlight seems to say:
> *Has thou then still the old unquiet breast,*
> *Which neither deadens into rest,*
> *Nor ever feels the fiery glow*
> *That whirls the spirit from itself away,*
> *But fluctuates to and fro,*
> *Never by passion quite possess'd*
> *And never quite benumb'd by the world's sway?—*
> And I, I know not if to pray
> Still to be what I am, or yield and be
> Like all the other men I see.
>
> [ll. 23–36]

But the moral decision has, in fact, been made. The poem ends with a description of a world of "clear transparency," set apart alike from the "brazen prison" of the "slave" majority and the storm-tossed world of the "madman," in which the soul of the speaker proposes to dwell. "A Southern Night," an elegy on his brother in which Arnold refers to the earlier poem of similar title, expresses more decisively the end of youthful agitations in the more stable world of stoic endurance.

> Ah! such a night, so soft, so lone,   •
>   So moonlit, saw me once of yore
> Wander unquiet, and my own
>   Vext heart deplore.

> But now the trouble is forgot;
>> Thy memory, thy pain, to-night,
> My brother! and thine early lot,
>> Possesses me quite.

[ll. 13–20]

The association of the moon alternatively with death and peace operates powerfully in Arnold's poems of morality.

Two narrative poems, "Tristram and Iseult" and "The Church of Brou," likewise have a tomb, or a tomb-like tableau, bathed in moonlight as the central image. In the 1877 edition of his poems Arnold suppressed the two less successful parts of "The Church of Brou," leaving Part III to stand by itself under the title "A Tomb Among the Mountains." The concluding image is that of "Palladium," the moonlight "shedding her pensive light at intervals" (III, 35) upon the "marble Pair" who "sleep" upon "cold white marble beds" (III, 27). In "Tristram and Iseult" the dying lovers are portrayed in a similar image, that of a sculptured monument upon which "the moon shines bright" (II, 101), as the Huntsman on the arras that hangs above the bed watches,

> And to himself he seems to say:
> *"What place is this, and who are they?*
> *Who is that kneeling Lady fair?*
> *And on his pillows that pale Knight*
> *Who seems of marble on a tomb?"*

[II, 163–167]

The cluster of values carried by the image of moonlight—peace, stasis, calm—shifts elsewhere in the poem to the passionless, innocent world of childhood associated with Iseult of Brittany and her children:

> Sweet flower! thy children's eyes
> Are not more innocent than thine.

But they sleep in shelter'd rest,
Like helpless birds in the warm nest.

✻ ✻ ✻

Full on their window the moon's ray
Makes their chamber as bright as day.
It shines upon the blank white walls,
And on the snowy pillow falls,
And on two angel-heads doth play. . . .

[I, 325–328, 333–337]

Still another passage suggests "Dover Beach," in which innocent love, moonlight, the sea, and the darkling plain of life
merge. The narrator, commenting on Tristram's feverish recollection of his youthful days with his innocent bride, observes:

Ah! 'tis well he should retrace
His tranquil life in this lone place;
His gentle bearing at the side
Of his timid youthful bride;
His long rambles by the shore
On winter-evenings, when the roar
Of the near waves came, sadly grand,
Through the dark, up the drown'd sand. . . .

[I, 211–218]

These poems of morality, so far as they contain poetry at
all, retain a residual element of the old tension; nostalgia, or
its memory at least, is still present negatively, in the strength
of willed decision required to control it. The moral element in
this tension is strongest in a poem like "The Voice," in which
the nostalgia is expressed within the context of a moral resistance that weighs down and exhausts the speaker. Moonlight
again dominates the scene:

As the kindling glances,
Queen-like and clear,

> Which the bright moon lances
>> From her tranquil sphere
> At the sleepless waters
>> Of a lonely mere,
> On the wild whirling waves, mournfully, mournfully,
>> Shiver and die.

[ll. 1–8]

The complication represented by the "voice" is close to the objectless regret of, say, Tennyson's "Tears, Idle Tears," a sudden stirring in the depths of the soul for some nameless and unattainable good:

> So sad, and with so wild a start
> To this deep-sober'd heart,
> So anxiously and painfully,
> So drearily and doubtfully,
> And oh, with such intolerable change
> Of thought, such contrast strange,
> O unforgotten voice, thy accents come,
> Like wanderers from the world's extremity,
>> Unto their ancient home!

[ll. 23–31]

Whether the "voice" be interpreted as that of the sirens of Romanticism—of George Sand or Sénancour or Byron or Wordsworth—or the voice, perhaps of Marguerite, of a lost love, or possibly even the silvery tones of Newman preaching at St. Mary's, the sudden up-welling of the "melancholy tones" both fails to break through the persona's moral resolve and yet at the same time drains that resolve of all joy; the experience is compared to the hearing of "strains of glad music at a funeral."

> In vain, all, all in vain,
> They beat upon mine ear again,
> Those melancholy tones so sweet and still.

Those lute-like tones which in the bygone year
    Did steal into mine ear—
Blew such a thrilling summons to my will,
    Yet could not shake it;
Made my tost heart its very life-blood spill,
    Yet could not break it.
                  [ll. 32–40]

The remote and self-sufficient soul, the Palladium of the speaker's "buried" life, remains unmoved, but the speaker experiences profound melancholy rather than joy in the fact.

The necessity of a joyless resistance of the will to the instinctive yearnings of the heart expressed in "The Voice" was a theme which had been forming in Arnold's mind for almost ten years prior to the letter to "K," that is, approximately from the time of his father's death in 1842. In "Fragment of an 'Antigone'" the myths recounted by the Chorus support those gods and heroes who "prefer obedience to the primal law" to their personal "self-selected good" (ll. 28–33). In "The Sick King in Bokhara" the lesson of self-renouncement is even clearer. The Vizier warns the young King that his grief over the man the King has sentenced to death is not wise; pity, once yielded to, can find no end of causes and thus becomes an intolerable burden. But the King replies:

O Vizier, thou art old, I young!
Clear in these things I cannot see.
My heart is burning, and a heat
Is in my skin which angers me.

But hear ye this, ye sons of men!
They that bear rule, and are obey'd,
Unto a rule more strong than theirs
Are in their turn obedient made.
                [ll. 181–188]

The Vizier's argument is politically wise, but the King's moral commitment has been made: no man can with impunity violate the eternal moral law.

But it is "Resignation," the subject of which had been on Arnold's mind since 1843, and which, by virtue of its length and position as the concluding poem in the 1849 volume, constitutes the most elaborate counterpoint to the poems with which the volume opened. The bleak doctrine of the title defines Arnold's response to the frenzied cry of the Romantic imagination in "The Strayed Reveller," the unresolved dialogue of "Mycerinus," and the blank void at the end of "The New Sirens." The moral doctrine of struggle within self-imposed limits had not yet attained the clarity and relevance which it was to have in "Empedocles on Etna," but the dialogue between romantic faith and scepticism, with their corresponding moralities of aspiration and resignation, had progressed to the point where Arnold was able to make distinctions.

The first two sections of "Resignation" set up an antithesis between the worldly activists, "whom labours, self-ordain'd, enthrall," and those "milder natures" who, either by schooling or by birth "resign'd," are "freed from passions." The former miss the true aim of life, for neither self-ordained action nor self-ordained suffering is man's end:

> Though he move mountains, though his day
> Be pass'd on the proud heights of sway,
> Though he hath loosed a thousand chains,
> Though he hath borne immortal pains,
> Action and suffering though he know—
> He hath not liv'd, if he lives so.

> [ll. 148–153]

In some ways superior to the active life of power or the heroic suffering of rebellion, though still far from satisfactory, is the passive, wandering life of the gipsies, who at least "move," and "see" the world although they "feel not" (l. 205). As a

"migratory race," "rubbing" through each day in a hereditary
fashion, they represent mankind as a whole.

> For them, for all, time's busy touch,
> While it mends little, troubles much.
>
> [ll. 126–127]

Finally there is the Poet, to whom Fate imparts "a quicker
pulse" (l. 145). Like the Poet in *Wilhelm Meister*, Arnold's
Poet shares the joys and sorrows of mankind by vicarious par-
ticipation in that "general life" of the universe which unrolls
before his impersonal gaze (ll. 186–199). But when Fausta,
whom the speaker is addressing, expresses envy of "the poet's
rapt security" (l. 246), his capacity for deep feeling and the
wide view, the narrator replies that both human affection and
the universe itself are "wider made" than most realize and
that even the Poet must "see, and see dismay'd, / Beyond his
passion's widest range, / Far regions of eternal change" (ll.
220–222). Life is greater than anything man, even the poet,
can say or feel about it. The speaker therefore recommends
for those like "Fausta" and himself, whom Fate has grudged
the "rapt security" of the Poet, the resigning of "passionate
hopes" in favor of "quiet, and a fearless mind."

> . . . they, believe me, who await
> No gifts from chance, have conquer'd fate.
> They, winning room to see and hear,
> And to men's business not too near,
> Through clouds of individual strife
> Draw homewards to the general life.
>
> [ll. 247–252]

This doctrine, which anticipates Empedocles' advice to Pausanias, is taught by Nature herself, since turf, hills, stream,
rocks, and sky "Seem to bear rather than rejoice" (l. 270).
There is "something infects the world" (l. 278), and neither

man's prayers nor his activities can alter its effect upon the "general lot." Arnold's difficulties in writing the poem and the lapses, in the final version, into prosaic verse suggest that the dispiriting Pausanian creed was already undermining his poetic powers.

The 1852 volume elaborates more frequently and more explicitly on the moral theme than does the 1849 volume. The narrator in "Stanzas in Memory of the Author of 'Obermann'" takes up the distinction, referred to also by Empedocles in the same volume (II, 111–117), between a poetry that serves merely as a "drug" or "charm" for escaping life and a poetry that tells the truth.

> Some secrets may the poet tell,
> For the world loves new ways;
> To tell too deep ones is not well—
> It knows not what he says.
>
> [ll. 41–44]

Obermann's poetry (like Arnold's own "Empedocles on Etna") was "fraught too deep with pain" (l. 38) to make an impression on the world and his resentment of the world's indifference has driven him into retirement. The "two desires" which now toss "the poet's feverish blood," the desire for society and the desire for solitude (ll. 93–96), can be reconciled only by the poet's embracing the loneliness of watching the world, and sharing vicariously, not actively, in its life.

> He who hath watch'd, not shared, the strife,
> Knows how the day hath gone.
> He only lives with the world's life,
> Who hath renounced his own.
>
> [ll. 101–104]

But such solitude, as Empedocles was to discover, was unbearable, and the attempt to bear it is the source of Obermann's despair. For all the pain of isolation, however, the speaker of the poem has found life in the modern world to be "colder" even than the solitude of the votary of Apollo; hence he has fled to Obermann's forest in order to listen once again for the "accents of the eternal tongue" (l. 125) which occasionally reach the lonely contemplative. Up to this point (approximately three fourths of "Stanzas in Memory of the Author of 'Obermann'" belong in the dialogue category) the conflicting desires of the protagonist remain unresolved. Suddenly, however, the speaker rejects "dreams that but deceive" (ll. 129 ff.). Apologetically, he tells his "sad guide" that "some unknown Power" forces him to return to the world and to "leave / Half of my life with you"; but he promises that he will at least be loyal to the ideals of "that small transfigur'd Band" with whom his guide now dwells, those "Children of the Second Birth" who have kept themselves "Unspotted by the world" (ll. 130–156). The dialogue is thus resolved by a moral decision imposed by circumstances. Like Pausanias, unable to bear the hopeless Romantic longing for what cannot be that has broken his master—"O unstrung will! O broken heart!"—the speaker in "Obermann" returns to the world determined at least to be loyal to his unhappy master's memory, but leaving half his life behind him. As in "Resignation," Arnold sees a personal morality of purity and unworldliness as a way of living in the world while preserving an inward sanctuary of silent attachment to the deeper movement of life itself, as distinguished from the mere bustle of contemporary civilization. Arnold thus marks his own passage into the modern world, accepting what seems inescapable but retaining the lesson of resistance to that world in the name of a higher life yet to be realized.

Other poems in the 1852 volume express the same stoic morality more tersely. "Human Life" refers to the folly and danger, as "unknown Powers" drive men "across the sea of life by night," of living "chance's fool" and following random desires. "Morality" portrays Nature praising those who fulfill "through hours of gloom" the tasks "in hours of insight will'd" (ll. 5–6). In "Self-Dependence" a clearer version of the same "voice" is heard in answer to the speaker's prayer to the sea and stars: "Resolve to be thyself" (l. 31). In "Consolation" the speaker sees his "own happy / Unalloy'd moments," which he "would eternalize" if he could, as being capable of prolongation only at the cost of "distress elsewhere" (ll. 60–62), in a kind of cosmic balance of pain and pleasure imposed upon the Powers that regulate life. Finally, in "The Second Best," the speaker's "natural" craving for a life of moderation, both in work and leisure, in pain and pleasure, is portrayed as having been "strangled" by his sustained reading, scheming, and wishful thinking (ll. 5–12); "so it *must* be," the poem concludes, but there is still something to be learned in the process:

> Who through all he meets can steer him,
> Can reject what cannot clear him,
> Cling to what can truly cheer him;
>   Who each day more surely learns
>
> That an impulse, from the distance
> Of his deepest, best existence,
> To the words, "Hope, Light, Persistence,"
>   Strongly sets and truly burns.
>
> [ll. 17–24]

These lines might serve as the somewhat austere Exultet of Arnold's hard-won morality, a morality which he himself labels a second best but which took on, as Arnold grew older, some measure of hope.

It is difficult to avoid the conclusion that Arnold's poems of morality as a whole reflect the defeat of Arnold the poet. Both the pastoral loveliness created by a poetic impulse in the service of "rural Pan," and the rebellious, aspiring passion of Empedocles are absent, and Arnold is left with the relatively chilling code of a resigned detachment awaiting better times. The melancholy of these poems is at times extreme, as in "Growing Old," with its startling Tennysonian echo ("the years that are no more" [l. 20]). What is it to grow old?

> It is to spend long days
> And not once feel that we were ever young;
> It is to add, immured
> In the hot prison of the present, month
> To month with weary pain.
> It is to suffer this,
> And feel but half, and feebly, what we feel.
> Deep in our heart
> Festers the dull remembrance of a change,
> But no emotion—none.
>
> [ll. 21–30]

The fact that some of these poems were written by a young man in his mid- or late twenties is all the more disconcerting. Their "message" unquestionably reflects what Arnold himself came more and more to believe and what no doubt impressed readers of like mind; the quality of the life which they render reveals a pain as deep and as incurable as Sénancour's, one that at times turned into an icy despair.

The triumph of the ethical element in his make-up, upon which Arnold drew to combat his despair, fulfilled the prophetic lamentation of Empedocles that reality would "Knead us in its hot hand, and change our nature" (II, 386). However important, even central, Arnold's ethical code was in his mature life, the emotional frigidity which it induced proved uncongenial to his aesthetic temperament and belied the expectations of his youth. There was always the memory of that "different world" he had once known:

> The smallest thing could give us pleasure then—
> The sports of the country-people,
> A flute-note from the woods,
> Sunset over the sea—

["Empedocles," II, 250–253]

but, once he had become "thought's slave," such spontaneous and pleasurable apprehension of beauty became impossible. Arnold the moralist, like an Empedocles who "has outlived his prosperous days," "whose youth fell on a different world,"

> in a world he loves not, must subsist
> In ceaseless opposition, be the guard
> Of his own breast, fetter'd to what he guards,
> That the world win no mastery over him—
> Who has no friend, no fellow left, not one;
> Who has no minute's breathing space allow'd
> To nurse his swindling faculty of joy—
> Joy and the outward world must die to him,
> As they are dead to me.

[II, 267–275]

The morality was the result of a forced retreat into the second best of *Entsagen,* and it remained throughout Arnold's life essentially what it was at the beginning, a necessary strategy to keep the "world" at a distance in order to preserve, so far as he could, his deepest inner life.

What we have seen thus far of Arnold's poetry reveals a pattern of disintegration, centered in the failure of the aesthetic consciousness to define a viable place for itself in the world of passion, thought, and action in mid-nineteenth century England. This pattern is confirmed by Arnold's later poems. In the general body of Arnold's poetry the early poems are consistently superior to those which he wrote later: the early to the late sonnets, for example; and "Sohrab and Rustum," "Stanzas in Memory of the Author of 'Obermann',"

"The Scholar-Gipsy," and "Stanzas from the Grande Chartreuse," to their later counterparts, "Rugby Chapel," "Obermann Once More," "Thyrsis," and "Westminster Abbey." It is
true that a late poem like "Balder Dead" comes alive in its
occasional touches of un-Homeric pathos, the familiar Arnoldian myth of aspiration, struggle, early defeat, and resignation emerging through the disguise of the Eddic saga, and
the accents of Empedocles and of the speaker of the stanzas
on the Grande Chartreuse reappearing in the voice of the dead
Balder:

> For I am long since weary of your storm
> Of carnage, and find, Hermod, in your life
> Something too much of war and broils, which make
> Life one perpetual fight, a bath of blood.
> Mine eyes are dizzy with the arrowy hail;
> Mine ears are stunned with blows, and sick for calm.
> Inactive therefore let me lie, in gloom,
> Unarm'd, inglorious; I attend the course
> Of ages, and very late return to light,
> In time less alien to a spirit mild,
> In new-recover'd seats, the happier day.

> [III, 503–513]

The voice is that of a buried Empedocles, speaking from the
world of the dead. When Arnold made one final attempt to
write poetry according to the critical ideal he had learned
from Goethe and had defended in the 1853 *Preface,* he composed *Merope,* a poem described by Sainte-Beuve as learned
but dead.[47]

As a summary assessment of Arnold's achievement as a poet,
we might say that he wrote minor poetry of a high order when
he rendered his nostalgia or the inner dialogue of his mind,
and concede that even the more starkly despondent moral
poems have the authenticity of anguish felt and resisted. But

the unevenness and instability of his creative power were evident from the beginning; as thought increasingly dominated feeling, a recitative verse gradually replaced Arnold's lyrical utterance; and when moral exhortation took over, poetry disappeared completely.

CHAPTER FIVE

Meta-Poems

There remains a small group of poems which are particularly useful in establishing a connection between Arnold's poetry and the theme and motive of his criticism. Though related, these poems are of two distinct kinds: several reflect Arnold's increasing optimism—what an unsympathetic critic has called his "dawnism";[48] the others reflect Arnold's undiminished faith in the aesthetic consciousness which continued to control his basic responses and judgments after he had stopped composing poetry. On the one hand, the "dawnism" relates to the assumption behind his criticism that the times were bad but not incurable and if rightly managed promised a new and perhaps even brilliant epoch. The aestheticism, on the other hand, explains the basis of this hope and the central concern of the criticism: the new role to be played by poetry in this promising future.

Unable in his poetry to penetrate the mystery of the "far regions of eternal change," Arnold postulated a universal general life of perpetual movement which in his criticism turned out to be progressive. The sources of this progressivism appear in a remark to Clough in 1848: "What you say about France is just about the impression I get from the accounts of things there—it must be disheartening to the believers in progress—

or at least in any progress but progress *en ligne spirale* which Goethe allows man ... [and which] is exactly Wordsworth's account of the matter."[49] This qualified optimism can be traced in several poems in which the basic impulse is not resignation, but aspiration; their subject not the coldness of the present world, but the possible beauty of a future world; their theme not the virtue of moral strength in resistance, but calm hope of a wholeness and harmony anticipated. The ideal to be sought was rooted in Arnold's memory of his childhood experience and analogous to it, but this ideal transcended the remembered harmony in its comprehensiveness and the remembered joy in its universality.

The concluding stanzas of "The Buried Life" contain a dim intimation of such a fulfillment, but the affirmative note in that poem, as we have seen, is so tentative and ambiguous and the experience through which Arnold leads up to it is so desolate, that the work belongs rather among the dialogue poems. "Revolutions," in which the repeated failure of past ages to attain the final "word" is mentioned, is less tentative; while hope is not quite dominant in the concluding stanzas, the speaker's gaze at least is fixed upon the future.

> One day, thou say'st, there will at last appear
> The word, the order, which God meant should be.
> —Ah! we shall know *that* well when it comes near;
> The band will quit man's heart, he will breathe free.
>
> [ll. 17–20]

"The Future," which concluded the 1852, 1853, 1854, and 1857 editions of the poetry, is more positive still, explicitly distinguishing between "the calm" of the "early mountainous shore" where man took his origin (ll. 75–76) and the new "solemn peace" envisioned for the future (l. 77). Like man himself, the River of Time originates in the mountains, and is seen as having reached in the present a circuitous wandering course on "the plain" (l. 51), very similar to that through which the River Oxus passes in the coda of "Sohrab and Rustum." It is

> Border'd by cities and hoarse
> With a thousand cries is its stream.
> And we on its breast, our minds
> Are confused as the cries which we hear . . . .
>
> [ll. 53–56]

But "haply," the speaker goes on, while men now say that "repose has fled / For ever the course of the river of Time" (ll. 58–59), no one can know for certain what shall succeed, and it "may" be (l. 75) that the River will acquire a new peace.

> And the width of the waters, the hush
> Of the grey expanse where he floats,
> Freshening its current and spotted with foam
> As it draws to the Ocean, may strike
> Peace to the soul of man on its breast—
> As the pale waste widens around him,
> As the banks fade dimmer away,
> As the stars come out, and the night-wind
> Brings up the stream
> Murmurs and scents of the infinite sea.
>
> ["The Future," ll. 78–87][50]

Most hopeful and affirmative of all in its argument, however, is the late poem that concluded the 1867 volume, "Obermann Once More," in which, after the religious history of Western civilization and the personal histories of "Obermann" and the speaker are rehearsed, the "sad Guide" of the first Obermann poem ends with this advice to his erstwhile disciple:

> "What still of strength is left, employ
> That end to help attain:

> *One common wave of thought and joy*
> *Lifting mankind again!"*
>
> [ll. 321–324]

The poem concludes with an analogue from the natural order to the mood of quiet expectation which the poem attempts to objectify.

> And glorious there, without a sound,
> Across the glimmering lake,
> High in the Valais-depth profound,
> I saw the morning break.
>
> [ll. 345–348][51]

Unique among Arnold's poems in its affirmative thrust—what "strength is left" to the speaker now emerges as a mere personal circumstance in the universal aspiration toward life and joy—"Obermann Once More" sets both Obermann's and the speaker's personal desolation in a larger perspective. Cleared of the dead-weight and hollow formalities of the old order by the French Revolution, the Europe of 1865 is seen as comparable to the Roman Empire of the fourth century on the verge of being renewed by the advent of Christianity.

On what basis and by what means was mankind to be lifted to new heights of thought and joy? The answer to this question is best sought in Arnold's prose, but "Obermann Once More" makes it clear that the renewal was not to come through a return to the Christian faith of the fourth century. Christ is dead, Obermann declares, and

> "In vain men still, with hoping new,
> Regard his death-place dumb,
> And say the stone is not yet to,
> And wait for words to come."
>
> [ll. 177–180]

Rather, as a transfigured Obermann tells his eager disciple,

> *"Unduped of fancy, henceforth man*
> *Must labour!—must resign*
> *His all too human creeds, and scan*
> *Simply the way divine!*

[ll. 185-188]

What is meant here Arnold later spelt out in considerable detail in his criticism, but the seminal idea of his criticism was already present in the other type of poem, which lies outside the general framework we have so far used in analyzing Arnold's "movement of mind," namely, poems which reflect on the nature of poetry itself.

The nucleus of Arnold's theory of poetry was contained in his remark to Clough on poetry's need to become a *magister vitae,* but Arnold's own poetry was, on the whole, a melancholy expression of the aesthetic consciousness at bay, increasingly weighed down and wearied by the intellectual and moral dialogue which attended the "melancholy passage" from nostalgia for the old to acceptance of the new world. Although he found, or said that he had found, a paradigm in Nature of that true harmony, wholeness, and activity which he craved, the claim is too often merely verbalized instead of realized in his poetry and too inconsistent with what he says of Nature elsewhere, to be altogether convincing.[52] But what he wanted to find in Nature, Arnold certainly found in poetry itself, in the poetry of Sophocles, for example,

> whose even-balanc'd soul
> From first youth tested up to extreme old age,
> Business could not make dull, nor Passion wild:
> Who saw life steadily, and saw it whole,

["To a Friend," ll. 9-12]

or of Shakespeare:

who didst the stars and sunbeam know
Self-school'd, self-scann'd, self-honour'd, self-secure.
["Shakespeare," ll. 9–10]

Sophocles and Shakespeare served Arnold as pre-eminent types of the poet, whom he described in "Resignation" as one who

sees life unroll,
A placid and continuous whole—
That general life, which does not cease,
Whose secret is not joy, but peace.
[ll. 189–192][53]

So far as Arnold could finally look to the future with some measure of hope, he was enabled to do so by his instinctive love of "the truth and beauty of things which make the Greek, the artist," and among artists the poet stood supreme. What distinguishes his criticism from that of his contemporaries is not his "dawnism," which was widespread at the time, but the means by which Arnold thought man would find happiness. Although the sources of his poetry ran dry, he neither rejected his early ideal of poetry nor abandoned the aesthetic temperament which he had assiduously cultivated throughout his formative years. What might be called Arnold's meta-poems are concerned with the nature of poetry as the highest manifestation of this temperament.

The group includes five poems: "The Strayed Reveller," the title-poem of the first volume of poetry in 1849; "The New Sirens," which carried the subtitle "A Palinode" in the first volume and again in the 1876 edition; "Resignation," which concluded the 1849 volume; "Memorial Verses," which first appeared separately in a magazine in 1850; and "Epilogue to Lessing's Laocoön," which did not appear until 1867.

The importance of "The Strayed Reveller" is indicated by the honor Arnold accorded it in making it the title-poem in his first volume. The bulk of the poem consists of the words which the Reveller of the title, who is seated on the portico of Circe's palace, addresses to Ulysses, a figure of heroic action. The youth's "sweet voice" has prompted Ulysses to ask him whether he is not a follower of "some divine bard," and the Strayed Reveller, in reply, dilates at some length on two themes: the gods, who are happy because they can witness the whole of life in calm detachment, without pain (ll. 130–206), and the "wise bards" who likewise attend the spectacle of life and who sing of it, but with "oh, what labour! / O prince, what pain!" (ll. 209–211). The poem thus presents two modes of existence: the detached Olympian mode of the gods, and the empathetic, involved mode of the Romantic bards, whose pain is the "price / The Gods exact for song: / To become what we sing" (ll. 232–234). The youthful Reveller explains that the wine of Circe which he is drinking enables him to have something of the divine vision without the human pain (ll. 270 ff.), and the poem concludes with his plea for more wine. The poem thus portrays Arnold's predicament as a poet aspiring to the total vision of the Olympians but fearful of the inevitable pain to mere men entailed by such a vision, a pain which includes the loss of personal identity.

It is as a palinode to "The Strayed Reveller" that "The New Sirens," which Arnold described to Clough as a "mumble,"[54] becomes intelligible. The poetic doctrine that it expresses is a retraction of the view expressed in the former poem. The persona's rejection of the New Sirens of Romantic love (as opposed to the old, pagan Sirens of sensual love) is, in effect, a rejection of the Keatsian poetic of empathetic identification in favor of a less illusory, if no less painful, acceptance of the truth. To the question

> Yet, indeed, this flux of guesses—
> Mad delight, and frozen calms—

> Mirth to-day and vine-bound tresses,
> And to-morrow—folded palms;
> Is this all? this balanced measure?
>
> [ll. 195–199]

the persona adds yet another question:

> Can your eyes, while fools are dozing,
> Drop, with mine, adown life's latter days?
>
> [ll. 209–210]

The speaker, however, is less sure of himself than the question implies:

> Shall you find the radiant lover,
> Even by moments, of to-day?
> The eye wanders, faith is failing—
> O, loose hands, and let it be!
>
> [ll. 221–224]

The poem wavers between identifying the rejection of the Romantic Sirens with, on the one hand, a gain in wisdom and, on the other, a loss of faith and love. In either case, the evasion carried out on Circe's portico is over:

> Long we wander'd with you, feeding
> Our rapt souls on your replies,
> In a wistful silence reading
> All the meaning of your eyes.
> By moss-border'd statues sitting,
> By well-heads, in summer days.
>   But we turn, our eyes are flitting—
> See, the white east, and the morning rays!
>
> [ll. 235–242]

The elegiac note dominates, the dawning is "unlovely," and the speaker is both confused and depressed:

> —Shall I seek, that I may scorn her,
> Her I loved at eventide?

> Shall I ask, what faded mourner
> Stands, at daybreak, weeping by my side?
>
> [ll. 271–274]

Only in the fifth, tenth, and eleventh stanzas is there a hint of the resolution which Arnold expounded to Fausta in "Resignation," the concluding poem in the 1849 volume.

"Resignation" was discussed earlier as a poetic statement of Arnold's decision to retreat into morality and character. What is of interest in the present context is the theory of poetry offered both in this poem and in "Memorial Verses." The theory is Goethe's rather than Keats's, and it describes a poetic of Olympian ("classical") detachment rather than of Romantic empathy and identification.

> The poet, to whose mighty heart
> Heaven doth a quicker pulse impart,
> Subdues that energy to scan
> Not his own course, but that of man.
>
> ["Resignation," ll. 144–147]

> ❋   ❋   ❋

> He sees the gentle stir of birth
> When morning purifies the earth;
> He leans upon the gate and sees
> The pastures, and the quiet trees.
>
> [ll. 170–173]

> ❋   ❋   ❋

> Lean'd on his gate, he gazes—tears
> Are in his eyes, and in his ears
> The murmur of a thousand years.
> Before him he sees life unroll,
> A placid and continuous whole—
>
> [ll. 186–190]

> ❋   ❋   ❋

Breathes, when he will, immortal air,
Where Orpheus and where Homer are.

[ll. 207–208]

Fausta, whose name suggests a restless energy which recognizes no limits, is warned by the speaker that it is only through the detachment exemplified in the great poets that men and women can hope to attain union with the general life. As children of the Second Birth who have died to themselves, the poets can contemplate the spectacle of life disinterestedly; and if Fausta and the speaker lack the special gift of the poet's rapt security, they can at least follow his example by dying to their fruitless yearning.

"Memorial Verses," which appeared in the following year and contained Arnold's first piece of extended literary criticism, reaffirms this classical poetic. It places Byron among those who have enacted in their writings the strife "of passion with eternal law" (l. 10), but who have "taught us little" (l. 8); it associates Wordsworth with Orpheus, a poet of nature who captured "the freshness of the early world" (ll. 38, 57); but it identifies Goethe, "Europe's sagest head" (l. 16), with those whose Olympian detachment enabled them to master the tumult and pain of life in art.

> He look'd on Europe's dying hour
> Of fitful dream and feverish power;
> His eye plunged down the weltering strife,
> The turmoil of expiring life—
> He said: *The end is everywhere,*
> *Art still has truth, take refuge there!*

[ll. 23–28]

Fifteen years later in "Epilogue to Lessing's Laocoön," poetry is again defined, in terms taken now from the *Laocoön,* both as a refuge from "the weltering strife" and as a vehicle of the highest truth. The speaker, addressing himself to the question raised by his companion in their discussion of Lessing's book—

> Why music and the other arts
> Oftener perform aright their parts
> Than poetry?

[ll. 9–11]

replies: because very few poets are sufficiently endowed to be
able to attend the "bright movement" of life as a whole (l. 191)
and at the same time, like the painter, to capture "in one
aspect" the "outward semblance" of things (ll. 56–57) and,
like the musician, to tap "some source of feeling" and inward
"passion" (ll. 82–83). In addition to this, he must be able to
discern

> The thread which binds it all in one,
> And not its separate parts alone.

[ll. 141–142]

The few poets who have done this (Homer and Shakespeare
are named) are true revealers; their work is a source of perpetual joy and a measure of life itself.[55]

The poetic defined in these latter poems attest to the validity
of describing the consciousness behind Arnold's criticism, and
the attitudes which inform it, as "aesthetic." This consciousness not only expressed itself spontaneously in verse but reflected an ideal of balance amidst tension, a reconciliation of
opposites through the fusion of imposed order, which takes
poetry as its model. Since there was no other "revelation" by
which modern man could live the full life, Arnold, when he
discovered that his own Muse could not sustain the Olympian
detachment required of the greatest poets, turned to prose in
order to explain the wholeness which he could not attain.
Arnold knew what he wanted, a Goethean harmony and power
in expressing the complex sensibility of an advanced, highly
civilized, post-Romantic "modern" culture. Unable in his early

years to realize this ideal either in his inner life or in his poetry, he accepted out of necessity what seemed to him the next best life and turned to prose in order to preach what he could not practice: the union of imagination and reason in an inward "culture" which found its supreme expression in the creative poetic act. As the next four chapters attempt to show, the main burden of Arnold's criticism is not a particular intellectual or moral gospel, but the exhibition and defense of this poetic temper and attitude. Whatever the ostensible topic or occasion, Arnold's criticism is consistently preoccupied with the nature and effects of the operation of the aesthetic consciousness, with explaining how art still had truth, and why modern man could find refuge there, indeed, could find in the best poetry a new religion.

CRITICISM: IMAGINATION, THE SOUL OF INTELLIGENCE

INTRODUCTION

I N S O F A R as Arnold's instinctive desire to make poetry out of his unsettling experiences furnished the unifying element in his movement from nostalgia, through dialogue, to resignation, his early career closely resembled that of Maurice de Guérin, to whom he later devoted an important essay. In spite of Guérin's "inner vicissitudes," Arnold wrote, few natures revealed "such essential consistency." "He says of himself, in the very beginning of his journal: 'I owe everything to poetry, for there is no other name to give to the sum total of my thoughts; I owe to it whatever I now have pure, lofty, and solid in my soul; I owe to it all my consolations in the past; I shall probably owe to it my future.' Poetry, the poetical instinct, was indeed the basis of his nature."[1] Unlike Guérin, however, whose wanderings were cut short by an early death, Arnold survived to find that the "effort to unite matter" in poetic composition was too painful to be sustained. Moreover, he was increasingly depressed by a feeling of "real humiliation" when he thought how little of what he had written was "calculated to give, to readers unacquainted with the great creations of classical antiquity, any adequate impression of their form or of their spirit."[2] Despite the pressures which eventually led to his abandoning poetry, however, and despite the subsequent vicissitudes of his long career as school inspector and critic, Arnold's poetic instinct remained the basis of his work, qualifying everything that he wrote and providing the consolation of his later years as it had of his youth.

The general course of Arnold's transition from poetry to criticism, whatever inner complications it may have involved, was simple enough. Once he had come to recognize the discrepancy between his actual fragmentation and melancholy and the poetic ideal which he had acquired from his readings, he made several attempts in the mid-fifties to write poems that would better illustrate the qualities of "Greek" poetry which he constantly had in mind. When this attempt failed, notably in *Merope,* he turned from poetry and began to explore the sources of failure in himself and in his environment to see if he might discover a remedy.[3] The consequence of this exploration was a fundamental change in his attitude towards his age; at the same time, it left his commitment to poetry essentially unimpaired.[4]

The letters to Clough show that until he was almost thirty Arnold had resisted with such resources as he could muster what he felt to be the alien pressures of his age. In 1848 this resistance threatened to lead to a complete break with his immediate circle of friends: "better that," he told Clough in later reporting his feelings at the time, "than be sucked for an hour even into the Time Stream in which they and [you] plunge and bellow"; for consolation, Arnold wrote, "I took up Obermann, and refuged myself with him in his forest against your Zeitgeist."[5] By the mid-fifties, however, the fateful decision to enter the Zeitgeist had been made; as a critic Arnold not only accepted the intellectual assumptions of his age as prerequisite for genuinely modern poetry, but, more hopefully, began to see in the modern "dialogue of the mind with itself" an instrument for persuading contemporary English society that there was a way out of the vulgarity, caprice, and confusion that threatened to overwhelm it. Unlike the early letters, in which he warned Clough that it was better to do and be nothing than to engage in philistercy, that the atmosphere of the present was like that in the age of Rome's decline, the later letters and the criticism were firmly set against "quietism," "a doctrine with a certain attraction for all noble natures," Arnold wrote in 1863, "but, in the modern world at any rate, incurably sterile."[6] This change in attitude first found public expression in Arnold's inaugural lecture of 1857, in which he censured Lucretius for having withdrawn from the world into sullen solitude: "how," Arnold asked, "can a man adequately interpret the activity of his age when he is not in sympathy with it?"[7] The desire to understand his age so that he might "interpret" it involved a fundamental reorientation in outlook of the kind described by Joubert, in a passage which Arnold cited with approval, concerning "the contrasting direction taken by the aspirations of the community in ancient and in modern states." "The ancients said *our forefathers,* we say *posterity*: we do not, like them, love our *patria,* that is to say, the country and the laws of our fathers, rather we love the laws and the country of our children; the charm we are most sensible to is the charm of the future, and not the charm of the past."[8]

But Arnold's *rapprochement* with the nineteenth-century Zeitgeist was only partial. The unifying theme of his criticism, implicit in his poetry in the words attributed to Goethe, "Art still has truth, take refuge there," reappeared in 1853 in a letter to Clough: "Stick to literature—it is the great comforter after all,"[9] and again, towards the end of his life, in his use of Guérin's term to answer the question of what made poetry a more important aid to the human spirit than art or science or philosophy or even religion: its "solidity."[10] Not only did images and themes carry over from the poetry into the prose, but the pattern of interrelationships established in "Empedocles on Etna" between the intellectual, ethical, and aesthetic consciousness of modern man remained intact. The intellectual dialogue experienced by Empedocles in Arnold's major poem operates in his prose as the same open-ended dialectic that leads, if unchecked, to loss of spontaneity and the "death" of the capacity to feel; similarly, the moral code of stoic endurance and the practical activity urged upon Pausanias serves in the criticism as a necessary but uninspiring discipline adopted to withstand uncongenial circumstances; and, finally, underlying both elements there is the controlling aesthetic consciousness, for which Callicles had been spokesman in the poem, which emerges in the prose as the one power capable of assimilating and surmounting both the intellectual dialogue and the austere morality of resignation in a vision of wholeness, order, and beauty to which Arnold's temperament and aesthetic education had early and permanently committed him. The spiritual *patria* of the criticism is Periclean Athens as conceived by the poetic imagination; the proposed England of the future is a projection into the future of the image of this idealized moment from the past.

The note of hope that characterizes Arnold's prose was thus produced by an inversion of the nostalgia that had inspired much of his poetry and was emotionally akin to it; the longings formerly attached to an irrecoverable past simply transferred themselves to an unattainable future. This explains why, beneath a newly acquired optimism, there persisted a deep vein of melancholy, noticed by Henry James, which gives to many of Arnold's better-known critical passages the peculiarly threnodic tone that had tinged his poetry.[11] The Periclean Greece of the criticism, like the Cumnor country and the green, happy places of childhood evoked in the poetry, provided Arnold with an ideal standard that embodied in the "unpoetical" world of mid-Victorian England those values which could satisfy his aesthetic instinct and needs.

A passage in Arnold's review of Curtius' *History of Greece* defines the objectives of his criticism and reveals its essential consistency with the theme and mood of the poetry. Writing in the midst of his religious campaign in the seventies, he particularly recommended to his readers Curtius' pages on Euripides, in which the Greek dramatist was described as "a lifelong sufferer from the unsolved conflict between speculation and art," a conflict that "possessed without satisfying him."[12] Arnold possessed the "quick sensibility," the "brilliant gift of finding the right word," and an "accurate knowledge of all the impulses moving his generation" which he found attributed to Euripides in Curtius' book. That these gifts had produced a similar conflict in himself is evident in his writings from the early letters to Clough down to the late·essay on "Literature and Science."[13] For this reason Curtius' remark (which Arnold cites in his review) that Euripides had managed under these trying circumstances to employ the "sophistry" of his generation "in order to bestow a new interest upon art"[14] provides an important clue to Arnold's critical method and objectives. Like Euripides, Arnold hoped to exploit the modern dialogue of the mind with itself, which possessed men without satisfying them, in order to establish a new role for poetry.

Significantly, in establishing this new role for poetry, Arnold identified the "intellectual deliverance" which was the announced intention of his criticism not with nineteenth-century positivist or idealistic philosophies, but with "Greek thought,"[15] and the lectures on Homer make it clear that, for Arnold, "Greek thought" meant not Thucydides, Plato, and Aristotle, but Homer, Pindar, and Sophocles—in short, Greek poetry. Religion and philosophy as England and Europe had known and practiced them would, in other words, have to make conditions with what Arnold conceived to be the "Greek" idea of poetry as a complete *magister vitae*. The audience for which he wrote, as well as the message he wished to deliver, pre-vented Arnold from stating his position aggressively and boldly, but the direction in which the "main movement of mind" led him in his criticism is unmistakable. The era of the teacher Jesus, he wrote, "was the hour of the religious sense of the East; but the hour of the thought of the West, of Greek thought, was also to come." And Arnold concluded "now is the hour of the West."[16]

The new relevance of poetry was dictated by the nature of the "unsolved conflict" which Arnold had diagnosed as early as 1848 when he told Clough that the English suffered from an inability either to follow "logical absolute reason" as the French did, or to sink themselves in the "solid" ground of their "individuality as spiritual, poetic, profound persons."[17] One need not read deeply in the criticism to discover that the "thought of the West" which Arnold brought to bear upon "the religious sense of the East," more particularly upon Christianity, operates in his critical argument as a very complex and sometimes ambiguous element. The complexity is especially evident in the rhetorical manipulation of the term "reason," which serves in Arnold's critical vocabulary as a protean term capable of widening or contracting to meet the *ad hoc* demands of argument and audience. The purpose of the following chapters is to show, through a close study of the interrelationships which obtain in Arnold's criticism between the analytic reason of science, the dialectical reason of modern philosophy, the moral reason of conscience, and the imaginative reason of poetry, how Arnold's instinctive attraction to "Greece," that is, to Greek poetry, gave consistency and weight to his prose and determined its central theme. For in spite of the large concessions which he was prepared to make both to the religious sense of the East represented by traditional Christianity and to the new thought of the West represented by modern empiricism and dialectical idealism, the overall objective of his criticism was to establish the primacy of the aesthetic over both the scientific and the ethical consciousness, and thereby to establish, as he hoped, a new "spiritual, poetic, profound" basis for modern civilization in poetry itself.

CHAPTER SIX

Pure Reason: Analytic
and Dialectic

The "logical absolute reason" to which Arnold referred in his letter to Clough served as the "pure" reason of his epistemology —intelligence functioning in a context uncomplicated by demands of the heart or the extenuating conditions of action. In this sense, reason had for Arnold two separate meanings which he did not take pains to distinguish clearly but whose relationship is important to an understanding of his argument.

In its first and less important meaning, "reason" appears in its orthodox eighteenth-century sense: as an instrument, based upon the model of Newtonian science, for breaking down phenomena into their irreducible elements. Arnold's respect for rational analysis in this eighteenth-century sense, and for its achievements in the natural sciences, was both genuine and persistent. In his late "Liverpool Address" he referred to his early encounter with analytic reason; he had once "had thoughts of studying medicine," he wrote, and he had been deeply impressed at the time by a remark made by Sir Ashley Cooper, the noted physician, to a student: "That, sir, is the way to learn your business; *look for yourself,* never mind what other people may say; no opinion or theories can interfere with information acquired from dissection."[18]

The concept of reason implicit in this advice appears in "The

Function of Criticism at the Present Time," in which Arnold contrasts the rational process of "analysis and discovery" with the quite different "creative" (but equally rational) process of "synthesis and exposition."[19] This association of the rational process with "discovery," a commonplace of the age, explains Arnold's frequent linking of truth with novelty; "true" and "profound" ideas tend to be equated in his criticism with ideas that are "new" and "fresh."[20] The lectures on Celtic literature describe the *science des origines* as lying "at the bottom of all real knowledge of the actual world,"[21] and in a late work, *God and the Bible,* he presented science as the one avenue to knowing the "real constitution of things."[22] Despite his respect for science and the analytical method, however, Arnold had little to say about them, and in his own analyses he made no pretension to scientific exactitude or thoroughness.[23] Arnold assumed the validity of scientific knowledge but was not interested in it.

This indifference had its roots deep in Arnold's poetic temperament. In the essay on Maurice de Guérin there is a description of the difference between the aesthetic and the scientific response to the world of physical objects which reveals this temperamental bias. "The interpretations of science," Arnold wrote, "do not give us [an] intimate sense of objects as the interpretations of poetry give it; they appeal to a limited faculty, and not to the whole man. It is not Linnaeus or Cavendish or Cuvier who gives us the true sense of animals, or water, or plants, who seizes their secret for us, who makes us participate in their life, it is Shakspeare . . . it is Wordsworth . . . it is Keats. . . ."[24] Arnold's implicit appeal to poetry and to the criterion of the "whole man" established the limitations of scientific reason by contrasting it with poetic, or as he called it, imaginative reason. It was on the basis of this contrast that he regarded as a serious error the tendency of his age to view the scientific consciousness as the highest mode of organizing experience. Where the scientific temperament was content to stay in its proper sphere, Arnold was convinced that its results were good; but where it was not so confined, as in a Faraday, it led to a fatal misreading and diminishing of life.[25]

Arnold did detect in analytic science, however, particularly in its constant accumulation of fresh knowledge, evidence for "the human spirit's general advance."[26] In this respect his prose reflects the nineteenth-century tendency to question, on the very basis of the new evidence always accruing, the Enlightenment's faith in the finality of discoveries made by analytical reason. The fixed reason and stable world of eighteenth-century science and philosophy had already shown signs at the end of the eighteenth century of giving way to a new concentration on process, a change which was evident in the writings of critics whom Arnold admired. Lessing, according to one historian, signalled a turning point in European intellectual history by replacing "analytical reason with synthetic reason, and static reason with dynamic reason";[27] Goethe himself, whom Arnold quotes, had written that "religion itself, like time, like life and knowledge, is engaged in a constant process of advance and evolution."[28] Consciousness of change and of the historical process was also available to Arnold in the writings of Coleridge, Carlyle, and Dr. Arnold.[29] In presenting culture itself as a process—"It is in making endless additions to itself, in the endless expansion of its powers, in endless growth in wisdom and beauty, that the spirit of the human race finds its ideal"[30]—Arnold simply incorporated into his criticism the nineteenth-century *Historismus* which had grown out of the general shift of attention at the beginning of the century away from the atomistic structure to the "dynamic" origin of things. Arnold could therefore argue that the "technical" conclusions of science had ultimately to be assimilated into a philosophical view capable of putting them into some perspective and thereby establishing their significance; philosophical ideas, in turn, which "come originally from the sphere of pure thought," were themselves "put into circulation by the spirit of the time."[31] Hence all knowledge was "relative." Arnold praised Heine precisely because the latter could treat a wide variety of figures from the past without ever attempting "to be *hubsch objectiv*, 'beautifully objective,' to become in spirit an old Egyptian, or an old Hebrew, or a Middle-Age knight, or a Spanish adventurer, or an English royalist; he always remains Heinrich Heine, a son of the nineteenth century."[32] This historicization of thought lay behind the second and more important meaning which Arnold attached to reason —as a dialectical instrument constantly expanding man's range of awareness.

As a dialectical instrument participating in as well as reflecting the "movement of mind" that characterized man's intellectual history, pure reason seemed to Arnold to be a constructive as well as a "dissolving" force. The "dissolving" effect was described in the essay on Heine. When a "modern" spirit was told "a thing must be so," that "there is immense authority and custom in favour of its being so, it has been held to be so for a thousand years, he answers with Olympian politeness"—asking Goethe's question—"But *is* it so? is it so to *me?*" "Nothing," Arnold observed, "could be more really subversive of the foundations on which the old European order rested."[33] The effects of this attitude in the intellectual order were manifest in the consequences which it entailed in the spheres of theology and politics. In his religious criticism Arnold rejected not only the traditional arguments from Design and First Cause but those from analogy and probability as well. The latter arguments had been advanced by religious thinkers, such as Butler and Newman, whom Arnold deeply respected, and he displayed greater patience in handling them than in treating philosophers, but this deference did not affect his essential judgment on the lack of cogency in their reason-

ings. Scrupulously refraining from direct attacks upon Newman's reputation and writings, Arnold nevertheless dismissed
Newman's religious solution as impossible; similarly, he judged
Bishop Butler's argument in support of the immortality of the
soul as simply unproven. "The positive existence of the world
to come must be proved, like the positive existence of the
present world, by *experience*," but "we have no experience of
a further different state beyond the limits of this life."[34] Again,
he described Butler's (and, by inference, Newman's) reliance
on "probability" as "vain and dangerous,"[35] and rejected the
attempt to establish by analogy a connection between moral
laws in this world and moral laws in a next on the grounds
that what had been assumed was precisely what required
proof. As for the argument from design, which Butler shared
with the Deists, Arnold commented that we are "in full metaphysics."[36]

Although the modern dialectic manifested itself in a nega-
tive, "dissolving" function, it had a positive liberating function
as well, not only politically, as in the French Revolution, but
also morally. In "The Literary Influence of Academies," when
contrasting Addison and Joubert as moralists, Arnold cited
Addison's remarks on the dangers to "fixedness in religious
faith" that resulted from a too free indulgence in speculation:
"Those who delight in reading books of controversy do very
seldom arrive at a fixed and settled habit of faith. The doubt
which was laid revives again, and shows itself in new difficulties; and that generally for this reason,—because the mind,
which is perpetually tossed in controversies and disputes, is
apt to forget the reasons which had once set it at rest, and to
be disquieted with any former perplexity when it appears in a
new shape, or is started by a different hand." Arnold cited the
passage in order to point out the obsoleteness of the point of
view which it expressed.

It may be said, that is classical English, perfect in lucidity, measure, and propriety. I make no objection; but, in my turn, I say that the idea expressed is perfectly trite and barren, and that it is a note of provinciality in Addison, in a man whom a nation puts forward as one of its great moralists, to have no profounder and more striking idea to produce on this great subject. Compare, on the same subject, these words of a moralist really of the first order, really at the centre by his ideas,—Joubert:—

"*L'expérience de beaucoup d'opinions donne à l'esprit beaucoup de flexibilité et l'affermit dans celles qu'il croit les meilleures.*"

With what a flash of light that touches the subject! how it sets us thinking! what a genuine contribution to moral science it is![37]

Arnold thus saw the highest fruits of the intellectual life not in certain knowledge based upon logical reasoning, but in that "experience" of a wide variety of "opinions" which liberated men from a false "fixity." The "flexibility, *ondoyant et divers,*" characteristic of the modern mind constituted the latter's superiority to an Addisonian "fixity" in ideas, and Arnold invoked it against all philosophical and theological fixities—whether Benthamite or Comtist or Christian—in the name of the higher ideal of dialectical open-endedness. Only in a completely free "play" of the mind could the modern thinker have that sense of "creativity" which, if different from and inferior to the creativity of the poet, nevertheless had its own compensations, Arnold believed, in providing an intellectual deliverance from "systems" and from the more chilling conclusions of modern science.

Yet even as a dialectical instrument, reason for Arnold was limited; although it liberated man from provincial ignorance, the dialectical process was itself inconclusive. When a great philosopher came upon a new, striking, and profound idea, "true" for the age in which he lived or even for aftertimes, this idea too was doomed to give way to still other, "truer"

ideas. As a subscriber to this view Arnold necessarily confined his category of "best ideas" to those which were "current
at the time," and it was for the same reason that "criticism"
appears in his work as a rational effort always "tending"—a
frequent and revealing term—"to establish an order of ideas,
if not absolutely true, yet true by comparison with that which
it displaces."[38] So far as they entered into and were conditioned
by the historical process, the conclusions of dialectical reason,
like those of analytic reason, were subject to the law of ob-
solescence. Popular responses to the speculations of philosophers "change very fast," Arnold told Clough in 1848, citing
for his friend's edification the remark of the Frenchman who
had observed, "oh . . . Comte—Comte has been quite passé
these 10 years."[39] A later reference to Positivism and to systematic philosophy generally in *Culture and Anarchy* viewed
the relationship between philosophy and "culture" from the
same dialectical point of view.

Culture is always assigning to system-makers and systems a smaller
share in the bent of human destiny than their friends like. A current
in people's minds sets towards new ideas; people are dissatisfied
with their old narrow stock of . . . ideas . . . , and some man, some
Bentham or Comte, who has the real merit of having early and
strongly felt and helped the new current, but who brings plenty
of narrowness and mistakes of his own into his feeling and help
of it, is credited with being the author of the whole current. . . . [40]

In conceiving the life of reason as "an eternal series of intellectual acts,"[41] Arnold saw the intellect in its higher function
as simply a faithful mirror of an endless becoming, which he
had extended in his poetry to the "far regions of eternal
change." Hegel was the significant philosophical figure of the
century because, Arnold wrote, he had seized Heraclitus' single
pregnant sentence and cast it "with a thousand striking applications, into the world of modern thought."[42] For Arnold, the

"thought of the West" thus included, in addition to and beyond the analytical knowledge gained by science, the Hegelian historical-dialectic which repeatedly appears in his own criticism, in a term which he borrowed from Goethe, as the "Zeitgeist."

It is worth noting that the futility of philosophical and theological argument had impressed itself upon Arnold as a result of his early readings in philosophy. After the death of his father, Arnold had turned to philosophy for help, and his readings not only failed to provide an answer to his doubts but severely inhibited the expression of his poetic gift. The lack of "solidity" in philosophies, he wrote later, argued "a dash of pedant in a man to approach them, except perhaps in the ardour of extreme youth, with any confidence." Recalling that in his late twenties, "we [in our doubt] . . . did betake ourselves once to Descartes with great zeal, and were thus led to an experience which we have never forgotten,"[43] Arnold makes clear that the experience was one of complete disillusionment, followed by similar experiences with other philosophers.[44] It is clear also that theology and philosophy, like mathematics, proved incomprehensible to a man of Arnold's temperament. The theorem which states that the sum of the angles in a triangle equals two right angles must be true, Arnold acknowledged, but he could not *see* the truth of it.[45]

The lasting effects of this disillusionment with philosophy are evident in *God and the Bible,* in which Arnold recalled his youthful crisis with a mockery that betrays an uncharacteristic bitterness: "At the mention of that name *metaphysics,* lo, essence, existence, substance, finite and infinite, cause and succession, something and nothing, begin to weave their eternal dance before us! with the confused murmur of their combinations filling all the region governed by *her,* who, far more indisputably than her late-born rival, political economy, has

earned the title of the Dismal Science."[46] So far as the idea of
God was concerned, Arnold wrote, he was forced to turn from
the abstractions of philosophy to the historical data of semantics,
in which the true science of "being" was shown to belong to
the science of physiology, not metaphysics.[47]

The appeal to semantics was characteristic. Arnold's poetic
temperament could accept abstract language only when the
metaphorical substructure of such language was rightly understood. "The moment we have an abstract word," he wrote,
"a word where we do not apprehend both the concrete sense
and the manner of this sense's application, there is danger."
The term "God," for example, was "a simple figure," the dec-
laration of "a perceived energy and operation, nothing more";
similarly, the term être designated a physical process, breathing.[48] Metaphysics, in short, was simply a disguised form of
poetry lacking the sensuousness and concreteness—and therefore the effectiveness—of essential poetry.

The bias of Arnold's temperament explains why, just as he
had argued for the superiority of the poetic over the scientific
approach in his discussion of the proper mode of apprehending
physical objects (citing Guérin as an example), so in his discussion of the proper way of treating ideas he again called for
an imaginative, poetic approach, this time citing Joubert, the
"French Coleridge," as a model. The beauty of Joubert's handling of ideas was "not in what is exclusively intellectual,—
it is in the union of soul with intellect," that is, "he has the
faculty of judging with all the powers of his mind and soul at
work together in due combination."[49] Joubert thus exhibited in
his handling of ideas the same wholeness that had characterized Guérin's response to physical nature. The way in which
"soul" corrected and enhanced "intellect" Arnold indicates in
another passage.

Even metaphysics [Joubert] would not allow to remain difficult
and abstract: so long as they spoke a professional jargon, the lan-

guage of the schools, he maintained,—and who shall gainsay him?—that metaphysics were imperfect; or, at any rate, had not yet reached their ideal perfection.

"The true science of metaphysics," he says, "consists not in rendering abstract that which is sensible, but in rendering sensible that which is abstract; apparent that which is hidden; imaginable, if so it may be, that which is only intelligible." [50]

The true philosopher moved the reader away from "abstract" intellectual considerations towards the concrete "imaginable," that is, towards the poetic. This conviction was the basis of Arnold's appeal to semantics in defining "God." Even when managed with grace and charm, the language of pure intellect lacked the concrete immediacy of poetic intuition. Contrasting Maurice de Guérin with his sister, Eugénie, Arnold wrote: "her words, when she speaks of the life and appearances of nature, are in general but intellectual signs; they are not like her brother's—symbols equivalent with the thing symbolised. They bring the notion of the thing described to the mind, they do not bring the feeling of it to the imagination." [51]

Because the exercise of dialectical reason was necessary to prevent narrowness, but incapable of attaining absolute certitude, Arnold postulated "disinterestedness" as the highest intellectual virtue. By being disinterested, man detached himself from inhibiting idiosyncracies of environment and education, put himself in touch with the world at large, and acknowledged the limits of reason both in its analytical and its dialectical functions. [52] At the same time the very extremity of his skepticism opened the way for Arnold's re-introduction of truth and religion on other grounds. On this point the Curtius review is again revealing. According to Curtius, Euripides had "contended for the right of every individual to approach in inquiring meditation all things human and divine; *but*"—and the italics were Arnold's—"*at the same time he was not blind to the dangers of this tendency. He openly declared them,*

. . . *representing the miserable end of a man who opposes his reason to the system of the gods.*"[53] The opposition of reason to the will of the gods, as Arnold understood the terms, occurred when, like Empedocles, man looked to reason for a certitude which reason could not supply. Yet once the inherent limitations of analytical and dialectical reason were recognized and accepted, it was still possible, Arnold concluded, to find within man, in his character and conscience, a "fixed, fatal, spiritual centre of gravity"[54] by which to check the dialogue of the mind with itself. Truth was to be found, Arnold believed, neither in history nor in scientific exploration of the external world, but within, in the heart and conscience and "soul." The highest wisdom was not rational and discursive but moral and intuitive.[55]

CHAPTER SEVEN

Ethical Reason: Stages
of Growth

The influence of his Victorian environment, and more particularly of his father, would be sufficient to explain why Arnold's
search for a solution to his inner conflict had from the beginning a strong ethical element. The inconclusiveness of his intellectual experience had given special urgency to what he believed to be the central question of life, "how to live." In 1849
he reported to Clough that he had been driven in upon himself,
and was "more snuffing after a moral atmosphere to respire
in than ever before in my life."[56] In the early fifties he turned
to "morality and character" in order to escape the dialogue of
the mind, with its disillusionments and ennui. Yet, as "Empedocles on Etna" makes clear, the moral life, so far as it was
characterized by mere endurance and stoic resistance, was to
Arnold a second best. Citing Thomas à Kempis, he had indicated his readiness to do violence to himself, but in breaking
"in large measure" with his vocation Arnold did so only because the age was uncongenial, the state of knowledge uncertain, and the struggle too lonely, *not* because the poetic
gift and the ambitions it inspired were unworthy. When Arnold turned to "morality and character" in the early fifties,
therefore, he did so with a characteristic difference which was
reflected in the fact that the key intellectual figure in the drama

of his "conversion" was not his father, but the philosopher Spinoza.

The ethical doctrine expounded in Arnold's later criticism both made use of and at the same time altered the "moral lesson" enjoined by Spinoza. Arnold described this lesson as one "not of mere resigned acquiescence, not of melancholy quietism, but of joyful activity within the limits of man's true sphere."[57] He had already embodied this lesson in his poems of morality, and it reappears in his criticism as the Hebraic-Biblical ethic based on the concept of God as "the eternal not-ourselves that makes for righteousness." In Arnold's interpretation, however, the Spinozan "moral" drawn from Nature not only permitted a "free play" of mind in the intellectual sphere but steadied and balanced and inspired the poetic temperament. Arnold's objective as a moralist, unlike Spinoza's, was both to stress the indispensability of morality and at the same time to bring it into connection with his view of reason as a disinterested, dialectical instrument making for the expansion of consciousness, and, more importantly, with his primary interest in poetry.

In the essay entitled "Spinoza and the Bible" Arnold defended Spinoza against the charge of atheism on the ground that wherever reason may have led him, even to the rejection of a personal God and of final causes, Spinoza nonetheless "impresses Goethe and any man like Goethe, and then he composes him; first he fills and satisfies his imagination by the width and grandeur of his view of nature, and then he fortifies and stills his mobile, straining, passionate, poetic temperament by the moral lesson he draws from his view of nature."[58] The joint reference to Goethe and the imagination is important, for it indicates what it was in Spinoza that attracted Arnold. According to his brother, when Arnold was suddenly thrown upon his own resources after the death of their father in 1842, he turned for guidance and inspiration to "Goethe's art and

Spinoza's mysticism."[59] The remark not only supplies further evidence regarding the link in Arnold's mind between Spinoza and Goethe, but suggests that Spinoza's role at a critical juncture in Arnold's life was much what it had been for Goethe in a similar situation.

A Balliol contemporary of Arnold's, Edward Caird, later wrote an essay on Goethe which indicates what that role was. After observing that Goethe's "apprenticeship" had ended, "when Spinoza took in his inner life that place which had hitherto been filled by Rousseau,"[60] Caird went on to describe Goethe's crisis in terms which suggest its similarity to Arnold's:

> Goethe's "storm and stress" period—the period of "unconditioned effort to break through all limitations"—was ended with *Werther,* and with it began a movement towards limit and measure . . . . If in this new phase of thought nature was still worshipped, it was no longer regarded as a power that reveals itself at once. . . . It was now the *natura naturans* of Spinoza—i.e., as Goethe conceived it, a plastic organizing force . . . which in human life reveals itself most fully as the ideal principle of art. . . . Demanding, as a poet, that the ideal should not be separated from the sensuous, he is now conscious that the poetic truth of the passions shows itself . . . only when their conflict leads to their 'purification,' and so reveals a higher principle.[61]

The change in Goethe's outlook effected by his reading of Spinoza is summed up by Caird as a movement from restless aspiration to the order of those who "cheerfully renounce" whatever is not granted: a movement "back through a kind of Stoicism to an Optimism which moves on a higher level."[62] Just as he encountered Rousseauism once removed through Byron, Arnold derived his Spinozism through Goethe; his own "apprenticeship" ended when, as his brother recalled, he opened his Goethe and closed his Byron at Oxford.[63]

Arnold's high regard for Spinoza is indicated in his remark that the latter's name and work "bid fair to become what they deserve to become,—in the history of modern philosophy the central point of interest."[64] Spinoza's influence may be seen in the two quite different aspects of Arnold's ethical doctrine which corresponded to the two elements which he had singled out in Goethe's response: the composing, moral lesson, and the inspiring, poetic, imaginative vision. The first had to do with *Entsagen* and obedience, with what had to be; the second, with the imaginative apprehension of what might be. On the one hand, a stoic note of retrenchment; on the other, a passionate yearning for the ideal.

So far as morality in general was concerned, Arnold followed Spinoza, first of all, in setting up a rigid separation between intellect and conduct. In the essay on Spinoza he argued in support of the "hidden secret," unknown to reason, that "obedience" to the "universal divine law" will save men whether or not they apprehend it aright intellectually.[65] Later, in *God and the Bible*, he cited Joubert on the utter separation of religion and "physics," that is, the natural sciences.[66] Thus theology and philosophy, religion and reason, conduct and speculation, were kept apart: "Theology demands perfect obedience, philosophy perfect knowledge," and on this assumption Arnold could conclude that "the truest speculative opinion about the nature of God is impious if it makes its holder rebellious; the falsest speculative opinion is pious if it makes him obedient."[67] But in these statements Arnold's criterion was public order and the common weal, not truth; the separation of speculative and moral reason was made necessary by the assumption that "old moral ideas leaven and humanise the multitude: new intellectual ideas filter slowly down to them from the thinking few; and only when they reach them in this manner do they adjust themselves to their practice without convulsing it."[68] Hence Arnold's separation of religion and intellect was a strategy rather than a principle: like Spinoza, he had in mind the masses of people who followed the universal divine law—"cease to do evil"—simply as moral reason gives it: "not from a sense of its intrinsic goodness, truth, and necessity, but simply in proof of obedience (for both the Old and New Testament are but one long discipline of obedience)".[69] This distinction served as the basis of Arnold's contrast between the religion of the few and the religion of the many. "The highly-instructed few, and not the scantily-instructed many, will ever be the organ to the human race of knowledge and truth. Knowledge and truth, in the full sense of the words, are not attainable by the great mass of the human race at all. The great mass of the human race have to be softened and humanised through their heart and imagination, before any soil can be found in them where knowledge may strike living roots."[70]

The second and more important aspect of Spinoza's influence on Arnold had to do with "knowledge and truth in the full sense of the words," that is, with the religion of the few which was also the religion of the future. At this higher level of awareness the gap between reason and conduct, Arnold believed, disappeared. As early as 1850, in the midst of his heavy readings in philosophy, he had written to Clough praising the "positive and vivifying" effect of Spinoza as compared to that of Locke,[71] and the appeal of this "vivifying" element indicates why Spinoza was the one philosopher between Anselm and Mill to escape Arnold's sweeping condemnation of theologians and philosophers in *God and the Bible*. We may recall that it was to Spinoza's "mysticism" that Thomas Arnold referred, an element in Spinoza's thought which presumably was absent from other philosophers whom Arnold read, even from such favorite ancient authors as Epictetus and Marcus Aurelius.

The nature of Spinozan "mysticism" and its "vivifying" effect were diagnosed by James Anthony Froude. In 1854, during a period when he and Arnold were especially close, Froude wrote a review of a new edition of the *Tractatus de Deo et Homine* for the *Westminster Review* in which, like Arnold, he stressed Spinoza's appeal to the imagination. "The power of Spinozaism does not lie . . . remote from ordinary appreciation, or we should long ago have heard the last of it. Like all other systems which have attracted followers, it addresses itself, not to the logical intellect, but to the imagination, which it affects to set aside."[72] Like Arnold, Froude was uneasy about Spinoza's "system" and "abstractions": "Things—essences—existences! these are but the vague names with which faculties, constructed only to deal with conditional phenomena, disguise their incapacity."[73] But Froude described as "unmixedly good" that influence of "Spinozaism" which he detected in the "more reverent contemplation of nature" displayed by modern landscape-painting and pre-eminently in the poetry of Wordsworth. Such reverence, he added, "if ever physical science is to become an instrument of intellectual education, must first be infused into the lessons of nature; the sense of that 'something' interfused in the material world"—and Froude went on to cite "Tintern Abbey."[74] It was this "Wordsworthian" aspect of Spinoza's identification of God with Nature which attracted Arnold as it had Goethe and which added a "mystical" dimension to Spinoza's otherwise austere geometrical metaphysics and stoic ethic.

The difference between a stoic and a mystical response to nature suggests the role played by Arnold's aesthetic temperament in his Goethean response to Spinoza and in his formulation of his ethical doctrine: "The two attitudes [stoic and mystical] are related in their origin since they are both attempts to escape from the domination of facts, but the methods of escape are fundamentally unlike. To transcend and transfigure a fact is different in psychological accompaniments as well as in effect from merely bearing it heroically. The former method is essentially that of the artist, and it was to the artist and emotionalist in Goethe that Spinoza in the last analysis appealed."[75] Arnold had provided a poetic statement of this distinction in his praise of Wordsworth in "Memorial Verses":

> Others will teach us how to dare,
> And against fear our breast to steel;
> Others will strengthen us to bear—
> But who, ah! who, will make us feel?
> The cloud of mortal destiny,
> Others will front it fearlessly—
> But who, like him, will put it by?
>
> [ll. 64–70]

Arnold was impressed by the appeal which Spinoza made to Goethe's imagination because as a poet Arnold, like Goethe and Wordsworth, was deeply committed to the world of the five senses; on more than one occasion he insisted that poetry was characterized by its being, in Milton's phrase, "simple, sensuous, and passionate." While Coleridge had felt it necessary, as a Christian, to condemn Spinoza's monism,[76] this monism was readily translatable by men like Arnold and Froude, who had given up Christianity, into a natural mysticism of the kind evident in Goethe's and Wordsworth's poetry. The Goethean-Wordsworthian interpretation of nature as a "plastic power" that moves and shapes things, including the mind of man, provided, in fact, the basic Romantic analogue for the activity of the poetic power itself.

In tracing the influence of Spinoza in Goethe's passage from pessimism to optimism, Caird's essay suggests another reason why Spinoza appealed to Arnold on temperamental as well as, or more than, on rational grounds: "his poetic faculty seemed to him something higher than his individual will and impulses —something that might claim kindred with the productive force of nature itself. Such a view of things we may call in a special sense Hellenic, since it was in ancient Greece that the higher spiritual interests of man seemed most directly to connect themselves with the gifts of nature . . . . they showed themselves artists not only in art, but in life, and escaped the painful division of the modern mind."[77] Although Spinoza's theodicy ruled out the supernatural, personal God of Christianity, it provided for a *natura naturans* which identified God with nature, and Arnold adopted this notion, with important alterations, in both his religious and his aesthetic doctrine. "Reason," Arnold wrote in his essay on Spinoza, "tells us that a miracle,—understanding by a miracle a breach of the laws of nature,—is impossible, and that to think it possible is to dishonour God . . . and to say that God violates the laws of nature is to say that he violates his own nature."[78] Spinoza's God-in-Nature could therefore be described by Arnold as the true "beatific vision"[79] of modern religion. It established a link between man and the physical universe which guaranteed the legitimacy of the aesthetic mode.

Spinoza's role in Arnold's movement of mind might be described as that of the agent by whose help Arnold passed from the Christian order of thinking in which he had been nurtured in childhood, an order centering in the personal Christian God whom Coleridge described as "an 'I' that is alone the Lord God—and *him* thou shalt personally worship,"[80] to a naturalistic order of thinking in which God and Nature were one. As early as Lessing, however, European naturalistic thought was moving toward a philosophy very different from Spinozism proper. If the Spinozan *Deus sive natura* was present in Arnold's thought in the idea of an impersonal Nature, an Eternal Not-Ourselves, which operated immanently through secondary causes, Arnold arrived at his own definition of God by applying to Spinoza's notion his own view of the life of "pure" reason as a dialectical series of speculative acts, the mirror in human consciousness of the flux of the universe flowing, as it were, through the mind. Spinoza's Infinite Substance thereby became for Arnold a dynamic "stream of tendency," more specifically, an "Eternal Power, not ourselves, by which *all things* fulfill the law of their being."[81] Arnold's "Not-Ourselves" was thus an externalization of the inner dialectic of reason as it manifested itself in an expansive, universal energy, but it was also the ground of all being, the One and the All. As a poet Arnold was searching for the unity between man and nature which he found most perfectly realized in Greek art and which he believed modern man had lost or was in danger of losing; Spinozan Nature, seen as an active energy, provided the most adequate guarantee of the legitimacy of the aesthetic experience by reasserting this unity.

The bearing of Arnold's Spinozism, as derived through Goethe, both on his view of poetry and on the general assumptions from which he spoke is suggested by a passage from his concluding lecture on Celtic literature: "When Goethe came, Europe had lost her basis of spiritual life; she had to find it again; Goethe's task was,—the inevitable task for the modern poet henceforth is—as it was for the Greek poet in the days of Pericles, not to preach a sublime sermon on a given text like Dante, not to exhibit all the kingdoms of human life and the glory of them like Shakspeare, but to interpret human life afresh, and to supply a new spiritual basis to it."[82] Spinoza's "mysticism" was essential to the poet because, in Arnold's reading of Spinozism, it was the only modern philosophical view which preserved a role for poetic activity through offering, in Caird's words, "a view of things we may call in a special sense Hellenic." After completing his lectures on Celtic literature, Arnold began working on the essays which eventually went into the making of *Culture and Anarchy,* and in them he presented his case for an Hellenic ideal of culture as the necessary and adequate spiritual basis for living in the modern world. This ideal was based on a concept of mankind's moral evolution which was the counterpart in his ethical doctrine to the dialectic which he saw as characteristic of man's rational experience. For Arnold mankind's moral evolution was quantitative as well as qualitative. It was qualitative in that its teleology was controlled by Arnold's concept of an historical moment—Periclean Athens—when a small segment of society had already substantially achieved the highest perfection attainable by men. It was quantitative in that the task of modern civilization was to disseminate this perfection through the whole of society, through the lower as well as the upper classes, through Eastern as well as Western cultures. In proposing the ideal of culture Arnold was guided by his analysis of man's past, and his poetic temperament led him to the conclusion that evolution was a process which culminated in what may be called the "aesthetic condition."

CHAPTER EIGHT

Imaginative Reason:
the Aesthetic Condition

In his review of a book on Jewish history by his friend Arthur Stanley, Arnold noted, with regard to the New Testament, that Christ had "adapted His teaching to the different stages of growth in His hearers."[83] This concept of ethical "stages" Arnold applied to the moral life of individuals and of nations as well as to the history of humanity as a whole. Like the modern intellectual consciousness, modern man's ethical consciousness was the fruit of a long, gradual process of growth, of a struggle towards human "fulness" that for Arnold constituted the "will of God" for men individually and collectively. The various levels in this evolution which Arnold discriminated in his criticism may be identified as the Hebraic, the Stoic, and the Aesthetic, respectively. Although the first two occupy a substantial place in his discussion, it is the last which gives to his criticism its originality and force. Like the limitations of speculative reason, the limitations of moral reason were for Arnold inherent and final, and this fact led him to invoke a third power—the "imaginative reason"—both to make good these limitations and to reconcile the other two faculties, which, by themselves, failed to attain the completely satisfying perfection which men seek.

At its lowest, "Hebraic" level Arnold saw the moral life

as a combat with what he called the "obvious faults of our animality."[84] Victory in this battle was indispensable for any sort of human life whatever; therefore, in judging between the relative importance of the discipline of intelligence and the discipline of the will Arnold argued that "the priority naturally belongs to that discipline which braces all man's moral powers, and founds for him an indispensable basis of character."[85] To this extent the moral instinct, which combats the lower self in man, deserved to "moderate." Arnold's repeated concessions to the achievement of "Puritanism," despite his profound temperamental aversion to it, bear witness to the importance which he attached to subduing the uninhibited sexual and aggressive impulses of the "raw natural man." Since he found sanctions for this morality among pagan as well as among Biblical writers, it was not for Arnold an exclusively Biblical morality, but he nevertheless saw the subduing of the lower self as the peculiar achievement of Hebraism, with its "governing idea" of "strictness of conscience," and success in this battle as the great contribution of the Christian religion to Western culture, for Christianity was simply "the later, the more spiritual, the more attractive development of Hebraism."[86] Greek culture, so far as it failed in this respect, eventually declined, although her greatest writers had likewise exalted the basic moral virtues postulated by Christianity.

Because it was a common Victorian practice to identify the obvious faults of human animality with the "lower orders" of Victorian society, Arnold felt free to stress morality in this rudimentary and conventional sense, giving to his prose an "Hebraic" emphasis that was closely connected with and appealed to a deep-seated fear of social anarchy that was widespread among thoughtful middle-class Victorians.[87] The priority thus enjoyed by conventional ethical criteria in Arnold's discussion of contemporary issues, given his background and circumstances, is understandable. Tested by their probable social consequences at the moment, ideas were less important for their truth than for their probable effect upon conduct. Even the educated minority, Arnold warned, although "curious to know the new ideas of their time," asked "to be edified, not informed only,"[88] and he later distinguished a healthy from a diseased "curiosity" precisely on the grounds that the latter was indifferent to the effects of ideas upon society.[89] But the Hebraic code of "strictness of conscience" and self-conquest, though indispensable, was not enough. Arnold indicated as much by absorbing the Hebraic code into the higher and more comprehensive stoic doctrine of *Entsagen,* what he called on one occasion the "freedom from all desire to subjugate destiny,"[90] and on another *"a sentiment of sublime acquiescence in the course of fate, and in the dispensations of human life."*[91]

This second, more advanced, stage of moral life found its appropriate moral virtue in "resignation," a virtue corresponding in Arnold's ethical doctrine to the intellectual virtue of "disinterestedness" which he recommended for the life of reason. Both involved a dying to the "self," in the one case the abandonment of the pretensions of reason, and in the other the suppression not only of the animal passions but even of those nobler but fruitless yearnings for perfect happiness which characterize youth. The danger of rebelling against a world in which perfect happiness was not to be had Arnold made clear in his analysis of the Celt, the Titan rebel, who seeks to fulfill desires which an "unknown Power" has no intention of satisfying. "Sentimental,—*always ready to react against the despotism of fact;* that is a description a great friend of the Celt gives of him; and it is not a bad description of the sentimental temperament; it lets us into the secret of its dangers and of its habitual want of success. Balance, measure, and patience, these are the eternal conditions, even supposing the happiest temperament to start with, of high success. . . ."[92]

By nature the Celtic spirit aspires "to be expansive, adventurous, and gay," but it always ends in "wistful regret," in "passionate, penetrating melancholy" when "the downs of life too much outnumber the ups."[93] Arnold saw in Celtism a characteristically "modern sentiment" which tended to impose itself everywhere, even—as in Ruskin's writings—upon the classical spirit of Homer, whereas the true clue to Homer was to be found in Goethe's remark to Schiller: "From Homer and Polygnotus I every day learn more clearly . . . that in our life here above ground we have, properly speaking, to enact Hell."[94] It is Homer who sees things as they truly are, life as it really is; because the downs of life do inevitably outnumber the ups, the Celt, unless he dies young, is doomed to Byronic melancholy. "They, believe me, who await / No gifts from chance, have conquer'd fate." This stoic ethic, which dominated Arnold's poems of morality, occupied an even more important place in his ethical doctrine than the fight against the raw natural man because it regulated man's relationship to a much larger portion of life, to his experience of external trials and the frustration of his nobler desires: in a word, to the experience of life as Hell.

Yet stoicism was not the final stage in man's moral evolution. Like Lucretius' poetry, stoicism was for Arnold too morbid, too gloomy, to be an adequate moral interpretation of life. If Hebraism lacked light, stoicism lacked hope and cheerfulness. Having subdued his animal passions, and having acknowledged the futility of youth's limitless aspirations and the inescapable limitations of reason, modern man still had not arrived at the goal; he had merely accepted the condition, the dying-to-self, which made the attainment of the true goal possible.

The final stage in the evolution of the ethical consciousness was for Arnold a state in which the flexibility of a free-playing mind, operating disinterestedly, is harmonized with a moral acquiescence capable of holding firm against the vicissitudes of life, while the poetic imagination conferred upon experience a form and beauty which lit up and, in its highest reaches, transfigured that experience. At this level human life presented the possibility of endless expansion from a poised center, a state in which the human spirit, like the action in a Greek tragedy, "rises, as the thought and emotion swell higher and higher without overflowing their boundaries, to a lofty sense of the mastery of the human spirit over its own stormiest agitations."[95] In its highest reach the ethical life was thus identified by Arnold with that intellectually disinterested and aesthetically active mode of responding to and organizing experience exemplified by Greek tragedy: "To combine, to harmonise, to deepen for the spectator the feelings naturally excited in him by the sight of what was passing upon the stage. . . ."[96] The greatness of Greek art and Greek beauty, rooted in an "impulse to see things as they really are," rested on its "fidelity to nature,—the *best* nature . . . ,"[97] and the "*best* nature," so far as humanity was concerned, was that "*best self*" by which "we are united, impersonal, at harmony."[98]

The residual Hebraism and Christianity in Arnold's ethical creed was thus subordinated, discreetly but decisively, to a higher morality of stoic acquiescence; and both were seen as preparatory to the disinterested contemplation of the spectacle of life characteristic of the aesthetic consciousness in its most sophisticated state.

That is why in its unelaborated form Arnold's moral doctrine has a truistic appearance, "Seek perfection." But in explaining his view of the nature of perfection—the full development of *all* the faculties, intellectual and aesthetic as well as ethical—he found the only adequate analogue in the world of Greek art, and in the "moral" experience which that art awakened in the reader or viewer.[99] If "righteousness" required the self-discipline of the Old Testament Law, the "bearing" of life evident in the "acquiescence" of the stoic, in the "obedience" of Spinoza, in the "necrosis" of Jesus, at a higher stage of culture the moral imperative commanded the development of the whole self. In addition, therefore, to the perfection sought by a purely Hebraic religion, with its God of righteousness, Arnold proposed in *Literature and Dogma* a more universal and comprehensive religious perfection, corresponding to a more comprehensive concept of God: "For the total man, therefore, the truer conception of God is as 'the Eternal Power, not ourselves, by which *all things* fulfil the law of their being' . . . so far as our being is aesthetic and intellective, as well as so far as it is moral." [100] In this larger view the proper object of "religious emotion" was the "stream of tendency," the *natura naturans* of Spinoza manifesting itself within man in reason, in conscience, and above all in that excess of energy which characterized poetic genius and enabled man, through art, to master the spectacle of the general life which surrounded him. Even the Hebrew God was something more than the author of the moral law, Arnold remarked, since as the author of *life* he was "the eternal and divine power from which *all* life and wholesome energy proceed." [101]

Yet the aesthetic faculty frequently appears in Arnold's criticism as merely one of several "sides" of human nature, requiring—like the other basic human impulses—development and expansion, and harboring peculiar dangers of its own when developed in isolation. This view raises the question of how the intellectual and moral concerns that play such a large role in Arnold's criticism are subordinated to the idea of poetry as the *magister vitae*. The way in which Arnold manages this becomes clear if we distinguish, as Arnold did, between the aesthetic faculty proper, which he called "sensibility," and what was previously referred to as the aesthetic condition, a mode of being which Arnold associated with the life of "imaginative reason."

The most detailed statement on the nature of "sensibility"

occurs in the lectures on Celtic Literature in the course of Arnold's analysis of poetic genius.

Of an ideal genius one does not want the elements, any of them, to be in a state of weakness; on the contrary, one wants all of them to be in the highest state of power; but with a law of measure, of harmony, presiding over the whole. So the sensibility of the Celt, if everything else were not sacrificed to it, is a beautiful and admirable force. For sensibility, the power of quick and strong perception and emotion, is one of the very prime constituents of genius, perhaps its most positive constituent; it is to the soul, what good senses are to the body, the grand natural condition of successful activity. Sensibility gives genius its materials; one cannot have too much of it, if one can but keep its master and not be its slave.[102]

Arnold linked the "magical" power of poetry in particular to the qualities here associated with "sensibility" ("perhaps the most positive constituent" of genius). It was "sensibility," under inspiration from the Muse—that is, when working in harmony with the plastic power, the shaping energy, of the Not-Ourselves—which raised the poet above the philosopher, the moralist, and the man of science. "Measure" and "harmony" Arnold associated with Goethe's "art," the *Architectonicè* which supplied the "classical" element in the Arnoldian doctrine. "Sensibility" provided the essential poetic insight and creative emotion and constituted the aesthetic faculty proper; "art" directed the disposition of the creative energy in a beautiful work. Sensitiveness of intelligence, openness, flexibility, *modus* and *ordo*, these characteristic qualities of a classical prose were invaluable qualities which ought to inform the intelligence and tact of the literary critic. But they fell short of the one thing needful which poetry exhibited, creativity, and hence for Arnold the highest function of criticism itself was to put the reader in touch with genius: "What is really precious and inspiring, in all that we get from literature, except this sense of an immediate contact with genius itself?"[103]

The nature of "imaginative reason" was thus implicit in Arnold's discussion of "genius." What was genius? It was, he wrote, "mainly an affair of energy, and poetry is mainly an affair of genuis," that is, of "an inventive power, a faculty of divination";[104] poetic genius was "the faculty of being happily inspired . . . by a certain order of ideas," of "dealing divinely with these ideas, presenting them in the most effective and attractive combinations,—making beautiful works of them, in short."[105] Of the two powers—the rational and the imaginative —included by the term "imaginative reason," poetry was therefore associated by Arnold primarily with imagination. Reason, the province of criticism, was necessary but insufficient; exercising a free play of intelligence, criticism could raise society to a certain plateau of intellectual awareness, just as moral reason could arm it against venality and the vicissitudes of life; but neither could inspire and transform ideas or morality by emotion. Indeed, since this transforming emotion was not within man's command, Arnold believed that the greatest poetry was not within the poet's command; "here is the part of the Muse, the inspiration, the God, the 'not ourselves'."[106] It was in his discussion of poetry and genius, that Arnold revealed the nature of his own deepest experience, and at the same time indicated the way in which Spinoza's "mysticism" supplemented Goethe's "art" in the formation of his mature critical doctrine.

If in one view of it, Arnold saw the aesthetic power, in the form of sensibility, as one element in man's total make-up— "we fulfill the law of our being so far as our being is aesthetic and intellective, as well as so far as it is moral"—the following passage from Culture and Anarchy indicates that the goal which Arnold posited was a state in which the aesthetic power assimilated and mastered a maximum of experience, overcoming the tensions created by practical, moral, and intellectual needs.

The best art and poetry of the Greeks, in which religion and poetry are one, in which the idea of beauty and of a human nature perfect on all sides adds to itself a religious and devout energy, and works in the strength of that, is on this account of such surpassing interest and instructiveness for us, though it was,—as, having regard to the human race in general, and, indeed, having regard to the Greeks themselves, we must own,—a premature attempt, an attempt which for success needed the moral and religious fibre in humanity to be more braced and developed than it had yet been. But Greece did not err in having the idea of beauty, harmony, and complete human perfection, so present and paramount. It is impossible to have this idea too present and paramount; only, the moral fibre must be braced too. And we, because we have braced the moral fibre, are not on that account in the right way, if at the same time the idea of beauty, harmony, and complete human perfection, is wanting or misapprehended amongst us; and evidently it *is* wanting or misapprehended at present.[107]

Arnold thus identified moral reason's profoundest intuition with "complete human perfection," with the Hellenic idea and Greek poetry, not with Hebraic morality and the Bible. The idea "of beauty and of a human nature perfect on all its sides" offered an ideal in which Hellenic "spontaneity of consciousness," the tendency "continually to enlarge our whole law of doing," occupied the summit in Arnold's hierarchy of values, incorporating the narrower Hebraic ideal of "strictness of conscience"[108] while at the same time going beyond it. Culture itself, although attainable only on condition of intellectual and moral effort, was in its perfection a state of effortless, immanent, and contemplative "fulness" in which man was at one with himself and with the world. The Hebraic virtue of self-conquest and the stoic virtue of resignation, coupled with the intellectual virtue of disinterestedness, prepared the soul for that simple, intuitive, spontaneous apprehension of the whole of experience which characterized great poetry.

This final state as Arnold describes it was identical with the aesthetic condition which Schiller had described in his *Letters*. A synopsis of Schiller's argument makes clear its affinity with Arnold's ideal of Culture.

In the free play of its powers human nature expresses itself on all its sides and as a totality, with the possibility of taking certain directions, which possibility, however, is never realized as long as the aesthetic condition persists. "All other exercises," says Schiller in his twenty-second letter, "give to the mind some particular aptitude, but for that very reason they impose upon it a particular limit; only the aesthetic leads to the unlimited. . . . Here alone we feel ourselves snatched out of time and our humanity expresses itself with a purity and integrity, as though it had as yet sustained no injury from the operation of external powers." Thus, the *aesthetic condition* which Schiller describes is one in which all the human powers work freely and harmoniously, without being set in motion by external needs, and without any single one becoming predominant. He regarded this condition as the perfection of culture, and not merely as a means to soften rudeness and mitigate discord.[109]

In order to distinguish the faculty involved in this experience from the analytical reason of science, the dialectical reason of philosophy, and the moral reason of ethics, Arnold invented the term "imaginative reason." He regarded the function of criticism highly enough to attribute to the critical act some measure of that "sense of creative activity" which he described as "the great proof of being alive,"[110] but poetry, and the genius of the poet, were the manifestations par excellence of the imaginative reason.

The relationship between the aesthetic faculty and the aesthetic condition, between "sensibility" and the life of "imaginative reason," Arnold treated from two distinct but related points of view in discussing the various levels of integration of the human faculties. One point of view he presented in his account of the history of religion, the other in his discrimination of the kinds and levels of poetic style.

In an analysis of mankind's religious history and of human progress generally, both of which he identified with the history of man's capacity to exercise his poetic gift over an ever-increasing range and accumulation of experience, Arnold established the hierarchy of values which informs his criticism. Translated into historical terms, the concept of the imaginative reason can be summed up in Arnold's own epithet "Indo-European." Commenting on the stages through which man had moved, he declared that it was

a higher state of development when our fineness of perception is keen than when it is blunt. And if,—whereas the Semitic genius placed its highest spiritual life in the religious sentiment, and made that the basis of its poetry,—the Indo-European genius places its highest spiritual life in the imaginative reason, and makes that the basis of its poetry, we are none the better for wanting the perception to discern a natural law, which is, after all, like every natural law, irresistible; we are none the better for trying to make ourselves Semitic, when Nature has made us Indo-European, and to shift the basis of our poetry.[111]

Perfection involved a union of East and West, of emotion ("Hebrew fire") and idea ("Greek thought"), of soul and intellect, of moral and dialectical reason. This union could be effected only by the imagination, not by logic or by strictness of conscience. The *"idea"* of *"*beauty, harmony, and complete human perfection" needed "a religious and devout *energy"* to supplement it; poetic genius alone had this combinative energy, the power of magically transfiguring the supposed facts of rational and moral experience into something lovely and satisfying.

This transfiguration, however, was illusory if the facts so transfigured were misapprehended. At a primitive stage in the development of human consciousness, Arnold argued, the poetic power had expressed itself in the great cosmic religions: "imagination coming in to help, [primitive men] make [the law of nature], as they make everything else of which they powerfully feel the effect, into a human agent, at bottom like themselves, however much mightier,—a human agent that feels, thinks, loves, hates. So they made the sun into a human being; and even the operation of chance, fortune." It was only at a later, more advanced stage that Israel had a moral intuition of the importance of conduct centered in the doctrine of obedience. "And what should sooner be thus made into a human being . . . than the operation which affects man so widely and deeply,—for it is engaged with conduct, with at least three-fourths of human life,—the *not ourselves* that makes for righteousness." Yet still later, there had been the Hellenic intuition of the importance of intelligence and of beauty. "What was the Apollo of the religion of the Greeks? The law of intellectual beauty, the eternal not ourselves that makes for intellectual beauty."[112]

In discussing the kind of poetry which would be appropriate to the state of human consciousness as it had evolved in the nineteenth century, Arnold, of course, rejected the primitive stage, in which poetry consisted of an unconscious naming of physical bodies, moral virtues, and natural laws, ignorant of what it was doing. Like the Celtic temperament in the modern world—only less culpably because less consciously—the primitive mind rebelled against the despotism of fact, and in a more sophisticated age it was therefore destined either to lose itself in unreality or to end in passionate melancholy. Israel's moral intuition of the importance of conduct, on the other hand, constituted a permanent acquisition of human consciousness; henceforth all higher poetry would have to assimilate the great moral insights of the Bible. In Christianity this morality had found poetic expression in the story of the

Nativity, the poetry with which the early Christians surrounded the moral intuition of the importance of purity, and in the story of Easter, in which the Christian liturgy poetically expressed the joy that followed from the practice of necrosis.[113] Poetry which thus expressed the joy attending sublime moral convictions and practices marked an important advance in the seriousness and value of poetry. The poetry of the cosmic religions, therefore, gave way in more advanced cultures to the ethical poetry of the Bible. After Israel and before Jesus, however, there had been the Hellenic intuition of the idea of man's total perfection, of his instinct for beauty and knowledge as well as for conduct. This Hellenic intuition had superseded that of the Bible, correcting Biblical preoccupation with conduct alone, which in Protestant Puritanism had ended by stifling the love of intellect and beauty. In the figure of Jesus the Bible also had recognized this higher ideal, but its purest embodiment was to be found, Arnold declared, in the poetry of Periclean Greece; in that "century in Greek life,—the century preceding the Peloponnesian war, from about the year 530 to the year 430 B.C.,—in which poetry made, it seems to me, the noblest, the most successful effort she has ever made as the priestess of the imaginative reason, of the element by which the modern spirit, if it would live right, has chiefly to live."[114]

It is no mere accident, therefore, that Arnold should have described the highest perfection of humanity as "Apolline," that is, as that "state of illumination and elevation of the human soul" of which Apollo, "the great awakener and sustainer of genius and intellect," was the appropriate deity. The Apollo of the "Hellas of Hellas," he wrote, was "not only the nourisher of genius, he was also the author of every high moral effort; he was the prophet of his father Zeus, in the highest view of Zeus. . . ."[115] Culture, therefore, in Arnold's conception of it, went beyond Christianity and constituted a higher kind of religion: "in determining generally in what human perfection consists, religion comes to a conclusion identical with that which culture . . . likewise reaches," with this difference, that culture seeks "the determination of this question through *all* the voices of human experience which have been heard upon it, of art, science, poetry, philosophy, history, as well as of religion, in order to give a greater fulness and certainty to its solution."[116] Hebraic-Christian resistance to "animality" is thus assimilated into a higher eudaemonistic ethic of full development in which the other "voices" of human nature are also heard, with all of these voices in subordination, finally, to the voice of poetry. "The characteristic bent of Hellenism, as has been said, is to find the intelligible law of things, to see them in their true nature and as they really are. But many things are not seen in their true nature and as they really are, unless they are seen as beautiful. Behaviour is not intelligible, does not account for itself to the mind and show the reason for its existing, unless it is beautiful. The same with discourse, the same with song, the same with worship, all of them modes in which man proves his activity and expresses himself."[117] Thus conduct, speech, and worship, as elsewhere in Arnold's criticism the physical world and ideas, must account for themselves to the mind and show the reason for their existence by being beautiful. Because poetry alone could evoke and educate this instinct and thus satisfy the needs of the imaginative reason, Arnold offered poetry as the chief instrument for the education of men.

It would be difficult, therefore, to overestimate the importance which Arnold attached throughout his criticism to the role of the "instinct for beauty" as the "connecting," "harmonizing," "perfecting" impulse in man.

I have called religion a yet more important manifestation of human nature than poetry, because it has worked on a broader scale for perfection, and with greater masses of men. But the idea of beauty

and of a human nature perfect on all its sides, which is the dominant idea of poetry, is a true and invaluable idea, though it has
not yet had the success that the idea of conquering the obvious
faults of our animality, and of a human nature perfect on the moral
side,—which is the dominant idea of religion,—has been enabled
to have; and it is destined, adding to itself the religious idea of a
devout energy, to transform and govern the other.[118]

Yet it is clear from Arnold's history of religion that not all
poetry was equally "religious," equally capable of satisfying
the "idea of a comprehensive adjustment of the claims of both
sides in man, the moral as well as the intellectual, of a full
estimate of both, and of a reconciliation of both,"[119] although
all poetry, so far as it was poetry, manifested something of the
basic aesthetic impulse towards unity and harmony. It is in
his analysis of poetic style that Arnold explicitly established
the various levels of poetry as these were reflected in levels of
style. First distinguishing between the "magical" and the
"moral" manifestation of the poetic consciousness, each con-
stituting an "interpretation" or "criticism" of life, and then
distinguishing between two kinds of "moral" interpretation, the
"severe" and the "simple," Arnold incorporated into his literary
criticism a threefold division which corresponded to the three
stages in evolution of man's consciousness as described in his
history of world religion. In the process he also elucidated his
claim regarding the religious function of poetry.

The "magical" interpretation of poetry had to do largely,
in Arnold's view of it, with man's relationship to external nature. "Sensibility" gave to poetic genius "a peculiarly near and
intimate feeling of nature and the life of nature"; the poet
"seems in a special way attracted by the secret before him,
the secret of natural beauty and natural magic, and to be
close to it, to half-divine it."[120] The essay on Maurice de
Guérin contains Arnold's clearest statement of the point. "To
make magically near and real the life of Nature, and man's

life only so far as it is a part of that Nature, was his [Guérin's] faculty; a faculty of naturalistic, not of moral interpretation. This faculty always has for its basis a peculiar temperament, an extraordinary delicacy of organisation and susceptibility to impressions; in exercising it the poet is in a great degree passive (Wordsworth thus speaks of a *wise passiveness*); he aspires to be a sort of human Æolian harp, catching and rendering every rustle of Nature. To assist at the evolution of the whole life of the world is his craving . . . ."[121] Although the "magical" temperament tends, in isolation, to become "morbid" and "devouring," Arnold argued that a poetry of natural magic "illuminates" man as well as, though differently from, a poetry of moral profundity. Like the latter, it gives the poet "a satisfying sense of reality; it reconciles him with himself and the universe"[122] in a way which science is unable to do. In certain critical passages on Wordsworth as well as in his essay on Guérin Arnold was on the very edge of the aesthetic experience as it was about to pass over into religious worship: the "sense of what there is adorable and secret in the life of Nature," he remarked, gave to Guérin's poems "something mystic, inward, and profound."[123] Arnold stopped short because the sense of possessing the "secret" of Nature elicited by the poetry of Guérin or even of Wordsworth could not, finally, be proved not to be illusory. For this reason he devoted most of his attention to poetry's other mode "of exercising its highest power," to be interpretative through "moral profundity."[124]

Whereas "magical" poetry interpreted life "by expressing with magical felicity the physiognomy and movement of the outward world," the poetry of "moral profundity" interpreted it "by expressing, with inspired conviction, the ideas and laws of the inward world of man's moral and spiritual nature."[125] This difference Arnold pursued in his analysis of style. The "Celtic" style, the expression of pure sensibility, was characterized mainly by quickness and delicacy; the "Greek" style, on the other hand, was characterized mainly by nobility. In Homer, for example, style was "something more than touching and stirring; it can form the character, it is edifying."[126] A delicate organization of great sensibility was the poetic gift proper, a gift of the gods; nobility, on the other hand, expressed "the individual personality of the artist"[127] and was a sign of character, of the "noble nature" that lies behind and works through the poetical gift.[128] But the poetry of moral profundity, Arnold goes on, may treat its "serious subject" in one of two ways, either with "severity"—"which comes from saying a thing with a kind of intense compression, or in an allusive, brief, almost haughty way,"—or with "simplicity"—which comes from saying a thing "with the most limpid plainness and clearness."[129] Although both the "severe" and the "simple" were alike "grand" styles, Arnold expressed, in an important passage, his preference for the "simple": "the severe seems, perhaps, the grandest, so long as we attend most to the great personality, to the noble nature, in the poet its author; the simple seems grandest when we attend most to the exquisite faculty, to the poetical gift. But the simple is no doubt to be preferred. It is the more *magical* . . . ."[130] Thus Arnold introduced into his discussion of the grand style that magical element which gave to poetry a dimension beyond that of edification, namely, its power of so dealing with things as "to awaken in us a wonderfully full, new, and intimate sense of them, and of our relations with them. When this sense is awakened in us, as to objects without us, we feel ourselves to be in contact with the essential nature of those objects, to be no longer bewildered and oppressed by them, but to have their secret, and to be in harmony with them; and this feeling calms and satisfies us as no other can."[131] Much as he admired the Miltonic grand-style-severe, Arnold preferred the Homeric grand-style-simple because the former was too *merely* personal, the earned product of moral and intellectual effort with the mark of that effort still upon it; the grand-style-simple, on the other hand, was absolutely effort-less, limpid, and transfiguring. It was the expression of the aesthetic condition in its perfection; it was Apolline.

Thus Arnold posited three levels of poetic activity which corresponded to the three stages in man's religious develop-ment. First, there was the level on which "sensibility," the most positive, most purely poetic element in genius, expressed itself without restraint, but which ended, for want of a fixed center, in "Celtic" melancholy. Secondly, at the level of the grand-style-severe, the poet mastered and organized his poetic gift (the Celtic element) by force of "character" and thus pre-vented his poetic instinct from expending itself in fruitless rebellion against the despotism of fact, but at this level traces of intellectual and moral struggle were still evident in the poetry. Finally, at the level of the grand-style-simple, the poet combined "sensibility" and "character" at a still higher level, having himself achieved a state of inner harmony and of union with himself and the world; at this level the veil of self-con-sciousness along with all doubts and disharmonies disappeared in an intense, absorbing, satisfying experience of the unity and harmony of existence. Arnold found the poetic power con-stantly at work, relieving and rejoicing the morality and knowledge characteristic of each stage in the evolution of human consciousness, whether individual or communal, and thereby providing the "religion" appropriate to that stage: the highest poetry of the primitive consciousness had appeared in the myths of cosmic religion; the highest poetry of the Hebraic moral consciousness was to be found in the prophetic utter-ances and *sententiae* of the Bible; but the highest poetry of all, the poetry of the Hellenic imaginative reason, was em-bodied in the Apollonian tragedy of Greek religion.

Arnold's judgment of particular poets was not rigidly de-termined by his evolutionary view of man's slow ascent towards perfection, but the pattern controls his generalizations about poetry and, with very little variation, his analysis of national cultures as well.[132] The pattern involved a movement from the unconscious exercise of poetic magic, through a conscious use of it, first, in the service of purifying ethical doctrine, and finally in the service of a higher ideal of perfect harmony and union which Arnold associated with Greece. Religion was seen as the product of the imagination operating on the ideas furnished by reason at various levels of self-consciousness and sophistication, and Arnold argued that modern poetry could do no better than match the poetry of Greece.

Arnold was understandably anxious to stress the similarities rather than the differences between traditional Christianity and the new morality and religion which he was recommending, but the differences were there and they were fundamental. They show themselves in the different moral qualities and general temper which distinguished the man of one book, even when that book was the Bible, from the man of Culture. In concluding "Pagan and Mediaeval Religious Sentiment" Arnold cited Sophocles as representing the highest religious wisdom,[133] and in the 1869 Preface to *Culture and Anarchy* he wrote: "Sophocles and Plato knew as well as the author of the Epistle to the Hebrews that 'without holiness no man shall see God,' and their notion of what goes to make up holiness was larger than his."[134] Towards the end of his religious campaign, after taking from the Bible several "religious examples" of morality touched with emotion, he added that "we might also find them elsewhere," citing a passage from Sophocles and concluding: "That is from Sophocles, but it is as much religion as any of the things which we have quoted as religious."[135] In arguing that any noble and serious imaginative work of art was religious, Arnold prepared the way for his final statement on the subject in "The Study of Poetry."

CHAPTER NINE

Poetry as Religion

In 1878, after having devoted almost a decade of his life to
religious discussion, Arnold acknowledged the close connection in his own mind between religion and poetry when he
announced that in "returning to devote to literature, more
strictly so-called," what remained to him of life, he was returning "to a field where work of the most important kind
has now to be done, though indirectly, for religion." "I am
persuaded that the transformation of religion, which is essential for its perpetuance, can be accomplished only by carrying
the qualities of flexibility, perceptiveness, and judgment, which
are the best fruits of letters, to whole classes of the community
which now know next to nothing of them."[136] In writing pref-
aces to the works of various literary figures in the 1880's, Arnold was therefore performing, indirectly at least, a religious
service. The manifesto of this final phase of his career appeared
in 1879 in the form of a brief introduction to an anthology
bearing the title *The Hundred Greatest Men.* In it Arnold
reaffirmed his faith in the superiority of poetry and of the poet
to other forms of human greatness.

Arnold's manifesto was, in some respects, simply a restate-
ment of Wordsworth's defense of poetry as "the breath and
finer spirit of all knowledge." Unlike Wordsworth, however,

Arnold emphasized the immense importance of poetry by pointing out the limitations of the other voices of human experience, of art, of science, of philosophy, and of religion itself. "Compare poetry with other efforts of the human spirit," he suggested. With art?—"poetry thinks, and the arts do not." With science?—"Poetry gives the idea, but it gives it touched with beauty, heightened by emotion." With philosophy?— "the philosophies, the constructions of systematic thought which have arisen, . . . are so perishable that to call up the memory of them is to pass in review man's failures." With religion?—"the strongest part of our religion to-day is its unconscious poetry." Poetry was not only a higher wisdom and of more serious worth than history, as Aristotle had said, but it surpassed the other modes of human experience as well. "The future of poetry is immense, because in conscious poetry, where it is worthy of its high destinies, our race, as time goes on, will find an ever surer and surer stay."[137] In poetry, as a synthesis of thought and emotion completely conscious of itself, man could find "the most adequate and happy" of all manifestations "through which the human spirit pours its force." "This is what we feel to be interpretative for us, to satisfy us—thought, but thought invested with beauty, with emotion. Science thinks, but not emotionally. It adds thought to thought, accumulates the elements of a synthesis which will never be complete until it is touched with beauty and emotion; and when it is touched with these, it has passed out of the sphere of science, it has felt the fashioning hand of the poet."[138]

In his important essay on Wordsworth, Arnold defined poetry as "nothing less than the most perfect speech of man, that in which he comes nearest to being able to utter the truth."[139] What he meant by "truth" appeared in a reference to his earlier claim in the lectures on Homer that "the noble and profound application of ideas to life [was] the most essential part of poetic greatness." The ideas in question, Ar-

nold explained, were "moral ideas"—"on man, on nature, and
on human life," in Wordsworth's phrase—applied, however,
not by "composing moral and didactic poems,—that brings us
but a very little way in poetry," but "under the conditions
fixed . . . by the laws of poetic beauty and poetic truth." And
he explains: "If it is said that to call these ideas *moral* ideas is
to introduce a strong and injurious limitation, I answer that it
is to do nothing of the kind, because moral ideas are really so
main a part of human life. The question, *how to live*, is itself
a moral idea; and it is the question which most interests every
man, and with which, in some way or other, he is perpetually
occupied. A large sense is of course to be given to the term
moral."[140] How large a sense is suggested by Arnold's citation
of Milton's "Nor love thy life, nor hate," Shakespeare's "We are
such stuff / As dreams are made of," and Keats's "For ever wilt
thou love, and she be fair," as examples of the poetic utterance of a "moral idea."[141] Arnold thus made it clear that in
using the term "moral" he had in mind not "doctrine such as
we hear in church" but doctrine which has "the character of
poetic truth,"[142] that is, doctrine which poetry teaches less by
what it says than by what it is: man celebrating a liturgy rooted
in the great human instinct for beauty.[143] "Poetry is the reality,
philosophy the illusion"[144] because "to see things in their
beauty is to see things in their truth, and Keats knew it."[145]
Ranking didactic poetry low on the scale of aesthetic value,
Arnold could nevertheless recommend poetry for its "edifying"
power because great poetry was constitutive; it created an
aesthetic world of poise, order, and beauty against which the
world of practical reality could be judged and by which readers
could be elevated above that reality.

Discussing the "literary" language of the prayers and services
of Catholic Christendom, Arnold observed in *St. Paul and
Protestantism* that for the modern man the "approximative part
of the prayers and services which he rehearses will be poetry,"

and concluded: "It is a great error to think that whatever is thus perceived to be poetry ceases to be available in religion. The noblest races are those which know how to make the most serious use of poetry."[146] If the most serious use of poetry was religious, this religious use was no longer to be confined to that fragment of the world's poetry which was to be found in the Christian Church. Shakespeare's works were more permanent than the Thirty-Nine Articles; Keats, Milton, and Wordsworth, Dante, Molière, and Goethe, Homer and Sophocles, served a religious function of a higher kind than either the "popular" or the "scholastic" poetry of Christianity. The "fulness" of the aesthetic experience as encountered in Sophocles, particularly, served Arnold as the ideal by which he tested human experience generally, for Sophocles not only dealt directly with human nature but with "human nature developed in a number of directions, politically, socially, religiously, morally developed —in its completest and most harmonious development in all these directions; while there is shed over this poetry the charm of that noble serenity which always accompanies true insight," the whole "idealized and glorified by the grace and light shed . . . from the noblest poetical feeling."[147]

With respect to "poetical feeling," Arnold located its two major sources in the two distinct points of view from which the "spectacle" of life could be regarded. In the lectures on Homer he had observed that "that great movement of life . . . that immense and magic spectacle of human affairs, which from boyhood to old age fascinates the gaze of every man of imagination . . . would be his terror, if it were not at the same time his delight."[148] The spectacle *was* terrifying; life was a hell in which men experienced frustration and sorrow, and eventually death. From this point of view the proper response, the lesson of nature itself, was resignation and the moderation of desire: a stoic "breasting" of life, the following of conscience despite frustration and sorrow, which produced that "testi-

mony of a good conscience" and had been not only a "source of
certitude" to the Hebrew prophets, but a source of joy as
well.[149] True religion in this sense, "whether we find it in
Sophocles or in Isaiah,"[150] could be attained through right conduct, issuing in the joy and peace which followed the exercise
of this self-control. Arnold believed that the conviction necessary to motivate such conduct would come from meditation in
the technical religious sense, that is, from "dwelling on the
matter," from "staying our thought on" moral principles and
holding them before the attention so as to obtain a "near and
lively experimental sense of their beneficence."[151] This source
of emotion was the basis of the "religion of righteousness"
which, quantitatively, dominates Arnold's religious criticism.
The importance of Jesus to religion lay less in his teaching an
ethics of necrosis, which the Old Testament and many classical
authors had also taught, then in the fact that "for him moral
action has liberty and self-knowledge; while the prophets of
the Jewish law inadequately conceived God's decrees as mere
rules and commands."[152] Because Jesus realized this law so
perfectly in his life, the record of his life and words could
awaken the requisite emotion vicariously in the devout reader.

There was, however, another and higher point of view from
which to regard the "spectacle" of life—to see it not as terrifying but as alluring. There was a joy proper to necrosis, but
there was also a joy proper to expansion and aspiration, to
that "sentiment after the ideal life" which Arnold had found
so impressive and memorable in the writings of George Sand.[153]
Here the analogy of Arnold's "poetical feeling" with Christian
grace in the theological sense is clear, for in this case the emotion was not earned, but given: "An influence, which we feel
we know not how, and which subdues us we know not when;
which, like the wind, breathes where it lists, passes here, and
does not pass there! Once more, then we come to the root and
ground of religion, that element of awe and gratitude which

fills religion with emotion and makes it other and greater than morality,—the *not-ourselves*."[154]

Discussing St. Paul's concept of righteousness, Arnold argued that "to the Hebrew, as to the Greek, the gift of life, and health, and the world, was divine, as well as the gift of morals."[155] By "this element in which we live and move and have our being, which stretches around and beyond the strictly moral element in us, around and beyond the finite sphere of what is originated, measured, and controlled by our understanding and will . . . by this element we are receptive and influenced, not originative and influencing; now, we all of us receive far more than we originate."[156] This experience Arnold saw as the peculiar province of poetry and for this reason, unlike Spinoza, he gave the key role to the passive, receptive powers, to imagination and to the emotions, as distinguished from active rational thought and voluntary action, in the process by which man brings himself into full harmony with the "stream of tendency." In great poetry the terror of life as hell was ameliorated and converted into delight by the "disinterested" poetic power which, inspired by the Muse, converted the spectacle of life into matter for delight by organizing experience in beautiful language. This was the consummation towards which Arnold's poetry and criticism reached out, the transfiguration of reality by the "Greek spirit." Rightly understood, the cures worked by Jesus were "eminently natural," Arnold wrote, "like the grace of Raphael, or the grand style of Phidias."[157]

Arnold thus developed his aesthetic position and solved the religious problem within an epistemological framework which placed the imaginative reason at the summit, connecting morality (religion's ethical element) with the Hellenic ideal of total perfection, dogma (the intellectual element) with the free play of dialectical reason, and ritual or liturgy (the aesthetic element) with that visitation of creative energy which organized man's noblest moral and intellectual experiences so as to make them beautiful. At its highest reach, poetry suspended the dialectic of thought and rose above the practical cares of life to witness with appropriate emotions the universal movement of life.[158] While for the uninstructed, poetry was primarily a means of edification (and that poetry best capable of edifying them was therefore to be preferred), for the initiated, poetry constituted the very life of life, becoming in its second and higher function an externalization of the aesthetic condition, the expression of the "beautiful soul" at one with itself and the universe.[159]

Arnold's ideal of Culture was moral, therefore, in a quite special sense. The morality was rooted in a religion of the Not-Ourselves that commanded the development of the whole man. Conduct was three fourths of life and the majority of mankind attained happiness through obedience; still, the ideal was total perfection, and as time went on more and more of mankind would be called to this higher perfection. The ideal of Culture was personal, but it was capable of carrying over into and transforming society, expressing itself, when widely shared, in national institutions; it was natural, but attained at the price of immense labor, hidden in the recesses of the poet's spirit, but where conditions allowed—Zeitgeist, discipline, genius, and the luck of the Muse—externalizing itself in perfect form, the *symmetria prisca* of Greece. Towards the end of his life Arnold cited with praise Amiel's description of *le grand monde,* "high society as the Old World knows it and America knows it not." The passage may be taken as a description of Arnold's own kingdom of God on earth, the goal, whether they knew it or not, of sensual Barbarian, hideous Philistine, and brutal Populace alike:

"By the instinctive collaboration of everybody concerned, wit and taste hold festival, and the associations of reality are exchanged for the associations of imagination. So understood, society is a form of poetry; the cultivated classes deliberately recompose the idyll of the past, and the buried world of Astraea. Paradox or not, I believe that these fugitive attempts to reconstruct a dream, whose only end is beauty, represent confused reminiscences of an age of gold haunting the human heart; or rather, aspiration towards a harmony of things which everyday reality denies to us, and of which art alone gives us a glimpse."[160]

In poetry men could find a prefiguration of this society to be. "Conscious" poetry, especially, by organizing the terror of experience into an aesthetic whole to delight the imagination, would serve mankind as a constant reminder of its highest possibilities and evoke in men the highest joy of which they were capable—the disinterested contemplation of the beauty of life and things. This aesthetic contemplation, "whose only end is beauty," was the *terminus ad quem* towards which the "main movement of mind" reflected in Arnold's poetry carried him in his criticism. His poetry recorded his evolution from a general mood of nostalgia to one of resigned acceptance, mediated by the poems of dialogue; his prose recorded his subsequent movement from resigned acceptance to a general mood of aspiration and hope for the future, mediated by a dialectical argument that culminated in a new religion of the imaginative reason. Though his Muse had departed, Arnold remained faithful to her to the end.

THE VIRGILIAN YEARNING

"—tendebatque manus ripae
ulterioris amore."

The Virgilian Yearning

Much of Arnold's prose touched on matters outside literature, and it has consequently been possible for readers to derive a variety of messages from his writings. Yet Arnold himself believed that religion, the "deepest thing in human life,"[1] contained the core of any writer's message. All roads, as he once remarked, lead to Rome.[2] T. S. Eliot noted that later critics have put two major religious constructions upon Arnold's works: that Religion is Morals, and that Religion is Art.[3] For the most part, twentieth-century criticism has tended to emphasize Arnold's equation of religion with morality and twentieth-century critics to value his achievement according to the value they attached to the morality. By some he has been regarded as a failed Romantic who was too Hebraic, and by others as a failed classicist who was too Romantic.[4] Still others, more approving, have seen a great modern humanist who delivered English literature from the excessive claims both of the moralistic Victorians and of the eccentric, if gifted, Romantic visionaries who preceded him.[5]

There are several reasons why, in both the favorable and the unfavorable views, Arnold's morality has provided the point of issue. Not only did he devote twice as many years to criticism as to poetry, but much of his criticism was directed to immediate issues in an age when the fear of social anarchy was widespread. The rhetorical manner of an "easy and un-polemical" style which Arnold devised in order to "get at" his reading public involved him in repeated affirmations of the indispensability of right conduct. These facts, together with the perspective provided twentieth-century readers by the *fin-de-siècle* aestheticism of the nineties and the impersonalist theory of poetry cultivated by influential writers like Pound, Joyce, and Eliot, have tended to make Arnold's work seem by comparison heavily moralistic.[6]

The present study attempts to balance this view by showing that Arnold's morality needs to be interpreted within the context both of his mid-Victorian environment and of his aesthetic temperament and training, which conditioned his response to that environment. The interplay between Arnold's temperament and his environment, understood in terms of William James's psychological distinction between the true self and the social self, may be seen as leading in Arnold's case to a position which, for a majority of his contemporaries, was revolutionary.[7] So far as he advocated the Hebraism of his age, it was Arnold's "social self" that spoke, the image which his environment imposed upon him and which Arnold, when truest to his own nature and vocation, wore as a mask in order that he might exploit it with telling irony.[8] For the life which most deeply attracted him was not moral but aesthetic: literature, he more than once insisted, was his proper *métier*, and throughout his career he never ceased to identify his "true self" with his vocation as poet. His aesthetic instinct, nurtured on the powerful currents of European Romanticism, led him to postulate, beyond the world of Hebraism which he shared with his father and many of his contemporaries, a higher and fundamentally different world regulated by a "Greek" ideal involving the development of all of man's faculties.

To this extent, despite the disillusionments and melancholy

which set him apart from his Romantic forebearers, Arnold remained faithful to the essential Romantic commitment. It was not that he regarded the "imaginative reason" as more important than moral reason. The one faculty was as necessary as the other, and to the extent that the masses of human beings persisted at the level of raw, natural man, the more immediate task of Culture was to inculcate standards of civilized behavior which were contained in the morality of the Bible and the higher pagan religions. But in describing the ideal to which humanity should aspire, Arnold gave priority to the imagination, a priority not of absolute merit nor of frequency (conduct remained three fourths of life), but of order and dignity. The tone of a man's life as set by the overall culture which controls his decisive tendencies Arnold repeatedly connected with qualities which he saw as peculiar to poetry and literary criticism; for while he believed that obedience by itself might "save" a man, he was convinced that poetry alone could transform his existence. Hence in the ideal represented by Arnold's concept of Culture the three terms of Eliot's formula —religion, morals, and art—draw together in a system of values in which art, represented in its most completely human mode of expression, that is, as poetry, occupied the central and moderating place.

In this respect Arnold's religion, one might argue, was the religion of the purest aestheticism possible, since it avoided both the ontological claims of earlier Romanticism as represented in Coleridge as well as the narrower Aestheticism, usually so-called, of the late Victorians. Judged against the attitudes of later writers like Pater, Yeats, Wilde, and Joyce, Arnold appears as a moralist in the classical tradition of stoicism, modified by the *Nachschein* of Christian sentiment; but in relation to the past which he inherited, he must be regarded as a Romantic advocate of the aesthetic consciousness, a critic who spelled out with greater effect than any previous English critic the central role of poetry in a pluralistic culture unsure of all ontological certainties. Identifying Culture with the realization of that inward aesthetic condition in which, as he believed, men could most perfectly attain their full humanity, Arnold extended into the major areas of human activity—education, history, politics, and religion—the basic Romantic thesis as described by Professor Gerard:

In romantic doctrine, the work of art, like the poetic experience which it expresses, owes its value as synthesis to a concert of the faculties which is orchestrated by the imagination. All the faculties (sensory, emotional, intellectual, imaginative, and moral) contribute to the elaboration of the work of art. They are all necessary for uniting the particular with the universal, the concrete with the ideal, the cognitive with the emotional, and for embodying the parent idea into organic sensuous forms which are both highly individualized and capable of touching the heart of the reader.[9]

For all his Hebraism, Arnold was a Romantic in the historical sense of that term, in the direct line of the tradition which holds the creative, unifying power of art above other forms of consciousness.

But it is also true that in his formulation of the basic tenets of that tradition Arnold made important adjustments which set off his work from that of earlier as well as of later Romantics. Wordsworth believed that the Romantics had in fact seen into the life of external things; Arnold was sure only of the sense that this was so, of the "feeling" of union and harmony to be found in poetry. Whether or in what sense the poetic experience was finally "true" he did not know for certain, beyond its testifying to the possibility of a better world than that in which he was compelled to live. This refusal to make Coleridgean claims for the cognitive functions of the imagination places him closer to later figures like I. A. Richards and Herbert Read than to Coleridge or Wordsworth. Richards' concluding statement in *Science and Poetry* is to this extent an accurate and revealing paraphrase of the position set out in Arnold's late criticism.

Our impulses must have some order, some organisation, or we do not live ten minutes without disaster. In the past, Tradition, a kind of Treaty of Versailles assigning frontiers and spheres of influence to the different interests, and based chiefly upon [moral self-] conquest, ordered our lives in a moderately satisfactory manner. But Tradition is weakening. Moral authorities are not as well backed by beliefs as they were; their sanctions are declining in force. We are in need of something to take the place of the old order . . . . a new order based on conciliation, not on attempted suppression. Only the rarest individuals hitherto have achieved this new order, and never yet perhaps completely. But many have achieved it for a brief while, for a particular phase of experience, and many have recorded it for these phases. Of these records poetry consists.[10]

It was not mere coincidence that Richards should have used as an epigraph to his influential book Arnold's famous statement on the future of poetry as the new religion, or that he should conclude his analysis with the words: "We shall then be thrown back, as Matthew Arnold foresaw, upon poetry. It is capable of saving us; it is a perfectly possible means of overcoming chaos." Arnold differed from his successors mainly in refusing to separate the various modes of awareness of which men had become increasingly conscious as the nineteenth century progressed. He turned to criticism precisely in order to combat the fragmentation of consciousness which he saw recorded in his own poetry and which was later to be widely accepted, in one form by Yeats's separation of will and imagination,[11] and in another form by Richards' distinction between the scientific and the emotive use of language.

The stress of maintaining such a position is evident in Arnold's criticism; his double view of Wordsworth, for example, reveals the tension which existed between that aspect of his thought which led him to assert that Wordsworth did not

know enough and a critical sensibility which led him to rank
Wordsworth among the great modern European poets. It was
almost as though, while recognizing them as the one thing
necessary, Arnold begrudged Wordsworth his wholeness and
joy on the grounds that no modern poet had an intellectual or
moral right to such things in an uncertain and "dissolving"
epoch. Yet his sense of the importance of Wordsworth's "deep
power of joy" grew upon him in his last years. What made
poetry religious to Arnold was something apart from and
beyond morality; it was not its ethical truth, which it shared
with morality, but its appeal to the "soul," that deepest self
which lay beyond mere intelligence and conscious will at the
very root of being, and of which reason and will were but
partial manifestations, that constituted poetry's special glory.
It was to the "soul," the source of life and energy and joy in
man, not to the mind or to the conscience, that religion likewise had ultimately to appeal, and for this task Arnold saw
poetry as the most adequate instrument in the modern world.
The connection between "soul," emotion, and religion, on the
one hand, and poetry and the imagination, on the other, he
defended by invoking Wordsworth: "For the power of Christianity has been in the immense emotion which it has excited;
in its engaging, for the government of man's conduct, the
mighty forces of love, reverence, gratitude, hope, pity, and
awe,—all that host of allies which Wordsworth includes under
the one name of *imagination*."[12] Beyond the moral teachings
of ethics and the rational conclusions of science there was
always for Arnold "that element of awe and gratitude which
fills religion with emotion and makes it other and greater than
morality,—the *not ourselves*."[13]

Such a statement helps to locate Arnold's underlying mysticism and to explain his profound sense of the analogy between
the religious worship which he had known in his youth and
the immanent and contemplative activity of the aesthetic con-

sciousness exercised in the creation or reading of poetry. In the words of a modern theologian:

Being an artist means wrestling with the expression of the hidden life of man, avowedly in order that it may be given existence; nothing more. It is the image of the Divine creation, of which it is said that it has made things "*ut sint.*"

The liturgy does the same thing. It too, with endless care, with all the seriousness of the child and the strict conscientiousness of the great artist, has toiled to express in a thousand forms the sacred, God-given life of the soul to no other purpose than that the soul may therein have its existence and live its life.[14]

The difference between the Christian worshipper and Arnold's man of Culture is the difference between the aesthetic consciousness operating in the service of a specific religious faith and the aesthetic consciousness operating on its own terms, simply in virtue of its innate needs and interests, according to a poetic faith in the transfiguring power of the imagination. For Keble and Newman and Hopkins the liturgy of Christianity united art and reality in a spiritual childhood before God the Father; for Arnold poetry united art and reality in a natural, creative innocence contemplating the spectacle of life—the Not-Ourselves. Arnold had a faith, therefore, but it was the instinctive faith of a poet who, wandering intellectually between the two worlds of religious faith and of radical doubt, trusted his poetic temperament and made that temperament the norm of experience.

So far as this faith could be given a rationale, Arnold made use of Spinoza and Goethe to formulate one, but his final appeal was to Greece. He did not recommend a reinterpretation of the Christian dogmas "as something universally salutary and indispensable, far less as any substitute for a practical hold upon Christianity and the Bible,"[15] but he nevertheless saw in the "Greek" idea of total perfection an ideal which would someday make literature and art as much "matters of public institution" as religion—an ideal higher than that of traditional religion, with its narrow and exclusive reliance upon Biblical precept.[16] Just as in Periclean Athens Greek literature had been more truly religious than Greek religion,[17] so in the modern world, Arnold believed, literature might be more truly religious than modern religion. Christianity as it existed in the nineteenth century was no longer an effective motive power among educated men, and the fact that it still motivated many among the uneducated was simply a sign of the latter's uninformed estate rather than of the truth of Christianity as it existed.[18]

Arguments against Arnold's position both as a religious and as a literary critic have come steadily and from various quarters ever since. The inconsistency of his argument was pointed out by contemporaries; others have protested against the "solemnity" which infects his evaluation of the "seriousness" of poets like Dante, Chaucer, and Burns; most telling, perhaps, have been the attacks of F. H. Bradley, T. S. Eliot, and others who questioned Arnold's range of experience as well as his theology and aesthetics. Judging Arnold by his poetry, Eliot concluded that he "had neither walked in hell nor been rapt to heaven," "the vision of the horror and the glory was denied him."[19] The validity of each of these criticisms must be allowed, but it seems probable that Arnold will survive them. In a critic there are more important virtues than consistency and more harmful prejudices than the requirement that poets be serious (Arnold's own criticism makes it clear that he did not confuse seriousness with solemnity). As to religion, and poetry, the present study has tried to show that Arnold's naive and sometimes tactless forays in the field of theology were a function of a deeper strain in his life and work which, if not itself touched by the heights or depths of religious experience, yet kept the way open for religion and could even allow a decisive place for it—namely, his life-long fidelity to poetry's own peculiar revelation.

If Arnold's message was ambivalent, as Eliot's summary indicates that it was, it was so in the same way and for much the same reason as the message of his chief mentor, Goethe. In both Goethe and Arnold there was a desire for what Arnold called "fulness," a desire which he once described to Clough as capable of becoming "almost maniacal" and which came into conflict with a simultaneous desire for simplicity, for what Arnold called "spontaneity of consciousness."[20] His desire for fulness notwithstanding, Arnold was never able to adopt wholeheartedly the "titanism" of some kinds of Romanticism (although "Empedocles on Etna" bears witness to its appeal) because his attraction to simplicity was even deeper. This desire had as its object that naive and spontaneous world of innocence, wholeness, and union which Arnold connected with his childhood, with Wordsworth, and with Homer, and which seems to be the more essential need and characteristic of the aesthetic temperament in any age. The attempt to validate intellectually the simultaneous desires for poetic fulness and for a spontaneous, creative innocence explains why for Arnold, as for Goethe, pantheism, God in nature, became his religion, and Spinoza the chosen prophet. This validating faith Arnold defined quite simply in his praise of George Sand's Wordsworthian sense of Divinity: "She does not attempt to give of this Divinity an account much more precise than that which we have in Wordsworth,—'a presence that disturbs me with the joy of animating thoughts'."[21]

Yet Lord Coleridge, who knew him well, once declared that Arnold always said what he thought, but "not perhaps all he thought." What he could not communicate discursively Arnold communicated by nuance, tone, and style; behind the urbane manner there was the melancholy. He was certainly aware that

neither Wordsworth nor Shakespeare nor Sophocles had an-
swered the central question of how to live purely in terms of
morality; morality was much, and it could bring contentment
to many, but it was not the whole of life nor was it, finally,
productive of the kind of life to which the greatest poets
aspired. Because he himself never attained the higher unity
for which he longed, having taken refuge in morality and character, his Hellenism was tinged with a nostalgia and sense of
loss and longing which the relative equilibrium of his later
years could never entirely quell.

The profound sadness of Arnold's deepest experience may
be illustrated by two prose translations made in his middle
years, one from Homer and the other from Maurice de Guérin.
The Homer translation, very brief, appears as a footnote to
the Greek lines cited in the text of the lectures on Homer.
"'A secure time fell to the lot neither of Peleus the son of
Æacus, nor of the godlike Cadmus; howbeit these are said
to have had, of all mortals, the supreme of happiness, who
heard the golden-snooded Muses sing, one of them on the
mountain (Pelion), the other in seven-gated Thebes.'"22
Here, as in "Empedocles on Etna," the insecure lot of man
finds relief in the happiness of hearing the Muses sing, in
beauty. The other translation, from Guérin's prose poem entitled "The Centaur," is longer and is again strongly reminiscent of the songs of Callicles in "Empedocles on Etna," touching indeed upon the same theme: "There I beheld [in the pale
clearness of the mountain-summits] at one time the god Pan
descend, ever solitary; at another, the choir of the mystic
divinities; or I saw pass some mountain nymph charm-struck
by the night." The translation concludes with Arnold's rendering of the words of Chiron, the aged centaur, to the youthful
Macareus (who, like Marsyas in Callicles' song, has been made
restless by his discovery of "the reed-pipe thrown away by
the god Pan"):

"Seekest thou to know the gods, O Macareus, and from what source men, animals, and the elements of the universal fire have their origin? But the aged Ocean, the father of all things, keeps locked within his own breast these secrets; and the nymphs, who stand around, sing as they weave their eternal dance before him, to cover any sound which might escape from his lips half-opened by slumber. The mortals, dear to the gods for their virtue, have received from their hands lyres to give delight to man, or the seeds of new plants to make him rich; but from their inexorable lips, nothing!"[23]

The aesthetic consciousness aspires to the wholeness both of comprehensiveness and of unity, remaining restless until it penetrates to that final insight which makes such wholeness possible; yet destiny withholds the necessary knowledge. Both passages, in distancing and controlling the "spectacle" of existence, combine stoic acquiescence in the dispensations of life with the pathos of an irrepressible longing. The latent terror, frustration, and confusion are subdued by the power of the lyre that gives delight, but it is the delight of melancholy and calm, not the animation of that deep power of joy for which Arnold searched.

In so far as he was unable himself to attain the fulness and joy which he repeatedly invoked in his criticism, Arnold may be said to have resembled two authors, not of Greece but of Rome, who, better than the Homer and Sophocles whom he commended to his readers in his criticism, represented his actual experience. The one, Marcus Aurelius, he described as a noble spirit whose moral precepts were of the best kind but whose "sense of labour and sorrow in his march towards the goal" constituted a relative inferiority, for "the noblest souls of whatever creed, the pagan Empedocles as well as the Christian Paul, have insisted on the necessity of an inspiration, a joyful emotion, to make moral action perfect." Because the Roman philosopher lacked this emotion, Arnold wrote, he "saved his own soul by his righteousness, and he could do no more. Happy, they who can do this! but still happier, who can do more!"[24] The qualified praise here given to Marcus Aurelius was extended, in almost identical language, to Virgil, Arnold's own poetic "master": if the former was "perhaps the most beautiful figure in history,"[25] the latter was "the most beautiful, the most attractive figure in literary history,"[26] a poet who lacked adequate spiritual mastery of his experience. In concluding his essay on Marcus Aurelius, Arnold brings the two classical figures together by borrowing a line from the *Aeneid*: "We see him wise, just, self-governed, tender, thankful, blameless; yet, with all this, agitated, stretching out his arms for something beyond,—*tendentemque manus ripae ulterioris amore*."[27] In Arnold, too, we feel a reaching out, a Virgilian "mystical yearning," for the spark that would loose the tongue, for the joyful emotion, the fulness, the faith, the idea, without which life was incomplete.

Arnold's melancholy, we may guess, was that of those who, like Marcus Aurelius, yearn "for something unattainable" and who await an uncertain day when "the religious life will have harmonized all the new thought with itself."[28] Meanwhile he was obliged to rest his case for modern poetry with the "faithful" mode of Goethe, with its "power of moral and spiritual emotion," at the same time offering to his contemporaries the achievements of classical Greece as a perpetual reminder of higher possibilities. The appeal to Goethe, in the light of a recent critic's evaluation of the German poet, is illuminating:

What was the nature of the experience in the face of which Goethe offered no help? It was the very kind of experience before which Goethe himself always proved helpless: the exposure to the manifestations of evil and sin. "The mere attempt to write tragedy might be my undoing," he once said, and it was the truth. . . . All of [his dramas] are potential tragedies, indeed so much so, that one may feel that the tragic conclusion could only be avoided at the price of complete artistic conclusiveness. They show a moving and yet unsatisfactory reluctance of mind and imagination to accept the rule of the road leading to the very centre of human destiny. This is not to imply that in that very centre there dwells, inescapably, tragedy. But once a man is compelled to penetrate to that central point in all seriousness, then there is only one region left that stretches, for the European, beyond tragedy. Beyond Hamlet and the rest that is silence, there stands only Prospero:

> And my ending is despair
> Unless I be reliev'd by prayer,
> Which pierces so that it assaults
> Mercy itself, and frees all faults.[29]

Arnold, trying late in life to come to terms with the writer to whom he was perhaps most deeply indebted, himself described *Tasso* and *Iphigenie,* which he thought Goethe's best plays, as "invented," "not natural," "devised," "something determined by the thinker, not given by the necessity of Nature herself."[30] Arnold thus seems to have felt what Goethe lacked: that *Iphigenie,* in the words of the critic just cited, "is dramatically not true because the objective world which is the scene of the play is not real," because "there is no real evil in that world," with the result that "the inexorable hardness of the Greek myth is dissolved into the softer substance of the goodness of human nature."[31] Arnold felt a deep affinity with Goethe because for Arnold, too, evil was not a tragic violation of the sacred but simply an impotence to be got rid of, a point of view which explains his dismissal of Sophocles' *Antigone* as out of date.[32]

What continues to attract readers to Arnold despite the absence from his work of the true tragic vision is, I would suggest, not the specifics of his message but the spiritual element which, in his own phrase, "lights up" everything he has to say and for which Greece served in both his poetry and criticism as the appropriate symbol. Arnold preserved in the depths of his inner life an innocence that went beyond the

physical chastity or intellectual naiveté with which he sometimes confused it, the creative innocence of the aesthetic consciousness itself which Schiller had found miraculously preserved in *Werther* and which has been called the original
innocence of those who do not know good and evil because
they "live, not beyond, but before that fatal rift."[33] This is
what Arnold meant, I believe, when he saw himself as born
under the sign of Pan, the deity who attended him from his
cradle upwards, that element in himself of the pure artist in
the sense of the artist defined by Thomas Mann, as one who
"is not originally a moral being, but an aesthetic one, his primary drive being not virtue but play—not virtue but virtuosity,
as it were." If Arnold attempted to improve his society and
himself, he did so most effectively when he worked in the only
way permitted to the artist, in Mann's words, "not by moral
precepts" but "by endowing [the world] with spiritual meaning; he uses thought, word, and image to set down his own
life and, figuratively, life as a whole. His task is to *animate*—
just that and nothing more."[34] When Arnold saw that his poetry
failed to animate, he took up criticism as one of those Children
of the Second Birth who, like Marcus Aurelius, have at least
kept themselves unspotted from the world.

    In summary, Arnold's place in English literary history was
in large measure determined by the general predicament of
the artist in the mid-nineteenth century. With Goethe and the
first-generation Romantics the aesthetic consciousness attained
an extraordinary awareness of its prerogatives and powers, and
as the century progressed and truth in other areas of experience seemed to become more and more problematical, the
aesthetic power took on with increasing explicitness the functions formerly borne by philosophy and religion. Arnold's place
in this process is indicated by his attempt to defend the aesthetic mode without allowing it to lose touch with these other
areas of human experience. But the task of assimilating and

mastering the accumulation of knowledge and experience proved more difficult in Arnold's generation than it had been for Goethe and the earlier generation of Romantics. Arnold's lot as a poet—as for most poets since—was to embody the pain of the struggle, to attempt to unify without pretending to solve the baffling experience of life in a multitudinous world, and thus to realize, "for a brief while and for some particular phase of experience," a measure of that order which in the modern world has come to seem increasingly difficult, rare, and precious. Both as a poet and as a critic, Arnold was the first writer in England to respond to this predicament by offering the aesthetic condition as the supreme achievement available to men in a civilization threatened by dehumanization. Unlike writers of the very first rank, Arnold lacked energy, scope, and final penetration to that area behind silence where Prospero dwells, but his writings retain the marks of an innocence and integrity which continue to make him one of the most attractive figures in literary history.

KEY TO ABBREVIATIONS

References to Arnold's writings in the notes are made in the abbreviated forms listed below. For the prose I have used the first four volumes of Professor Super's complete edition (now in process) of the prose, J. Dover Wilson's edition of *Culture and Anarchy*, Professor Neiman's collection of fugitive materials, and, for all other items, the relevant volumes of the Edition de Luxe. Note numbering is consecutive through each of the three Parts. Full bibliographical information is listed after the abbreviations.

CA: *Culture and Anarchy*, ed. J. Dover Wilson (Cambridge, 1932).

Commentary: C. B. Tinker and H. F. Lowry, *The Poetry of Matthew Arnold: A Commentary* (London, 1940).

Letters: *Letters of Matthew Arnold, 1848–1888* collected and arranged by George W. E. Russell (New York and London, 1896).

Lowry: *The Letters of Matthew Arnold to Arthur Hugh Clough*, ed. with introd. by Howard Foster Lowry (London and New York, 1932).

NB: *The Note-Books of Matthew Arnold*, ed. H. F. Lowry, K. Young, and W. H. Dunn (London, 1952).

Neiman: *Essays, Letters, and Reviews by Matthew Arnold*, ed. Fraser Neiman (Cambridge, Mass., 1960).

PW: *The Poetical Works of Matthew Arnold*, ed. C. B. Tinker and H. F. Lowry (London, 1950).

Super: *The Complete Prose Works of Matthew Arnold*, ed. R. H. Super (Ann Arbor, 1960——). (Vols. I–IV were available at the time of writing.)

UL: *Unpublished Letters of Matthew Arnold*, ed. Arnold Whitridge (New Haven, 1923).

Works: *The Works of Matthew Arnold*, Edition de Luxe (15 vols.; London, 1903–1904).

Notes

1. Wilhelm Windelband, *A History of Philosophy*, tr. James H. Tufts (2 vols.; New York, 1958, from rev. ed., 1901), II, 530. See also Katherine E. Gilbert and Helmut Kuhn, *A History of Esthetics*, Revised and Enlarged (Bloomington, Ind., 1954), Chs. XI-XIV, and Harold Höffding, *A History of Modern Philosophy*, tr. B. E. Meyer (2 vols.; New York, 1955), II, Bks. VI-VIII.

2. *The Works of Thomas Carlyle*, Centenary Edition (London, 1898), XXI, 260–261.

3. Friedrich Schiller, *On the Aesthetic Education of Man*, trans. with introd. by Reginald Snell (New Haven, 1954), p. 132. The eighteenth-century origins of the new aestheticism are discussed at length by Ernst Cassirer in *The Philosophy of the Enlightenment*, tr. Fritz C. A. Koelln and James P. Pettegrove (Boston, 1955), Ch. VII. The history of the idea of an "aesthetic attitude" in English eighteenth-century thought is discussed by Jerome Stolnitz in "'Beauty': Some Stages in the History of an Idea," *Journal of the History of Ideas*, XXII (1961), 185–204.

4. Edward Bullough, *Aesthetics: Lectures and Essays*, ed. Elizabeth M. Wilkinson (Stanford, Calif., 1957) p. 89.

5. *The Letters of John Keats*, ed. Maurice Buxton Forman, 3rd ed. (London, 1947), p. 317.

6. Bullough, *Aesthetics*, p. 70.

7. *The Poetical Works of William Wordsworth*, ed. Ernest de Selincourt (3 vols.; Oxford, 1952), II, 396.

8. "For Keats, the opposition between beauty and utility, like that between beauty and truth, seems to have been one more aspect of the division against himself which was resolved only by his premature death. He is the first great poet to exhibit that peculiarly modern malady—a conscious and persistent conflict between the requirements of social responsibility and of aesthetic detachment."

M. H. Abrams, *The Mirror and the Lamp: Romantic Theory and the Critical Tradition* (New York, 1953), p. 328.

9. William James, *Principles of Psychology* (2 vols.; New York, 1918), I, 310.

10. Murray Krieger, " 'Dover Beach' and the Tragic Sense of Eternal Recurrence," *University of Kansas City Review*, XXIII (1956), 73–79.

NOTES: PART ONE

1. "A Speech in Response to a Toast to 'Literature' " (1875), Fraser Neiman, ed., *Essays, Letters, and Reviews by Matthew Arnold* (Cambridge, Mass., 1960), p. 200—hereafter cited as "Neiman."

2. "Sainte-Beuve" (1869), Neiman, p. 165.

3. March, 1862, *Letters of Matthew Arnold, 1848–1888*, collected and arranged by George W. E. Russell (New York and London, 1896), I, 166—hereafter cited as "*Letters.*"

4. February, 1849, *The Letters of Matthew Arnold to Arthur Hugh Clough*, ed. with an introductory study by Howard Foster Lowry (London and New York, 1932), p. 99—hereafter cited as "Lowry."

5. "Stanzas in Memory of the Author of 'Obermann' " (ll. 131–132) and "To a Gipsy Child by the Seashore" (ll. 53–56), *The Poetical Works of Matthew Arnold*, ed. Chauncey B. Tinker and Howard F. Lowry (London, 1950), pp. 310 and 43—hereafter cited as "*PW.*"

6. See note 1 above.

7. For Arnold's discovery of Virgil see E. V. Lucas, *The Colvins and their Friends* (New York, 1928), p. 193. The *Eclogues* were read in the Fourth Form at Rugby; see Arnold Whitridge, *Dr. Arnold of Rugby* (London, 1928), p. 112. Arnold's mature view of Virgil is discussed below, pp. 42–43. For Arnold's classical readings at school see Warren D. Anderson, *Matthew Arnold and the Classical Tradition* (Ann Arbor, 1965), pp. 1–14.

8. Thomas Arnold, *Passages in a Wandering Life* (London, 1900), p. 63.

9. For Arnold's dandyism see Lowry, pp. 24-25. The biographers of Jowett, tutor at Balliol during Arnold's years there, record a barb which may have been aimed at Arnold: "He said of one who was known amongst his comrades as 'the poet' (1846): 'He is a very clever fellow and with considerable powers of mind, but obscured a little by the haze of Emerson and Wordsworth' " (Evelyn Abbott and Lewis Campbell, *The Life and Letters of Benjamin Jowett, M.A.* [London, 1897], I, 80). Jowett could not take Arnold seriously until long afterwards (I, 88-89). On life at Balliol during Clough's and Arnold's years there see H. W. Carless Davis, *Balliol College* (London, 1899), pp. 209-210.

10. May 1, 1853, Lowry, p. 135. I have retained Lowry's transcription of "philistercy." The German *Philisterei* suggests that Lowry may have misread Arnold's "e" as a "c."

11. Arnold observed that Maurice de Guérin, with whom he had considerable sympathy, had found the drudgery of teaching less irksome than the drudgery of journalism "inasmuch as to a sensitive man like Guérin, to silence his genius is more tolerable than to hackney it." *The Complete Prose Works of Matthew Arnold*, ed. R. H. Super (Ann Arbor, 1960—), III, 28-29—hereafter cited as "Super."

12. Lowry's summary is excellent: "The conclusion I should draw is, not that his poetic talent was constrained by the critical instinct, but that his output was sharply curtailed by the high standard he set himself." Among contributing causes Lowry lists the political interests which Arnold picked up at Lansdowne House, the later burden of the school inspectorship, heavy reading, and the poor reception accorded Arnold's early poems (Lowry, pp. 37-38). Lionel Trilling, however, stresses the uncongeniality of the age generally and the pressures of Arnold's critical intelligence (*Matthew Arnold* [New York, 1955], pp. 24 ff.). H. W. Garrod makes the "Marguerite" affair central (*Poetry and the Criticism of Life* [Cambridge, Mass., 1931], pp. 44-45).

13. *PW*, p. 227. Arnold later gave this stanza a title, "Persistency of Poetry."

14. On Arnold's sense of his unpopularity see William E. Buckler, *Matthew Arnold's Books: Towards a Publishing Diary* (Geneva, 1958), p. 67, and Sidney M. B. Coulling, "Matthew Arnold's 1853 *Preface*: Its Origin and Aftermath," *Victorian Studies*, VII, (1963–64), 240–247.

15. See Trilling, *Matthew Arnold*, p. 24.

16. October 28, 1852, Lowry, p. 124.

17. For Arnold's early readings see *The Note-Books of Matthew Arnold*, ed. H. F. Lowry, K. Young, and W. H. Dunn (London, 1952)—hereafter cited as "*NB*"—pp. 551 ff.; Alan Harris, "Matthew Arnold: The Unknown Years," *Nineteenth Century and After*, DCLXXIV (April, 1933), 498–509; and Kenneth Allott, "Matthew Arnold's Reading-Lists in Three Early Diaries," *Victorian Studies*, II (1958–59), 254–266.

18. Mrs. Humphry Ward, *A Writer's Recollections* (London, 1918), p. 12. Emerson's effect upon Arnold is explored by R. H. Super, "Emerson and Arnold's Poetry," *Philological Quarterly*, XXXIII (1954), 396–403. George Sand's influence is discussed by Iris Sells in *Matthew Arnold and France* (Cambridge, 1935), Ch. II.

19. For Carlyle's influence on Arnold see C. B. Tinker and H. F. Lowry, *The Poetry of Matthew Arnold: A Commentary* (London, 1940)—hereafter cited as "*Commentary*"—p. 300; Kathleen Tillotson, "Matthew Arnold and Carlyle," *Proceedings of the British Academy*, XLII (1956), 133–153; and David J. De Laura, "Arnold and Carlyle," *PMLA*, LXXIX (1964), 104–129.

20. There is no adequate study of Schiller's reception in England. See notes 26 and 27 below.

21. *Works of Thomas Carlyle*, Centenary Edition (London, 1898), XXV, 200.

22. Ibid., XXVII, 174–175.

23. Ibid., p. 186.

24. Ibid., p. 213.

25. Ibid., XXV, 113. For Carlyle's own early tentative aestheticism see "The State of German Literature," *Works*, XXVI, 56.

26. *The Life of Edward Bulwer, First Lord Lytton, by His Grandson* (London, 1913), II, 446. Arnold took from Schiller the epigraph for his early prize-poem "Cromwell." A possible source,

in addition to Carlyle and Bulwer-Lytton, of Arnold's knowledge of Schiller is John Herman Merivale, the third volume of whose *Poems Original and Translated* (London, 1844) contained a number of Schiller's lyric poems, including "The Gods of Greece," a lament for the passing of the happy Greek world of mythological presences, and "The Artists," which Merivale said required a knowledge of Schiller's *Aesthetic Letters* to be fully understood. The volume also contains an awkward version of Thekla's answer from Schiller's *Piccolomini*, which Arnold also translated, and a poem entitled "Resignation." Merivale saw Schiller as juxtaposing the aesthetic world of Beauty to the moral world of Duty, to the advantage of the former, which embodied the ideal towards which morality tended.

27. Edward Bulwer, Lord Lytton, "The Life of Schiller: A Biographical Sketch," *Miscellaneous Prose Works* (3 vols.; London, 1868), I, 468. This essay originally served to introduce translations of Schiller's poems which Bulwer published in 1847.

28. Ibid., p. 475. Arnold's quotation from Schiller in his own 1853 *Preface* is from Schiller's Preface to the *Bride of Messina*.

29. Ibid., pp. 486-487.

30. The name of Hölderlin does not occur in Arnold's writings, but the great German author's poems on Empedocles suggest at least a similarity of interests and outlook. Hölderlin's life and poems are discussed in E. M. Butler, *The Tyranny of Greece over Germany* (Boston, 1958), pp. 223-224, which also contains a chapter on Heine of interest to students of Arnold.

31. "Preface to First Edition of *Poems*" (1853), Super, I, 1-4.

32. *The Works of Thomas Carlyle*, XXIII, 332. In an early study James Bentley Orrick argued that Arnold read, or rather misread, Goethe through Carlyle ("Matthew Arnold and Goethe," *Publications of the English Goethe Society*, n.s., IV [1928], 5-54). My own somewhat different view of the relationship is discussed in Part Three and in the Conclusion below.

Crabb Robinson notes that Goethe was a topic of conversation in the Arnold household; under the date January 4, 1836, at Fox How, he wrote: "The main subject of conversation was one on which I have no pleasure in hearing Wordsworth talk—Goethe, whom he depreciates in utter ignorance. Dr. Arnold seems to be aware of the real objections to Goethe's moral character and is likely to overrate their importance" (*Harry Crabb Robinson on Books and their Writers*, ed. Edith J. Morley [London, 1938], II, 478). In 1839 Robinson read Goethe's poetry to the Fox How ladies (II, 566), and in 1850, at a breakfast with Clough, Arnold, and others, he records: "I talked with Arnold on German matters, particularly Goethe" (II, 699). It is unlikely, therefore, that Arnold's view of Goethe was exclusively determined by Carlyle. In any case, whatever the moralizing influence of Dr. Arnold, Wordsworth, and Carlyle on Arnold's early view of Goethe, he was reading his own copy of *Dichtung und Wahrheit* in the late forties (see Kenneth Allott, cited in note 17, p. 210), and his personal library included many of Goethe's other books and letters, including the correspondence with Schiller (see *NB*, p. 640). He later deprecated Wordsworth's disparagement of Goethe, and continued to praise Goethe long after he had lost faith in Carlyle (see Lowry, p. 47, and E. K. Brown, *Matthew Arnold: A Study in Conflict* [Chicago, 1848], p. 85).

33. "Preface to First Edition of *Poems*" (1853), Super, I, 7.

34. *NB*, pp. 346, 392, 428, 515.

35. Super, I, 13, 15. For additional evidence of Arnold's debt to Goethe see Kenneth Allott's annotations to the *Preface* in *The Poems of Matthew Arnold* (London, 1965), Appendix A, pp. 589-609 passim.

36. Trilling, *Matthew Arnold*, p. 139.

37. The 1853 *Preface* is related to contemporary issues by Coulling (see note 14, p. 210), H. W. Garrod ("Matthew Arnold's 1853 *Preface*," *Review of English Studies*, XVII [1941], 310-321), and Alba H. Warren, Jr. (*English Poetic Theory, 1825-1865* [Princeton, 1950], Ch. IX).

38. *The Works of Thomas Carlyle*, XXIII, 352.

39. "Preface to Second Edition of *Poems*" (1854), Super, I, 17.

40. *The Works of Thomas Carlyle*, XXV, 114.

41. Edward Bulwer, *Miscellaneous Prose Works*, I, 443.

42. September, 1849, Lowry, p. 111.

43. June 7, 1852, Lowry, p. 123.

44. February, 1853, Lowry, p. 130.

45. 1845?, Lowry, p. 59.

46. February, 1848, Lowry, p. 66.

47. 1845?, Lowry, p. 59.

48. February, 1849, Lowry, p. 99.

49. February, 1849, Lowry, pp. 98–99.

50. December, 1847, Lowry, p. 63.

51. February, 1849, Lowry, p. 99.

52. *Passages in a Wandering Life*, p. v.

53. Cited from *Memorials of William Charles Lake* (p. 161) in *The Library of Literary Criticism of English and American Authors*, ed. Charles Wells Moulton (Buffalo, N. Y., 1904), VIII, 628.

54. Whitridge, *Dr. Arnold of Rugby*, p. 206.

55. Arthur Penrhyn Stanley, *Life and Correspondence of Thomas Arnold, D.D.*, Minerva Library, New Series (London, n.d.), p. 106.

56. Quillinan's remark is cited in *Commentary*, p. 222. Crabb Robinson's comment was provoked by a review of Wordsworth's poetry which he thought Arnold had written: "I had not ascribed so much of Wordsworth feeling to any of the Arnold race" (*Books and their Writers*, II, 812).

57. Dr. Arnold's remark is cited by D. G. James in *Matthew Arnold and the Decline of English Romanticism* (Oxford, 1961), p. 2, Matthew's by Whitridge, *Dr. Arnold of Rugby*, p. 15. Arnold's sense of his difference from his father is also expressed in a letter to his brother William in March, 1856: "I too have felt that absurdity and disadvantage of our heredity connexion in the minds of all people with education, and am always tempted to say to people, 'My good friends, this is a matter for which my father certainly had a spécialité, but for which I have none whatever.' . . . I am inclined to think it would have been the same with any active line of life. . . ." *Unpublished Letters of Matthew Arnold*, ed. Arnold Whitridge (New Haven, 1923), pp. 31–32—hereafter cited as "*UL*." For a balanced account of Arnold's relationship to his father and the "strain of antipathy that seems to go back almost to Matthew's infancy," see Patrick J. McCarthy, *Matthew Arnold and the Three Classes* (New York and London, 1964), pp. 1–47. The phrase cited is from p. 25.

58. *Passages in a Wandering Life,* p. vi.

59. James Martineau, *Essays, Reviews, and Addresses* (London, 1890), I, 65. The first chapter of Francis J. Woodward's *The Doctor's Disciples* (London, 1954) contains a useful survey of first-hand responses to Dr. Arnold which supports Martineau's analysis.

60. Cited by Woodward, *The Doctor's Disciples,* p. 3.

61. *New Review,* I (1889), 113.

62. In 1847 Arnold purchased a copy of Béranger in Paris for Clough. The nature of the French poet's appeal for the young Arnold is suggested by Walter Bagehot's comments: "Goethe, who certainly did not undervalue the most elaborate and artful cultivation, at once pronounced Béranger to have 'a nature most happily endowed, firmly grounded in himself, purely developed from himself, and quite in harmony with himself.' In fact, as these words mean, Béranger, by happiness of nature or self-attention, has that *centrality* of mind which is the really valuable result of colleges and teaching" (*Literary Studies* [2 vols.; London, 1911], II, 250). Earlier in this essay Bagehot cited the concluding four lines of Arnold's "Youth and Calm" as illustrative of Béranger's "poetry of equanimity" (II, 238). Both Arnold and Bagehot linked Béranger with the Latin poet with whom Clough linked Arnold's poetry, Horace (Lowry, pp. 126, 127n). See also Warren D. Anderson, *Matthew Arnold and the Classical Tradition,* pp. 135–136.

63. March, 1845, Lowry, p. 56.

64. See *Letters,* I, 162 (March, 1862) and 392 (June 13, 1868). William S. Peterson, in a suggestive analysis of the landscape imagery in "Rugby Chapel," concludes: "The break in the governing metaphor . . . is profoundly significant: the two landscapes reveal the difference not only between two categories of men . . . but also between a father and a son" ("The Landscapes of 'Rugby Chapel'," *Victorian Newsletter,* No. 25 [Spring, 1964], pp. 22–23).

65. Lowry, p. 7.

66. Wendell Stacy Johnson has suggested that the debate between Clough and Arnold extended to their poetry ("Parallel Imagery in Arnold and Clough," *English Studies,* XXXVII [1956], 1–11).

67. *The Poems of Arthur Hugh Clough,* ed. H. F. Lowry, A. L. P. Norrington, and F. L. Mulhauser (Oxford, 1951), pp. 25, 43.

68. *The Portable Arnold,* ed. Lionel Trilling (New York, 1949), p. 18.

69. *Miscellaneous Works* (London, 1845), pp. 252-253.

70. Stanley, *Life and Correspondence of Dr. Arnold,* p. 41.

71. Ibid., p. 35.

72. Ibid., p. 172.

73. Ibid., p. 288.

74. Comments on the autobiographical element in "Sohrab and Rustum" appear in Maud Bodkin, *Archetypal Patterns in Poetry* (New York, 1958), pp. 63-65; J. D. Jump, "Matthew Arnold," in *From Dickens to Hardy,* ed. Boris Ford (Hammondsworth, 1958), p. 309; W. Stacy Johnson, *The Voices of Matthew Arnold* (New Haven and London, 1961), pp. 127-128; and, especially, Kenneth Burke, *A Rhetoric of Motives* (New York, 1950), pp. 7-10.

75. The similarity of "ironic quality" in "Sohrab and Rustum" and "Balder Dead" is noted by Johnson, *The Voices of Matthew Arnold,* p. 127. The close connection between the two poems in Arnold's own mind is documented by Tinker and Lowry (*Commentary,* pp. 89-91). The following lines (20-22) from the later poem reveal a similarity in theme:

> If any here might weep for Balder's death,
> I most might weep, his father; such a son
> I lose to-day, so bright, so loved. . . .

76. *Commentary,* pp. 73, 84-85.

77. Ibid., p. 76.

78. Kenneth Allott believes that Arnold's interest in the *Bhagavad Gita* was awakened in 1845 by Victor Cousin's *Introduction à l'histoire de la philosophie* (see note 17, p. 210). The note-book for 1860 has several entries bearing on Arnold's continued interest in Oriental religion (*NB,* pp. 9, 10, 11, 12), and a late essay entitled "A Persian Passion Play" (1871), eventually incorporated into the third edition of *Essays in Criticism,* brings this interest down to the period of Arnold's religious writings.

79. September 23, 1849, Lowry, p. 110.

80. "There is no doubt such religions as the Egyptian or Judaic being mainly ethical systems. The aesthetic type might, on the

other hand, be illustrated by Hindooism and by its purest representative, Greek religion. On the whole, pantheistic religions seem to point to the aesthetic attitude, while the conception of a personal God . . . belongs essentially to the ethical category" (Edward Bullough, *Aesthetics: Lectures and Essays*, ed. Elizabeth M. Wilkinson [Stanford, 1957], p. 80). Arnold's meditative habit of mind has been noticed by many critics; see, for example, the editors' Introduction to the *Note-Books*, Trilling, *Matthew Arnold*, pp. 26–31, 83, and John Shepherd Eells, Jr., *The Touchstones of Matthew Arnold* (New York, 1955), pp. 23–26.

81. March 4, 1848, Lowry, p. 71.

82. *PW*, p. 62 (ll. 49–52). Hereafter line references to Arnold's poetry will be given in the text, in brackets, immediately following quotations.

83. Cited by Lowry, p. 5.

84. Ibid., p. 130. Letter written in February, 1853.

85. Stanley, *Life and Correspondence of Dr. Arnold*, pp. 214–215.

86. Ibid., p. 373.

87. James Insley Osborne, *Arthur Hugh Clough* (London, 1920), p. 64.

88. See Louis Bonnerot, *Matthew Arnold, poète: Essai de biographie psychologique* (Paris, 1947), p. 18, and Merton A. Christensen, "Thomas Arnold's Debt to German Theologians: A Prelude to Matthew Arnold's *Literature and Dogma*," *Modern Philology*, LV (1957), 14–20.

89. "A susceptible, serious, intellectual boy may be injured by the incessant inculcation of the awfulness of life and the magnitude of great problems" (Bagehot, "Mr. Clough's Poems," *Literary Studies*, II, 275).

90. (June 13, 1868): "I do not say . . . that papa would have given Hellenism the prominence I give it; I know he would not; but time orders these things" (*Letters*, I, 392). After citing this letter, Bonnerot comments: "Cette réserve capitale marque que leurs sympathies furent imparfaites, surtout dans le domaine où l'Hellénisme a le plus d'influence: la sensibilité" (*Matthew Arnold*, p. 18). Another way to put the relationship is to say that Matthew

played the role of Schiller to his father's Kant in a temperamental reorientation of outlook of the kind described by Edward Bullough: "In Schiller's recasting of Kant's rigoristic ethical ideal into the conception of the 'schöne Seele,' a transition from the ethical to the aesthetic standpoint . . . can almost be observed in the making" (*Aesthetics*, p. 80).

91. There is an extended analysis of Arnold's temperament in D. G. James's *Matthew Arnold and the Decline of English Romanticism*, pp. 1–29, in the course of which the following passage from Arnold's essay on Maurice de Guérin is cited by James as unconsciously self-revealing: "Strong and deep religious feelings he had, implanted in him by nature, developed in him by circumstances of childhood: but he had also (and here is the key to his character) that temperament which opposes itself to the fixedness of a religious vocation, or any vocation of which fixedness is an essential attribute . . . a temperament common enough among artists." From this and related materials Professor James concludes that Arnold, too, had a natural tendency to "remain fluid, uncommitted, and imprecise," and this he relates to Arnold's poetic temperament.

The present study rests on the same inference, namely, that Arnold's temperament was innately poetic. My own position differs from Professor James's, however, in several respects, most importantly in regard to the assumption that the "Romantic" view of poetry was wedded to a doctrine of poetic "autonomy" and of poetry's inherently "profane" nature (p. 51), and his related argument that Arnold contributed to the decline of Romanticism by his willingness to make the "autonomous" poetic power subservient to extrapoetic interests (p. 81). The issues are too complex to be discussed adequately in a note; I have tried in Part Three and the Conclusion below to make a distinction which seems to me essential. James fails to make this distinction and is thereby led, I believe, to overlook the difference between Arnold's view of the poetic nature as it is in itself, on the one hand, and his view, on the other hand, of the conditions under which the poetic nature can normally and fully realize itself. As applied to the passage from the Guérin essay cited by James, the distinction suggests several points.

Arnold refers to a want of "fixedness," not as inherent in the poetic nature itself, but as "common enough among artists." What Arnold had in mind, I believe, is the poetic temperament as it tends to operate either in an age of intellectual and moral confusion or in an individually defective sensibility. Arnold criticizes Guérin precisely because, having a religious faith, he permitted it to exist apart from his poetic life, so that the latter did not, as Arnold told Clough poetry ought to, include "religion with poetry." In short, Guérin suffered from the modern disease of a dissociated sensibility.

Far from denying "fixedness" to the poet, Arnold thought of himself as most faithful to his own deepest personal needs precisely so long as he was composing poetry; however "fluid" he appeared to be to his friends or to members of his family, poetry *was* his vocation. The poetic temperament, it is true, resists the "fixedness" of other vocations, but only in order to remain faithful to the "fixedness" proper to the poet, who as a "spectator" rather than a participant is disinterested and flexible in the aesthetic sense, but not therefore necessarily "uncommitted" or inconstant at the deepest level of his experience. Elsewhere in the Guérin essay Arnold cites Guérin's claim that poetry saved him (see p. 133).

It was because his own inner restlessness infected his poetic life that Arnold eventually abandoned the writing of poetry. Far from being content with his own fluctuating, he suffered great anguish because of his inability to find an Idea by which to overcome it and was deeply resentful of an age which failed to provide its poets with such an Idea. This Idea Arnold believed to be inherent in poetry itself, when it was truest to its own *élan*, the greatest poets being characterized by a centrality which enabled them to subdue *all* of life to laws of poetic truth and poetic beauty. In all this Arnold, I believe, is much closer to the English Romantics than is Professor James, whose description of the "autonomy" of poetry and of its "profane" nature sounds more like Joyce than like Wordsworth.

NOTES: PART TWO

1. *The Works of Matthew Arnold*, Edition de Luxe (15 vols.; London, 1903–1904), IV, 5—hereafter cited as *"Works."*

2. November 30, 1853, Lowry, p. 146.

3. Ibid.

4. June 5, 1869, *Letters,* II, 9.

5. Arnold's attitude toward the use of biography in criticism is suggested in his proposal to Clough in 1852 regarding a series of studies of English poets which would be "biographical but above this *critical*: presupposing detailed lives of each poet," and for a series of Greek translations with each poet's work "preceded by his life" (Lowry, p. 121). The variety of Arnold's own critical methods is emphasized by Stuart Sherman in *Matthew Arnold: How to Know Him* (Indianapolis, 1917), pp. 150–165. See also R. A. Donovan, "The Method of Arnold's *Essays in Criticism*," *PMLA,* LXXI (1956), 922–931, and A. Dwight Culler, *Poetry and Criticism of Matthew Arnold* (Boston, 1961), pp. ix–x.

6. February 12, 1853, Lowry, p. 128.

7. Ibid., p. 129.

8. Ibid.

9. June 26, 1887, E. V. Lucas, *The Colvins and their Friends,* p. 193.

10. "Address to the Wordsworth Society" (1883), Neiman, p. 251.

11. "On the Modern Element in Literature" (1857), Super, I, 34, 36.

12. Ibid., p. 35.

13. W. Y. Sellar, a friend of Arnold's at Oxford and later (Lowry, p. 96), sheds light on Arnold's response to Virgil and on contemporary responses to both Arnold and Virgil in his study *The Roman Poets of the Augustan Age: Virgil,* 3rd ed. (Oxford, 1908). Sellar argues that at the beginning of the nineteenth century "The whole tone of the criticism which arose out of admiration for German thought and poetry" was opposed to the spirit of Latin literature of which Virgil was the great exemplar. He connects this revolt with the revival of interest in the Greeks in Germany and England and with the desire of the Romantics to escape the eighteenth-century literary tradition (pp. 72–75). Yet the Virgilian influence persisted, Wordsworth and Keble in England and Sainte-Beuve in France being among Virgil's admirers. Two nineteenth-century writers,

both relevant to Arnold, are seen by Sellar as especially Virgilian: Newman and George Sand. Sellar refers to Newman's *Grammar of Assent* (pp. 91, 422) and to George Sand's prose idyls, which "better than any modern poet . . . reproduce the Virgilian feeling of Nature" (p. 250). For a "pastoral melancholy" similar to Virgil's in English literature Sellar cites Arnold's "Thyrsis" (p. 155), and describes the Dido allusion in "The Scholar-Gipsy" as faithful to the Virgilian mood (p. 408). See Anderson, *Matthew Arnold and the Classical Tradition*, pp. 180–182: "[Arnold's] attempts to be Homeric come out more often than not as Vergilian" (p. 180).

14. Late 1847 or early 1848, Lowry, p. 65.

15. July 20, 1848, ibid., p. 86.

16. Late 1848 or 1849, ibid., p. 97.

17. October 28, 1852, ibid., p. 124.

18. 1853?, *UL*, p. 18.

19. September 6, 1853, Lowry, p. 143.

20. 1849, ibid., pp. 102–103.

21. *Commentary*, p. 270.

22. Describing Winchester life during his and Matthew's years there, Thomas Arnold wrote: "On Sundays the school went to cathedral for the communion service, occupying seats in the choir near William Rufus's tomb. Dr. Williams, the former head-master, usually chanted the service; his magnificent voice I can never forget, nor the beautiful rolling melody of the responses sung by the choir" (*Passages in a Wandering Life*, p. 18).

23. December 6, 1847, Lowry, p. 63.

24. *Views and Reviews* (Boston, 1908), p. 97. The review originally appeared in the *North American Review* for July, 1865.

25. *The Works of Thomas Carlyle*, XXV, 116.

26. Culler, *Poetry and Criticism of Matthew Arnold*, p. x.

27. The voice of the personae in Arnold's poetry is consistently that of experience looking back on innocence or on disillusioning events, a perspective which Arnold may have got, in part, from Wordsworth, whose poems frequently embody the voice of maturity reflecting on life as already lived. Arnold's tone, however, is that of the young man preternaturally weary rather than that of the sage.

28. Possible religious and political implications have been associated with the selection of Cromwell as the subject of the Newdigate competition for 1842–43. See Tinker and Lowry, *Commentary*, pp. 323–324, and Kathleen Tillotson, "Matthew Arnold and Carlyle," *Proceedings of the British Academy*, XLII (1956), 139.

29. Trilling, Bonnerot, and D. G. James discuss Arnold's relationship to Wordsworth in the works cited earlier. For recent specialized studies see Leon Gottfried, *Matthew Arnold and the Romantics* (London, 1963), Ch. II, for Arnold's debt to Wordsworth in the areas of morality, politics, and religion; U. C. Knoepflmacher, "Dover Revisited: The Wordsworthian Matrix in the Poetry of Matthew Arnold," *Victorian Poetry*, I (1963), 17–26, on their relationship as poets; and William A. Jamison, *Arnold and the Romantics* (Copenhagen, 1958), pp. 50–53, for Arnold's edition of Wordsworth's poetry.

30. *Poetical Works*, II, 260.

31. The following appears among Arnold's notations of possible subjects for poetic treatment: "Thun & vividness of sight & memory compared: sight would be less precious if memory could equally realize for us" (*Commentary*, p. 12).

32. J. P. Curgenven's "*The Scholar-Gipsy*: A Study of the Growth, Meaning, and Integration of a Poem," *Litera*, II (1955), 41–58; III (1956), 1–53, seems to me the best reading of the poem.

33. G. Wilson Knight emphasizes the Oriental element in "*The Scholar-Gipsy*: An Interpretation," *Review of English Studies*, n. s., VI (1955), 53–62.

34. The impact of the lesson learned from the "teachers" is slightly meliorated in Arnold's later revision of l. 67: "And purged its faith and trimm'd its fire."

35. The concluding line of the original version of the poem, published in *Fraser's* in 1855, reads "forest" instead of "desert." The change reflects, I believe, Arnold's movement of mind in the late fifties: as a "forest" the abbey is a wooded and secluded retreat; as a "desert" it is uninhabitable. If the authors of the *Commentary* are correct in their assumption (pp. 11–12) that the poem represents Arnold's final handling of a topic which he had first proposed to himself in 1849 under the rubric "To Meta—the cloister

& life liveable," there seems to have been some ambiguity in Arnold's attitude towards the topic from the beginning. The authors of the *Commentary* read the poem as one of "a series of poems on the various restraints imposed upon the human spirit by the religious sentiment, by the sentiment of love, and by the cloistered or regular life" (p. 338). Were these restraints good or not? Is the phrase "the cloister & life liveable" an equation or a contrast? The former interpretation seems applicable to the verses in the Yale Manuscript to which Tinker and Lowry give the title "To Meta: the Cloister" (*Commentary*, pp. 339–340) as well as to the original version of "Stanzas from the Grande Chartreuse"—at least, decision has been suspended. With the substitution of "desert," an image of death holds the final and decisive place: the cloister has become unliveable.

36. *The Use of Poetry and the Use of Criticism* (Cambridge, Mass., 1933), p. 100.

37. Kenneth Allott refers to Arnold's "time-ridden sensibility" in *Matthew Arnold: A Selection of His Poems* (Hammondsworth, 1954), p. 24.

38. In his introduction to the Oxford edition, Quiller-Couch suggests that Arnold, for once, missed an opportunity to italicize, and should have written, "And then he *thinks* he knows" (*The Poems of Matthew Arnold, 1840–1867* [London, 1909], p. xvi).

39. September 29, 1848, Lowry, p. 93.

40. In two senses: that love itself is inconstant, and that the sentiment of love inhibits the search for Truth.

41. December, 1847, Lowry, p. 63.

42. I am particularly indebted, in the discussion that follows, to Walter E. Houghton's helpful essay, "Arnold's 'Empedocles on Etna,'" *Victorian Studies*, I (1957–58), 311–336, and to Frank Kermode's *The Romantic Image* (London, 1957). Arnold published "Empedocles on Etna" prior to "Stanzas from the Grande Chartreuse," and he almost certainly composed it earlier as well. The earlier poem, however, falls later in the pattern of Arnold's development. Arnold, I suspect, found it more difficult to render in poetry his break with the past, which had deep roots in his childhood ex-

perience, than his rejection of the dialogue of the mind, which came later and involved less powerful emotional ties.

43. Howard W. Fulweiler has argued the close connection between Arnold's personal tensions and two poems in the Arnold canon that many critics have felt to be anomalous, "The Forsaken Merman" and "The Neckan." Fulweiler relates the latter poems to the "Marguerite" poems and to "Dover Beach" in the general pattern of Arnold's withdrawal and defeat as a poet ("Matthew Arnold: The Metamorphosis of a Merman," *Victorian Poetry*, I [1963], 208–222). The identification of the Merman and the Neckan as types of the poetic power seems to me illuminating and suggests an obvious connection with Callicles; the pattern Fulweiler traces in these poems is essentially the same as that which I have traced in "Empedocles on Etna." Particularly significant, so far as the present study is concerned, is the survival of the Neckan and the Merman as well as of Callicles as alien "wanderers" in a cruel land who are haunted by the sea. For Heine's probable influence, see Kenneth Allott, "Matthew Arnold's 'Neckan': The Real Issues," *Victorian Poetry*, II (1964), 60–63.

44. December 26, 1872, *Letters*, II, 104.

45. Ibid., I, 14–15.

46. A. G. Lehmann, *Sainte-Beuve: A Portrait of the Critic, 1804–1842* (Oxford, 1962), p. 257. Professor Lehman notes, immediately following this passage, that Sainte-Beuve "had found an image which summed up the outcome of his long quest (Matthew Arnold, reading it, made of it something more familiar): 'My soul is like these shores [at Aigues-Mortes] from which they say Saint Louis once took ship. The sea—and Faith—have long since slipped away, alas: it is as much as I can do to find a solitary tamarinth to shelter under from the arid noon heat. . . .' "

47. *UL*, pp. 68–69.

48. "Hugh Kingsmill," *Matthew Arnold* (New York and Toronto, 1928), pp. 207–227.

49. May 24, 1848, Lowry, p. 80. Professor Lowry provides relevant passages from Goethe and Wordsworth to explain Arnold's allusion; they compare human progress to the patterns of a spiral

and a river, respectively (p. 82). A qualified progressivist outlook is also evident in the writings of Dr. Arnold: "Those who vainly lament that progress of earthly things which, whether good or evil, is certainly inevitable, may be consoled by the thought that its sure tendency is to confirm and purify the virtue of good . . . " (*Introductory Lectures on Modern History*, ed. Henry Reed [New York, 1878], pp. 61–62).

50. For the abrupt shift of the river metaphor at the end of the poem, see *Commentary*, pp. 200–201.

51. This "dawning" contrasts strikingly with that in "The New Sirens" discussed below.

52. Notably in "In Harmony with Nature: To a Preacher" (*PW*, p. 5)—"Know, man hath all which Nature hath, but more," so that "Man must begin, know this, where Nature ends" (ll. 5 and 12). Cf. Lord Coleridge's remark in his obituary of Arnold: "He saw in the adamantine, undeviating, relentless, horrible cruelty of nature, not only towards vast masses of men and women, but to the blameless creatures of earth and sea and sky, an entire inconsistency with what we are told in the Bible of Bible's God" (*New Review*, I, [1889], 226).

53. Professor Brown's comment is pertinent here: "The detachment [recommended in "Resignation"] is not a hermit's, it is not exclusive; it is that of man who has no personal end which absorbs him, no ambition or passion which directs his course and puts blinkers upon his eyes. The disinterested man remains clear of vision and able imaginatively to enter into the manifold experiences of other men and even of natural objects. His impersonality is not a loss of contact with the stream of life but rather a qualification for feeling and understanding its currents" (*Matthew Arnold*, p. 26). Brown suggests, rightly I believe, that this was the appeal which the great poets—Homer, Shakespeare, Goethe, Wordsworth —held for Arnold.

54. March, 1849, Lowry, p. 104.

55. In 1848 Arnold wrote to Clough: "I recommend you to follow up these letters [of Keats] with the Laocoon of Lessing: it is not quite satisfactory . . . but very searching" (Lowry, p. 97). Sainte-Beuve described Arnold's 1853 *Preface* as "un vrai critique

classique de l'école de Lessing" (Bonnerot, p. 351 n.), and in both
the Preface to *Merope* and *Culture and Anarchy* Arnold praises
highly Lessing's sagacity (Super, I, 40, 48; *Culture and Anarchy,*
ed. J. Dover Wilson [Cambridge, 1832], pp. 70-71). Elsewhere
he linked Lessing with Goethe and Voltaire as the three "chief
sources of intellectual influence in Europe, during the last century
and a half" (Super, III, 41). It is perhaps worth noting here that
in 1841, in taking exception to Dr. Arnold's claim—in the latter's
inaugural lecture as Professor of Modern History—that the present
age was the last of progress, Crabb Robinson referred Arnold's
father to Lessing (*Writers and their Books*, II, 604).

NOTES: PART THREE

1. "Maurice de Guérin," (1863), Super, III, 30.
2. "Preface to *Merope*" (1858), ibid., I, 38.
3. E. K. Brown sees *Merope* as reflecting "a crushing defeat"
in Arnold's creative life, "a failure in the deepest places of his art
and character" (*Matthew Arnold: A Study in Conflict*, pp. 49-51).
4. A brief statement of the thesis defended in this part is contained in Lowry's statement that "the poet in Arnold never died."
The paragraph in which this statement appears (pp. 36-37) is worth
reading.
5. November, 1848, Lowry, p. 95.
6. Super, III, 98.
7. "On the Modern Element in Literature" (1857), ibid., I, 33.
8. "Joubert" (1864), ibid., III, 206-207.
9. May 1, 1853, Lowry, p. 135.
10. "For us to-day, what ground of the superiority of poetry is
the most evident, the most notable? Surely its solidity" ("Introduction to Poetry" [1880], Neiman, p. 238).
11. For a sensitive analysis of Arnold's prose which distinguishes
Arnold's "lyric" style from his other more frequent veins see Lewis
E. Gates's introduction, *Selections from the Prose Writings of Matthew Arnold* (New York, 1898).
12. "Curtius's *History of Greece* [III]" (1872), Neiman, p. 147.

13. See E. K. Brown, *Matthew Arnold: A Study in Conflict,* p. 141, on this tension in the late essays.

14. See note 12 above.

15. "On the Modern Element in Literature" (1857), Super, I, 20. On first publishing his inaugural lecture as Professor of Poetry in 1869 Arnold observed that he did so in the hope that it might "give some notion of the Hellenic spirit and its works, and of their significance in the history of the evolution of the human spirit in general" (Super, I, 18).

16. "Dr. Stanley's Lectures on the Jewish Church" (1863), Super, III, 81. See also Arnold's poem "East and West" *(PW,* p. 170).

17. March 6, 1848, Lowry, p. 73.

18. "A Liverpool Address" (1882), *Five Uncollected Essays of Matthew Arnold,* ed. Kenneth Allott (Liverpool, 1953), pp. 86–87.

19. "The Function of Criticism at the Present Time" (1864), Super, III, 261.

20. Ibid., pp. 270, 283.

21. *On the Study of Celtic Literature* (1866), ibid., p. 299.

22. *God and the Bible* (1875), *Works,* VIII, 83. Cf. a remark to Clough in 1848: "since the Baconian era wisdom is not found in desarts [sic]" (Lowry, p. 88).

23. Arnold's use of the current anthropological and ethnological theories is traced by Frederic E. Faverty in *Matthew Arnold the Ethnologist* (Evanston, Ill., 1951). His overall—rather loose—view of science in general is discussed in Fred A. Dudley's "Matthew Arnold and Science," *PMLA,* LVII (1942), 275–293.

24. 1863, Super, III, 13.

25. " . . . to be, like our honoured, and justly honoured Faraday, a great natural philosopher with one side of his being and a Sandemanian with the other, would to Archimedes have been impossible" *(CA,* p. 155).

26. "The Literary Influence of Academies" (1864), Super, III, 239.

27. Ernst Cassirer, *The Philosophy of the Enlightenment,* tr. F. C. A. Koelln and J. P. Pettegrove (Boston, 1955), p. 195.

28. "Endowments" (1870), Neiman, p. 178.

29. See Robert Preyer, *Bentham, Coleridge and the Science of History* (Bochum-Langendreer, 1958), esp. Chap. IV, for the sources and nature of Dr. Arnold's historiography.

30. *A French Eton* (1864), Super, II, 318.

31. "Dr. Stanley's Lectures on the Jewish Church" (1863), Super, III, 69.

32. "Heinrich Heine" (1863), ibid., pp. 125–126.

33. Ibid., p. 110.

34. "Bishop Butler and the Zeit-Geist" (1876), *Works*, IX, 319–320.

35. *God and the Bible* (1875), ibid., VIII, 58.

36. "Bishop Butler and the Zeit-Geist," ibid., IX, 324.

37. "The Literary Influence of Academies" (1864), Super, III, 248.

38. Ibid., p. 261.

39. Lowry, p. 74.

40. *CA*, p. 66.

41. "Dr. Stanley's Lectures on the Jewish Church" (1863), Super, III, 65–66.

42. "Spinoza and the Bible" (1863), ibid., p. 181.

43. *God and the Bible* (1875), *Works*, VIII, 60.

44. Ibid., pp. 64–65.

45. Ibid., pp. 66–67.

46. Ibid., p. 55.

47. Ibid., p. 81.

48. Ibid., pp. 76–80.

49. "Joubert," Super, III, 208, 205.

50. Ibid., p. 194.

51. "Eugénie de Guérin" (1863), ibid., p. 86.

52. Arnold's most dogmatic statement of his distrust of reason comes in a quotation from Goethe to the effect that "all which was really worth knowing in all the sciences he had ever studied would go into one small envelope," a statement which Arnold believed was especially applicable to Biblical criticism. *God and the Bible, Works*, VIII, 173.

53. "Curtius's *History of Greece* [III]" (1872), Neiman, p. 147.

54. *On the Study of Celtic Literature* (1866), Super, III, 382.

55. Cf. the remark in an 1848 letter to Clough: "The difference between Herodotus and Sophocles is that the former sought all over the world's surface for that interest the latter found within man," Lowry, p. 90.

56. September 23, 1849, ibid., p. 109.

57. "Spinoza and the Bible" (1863), Super, III, 177.

58. Ibid.

59. Cited by K. Allott, "Matthew Arnold's Reading-Lists in Three Early Diaries," *Victorian Studies*, II (1958–59), 255, from *The Manchester Guardian*, May 18, 1888.

60. Edward Caird, *Essays on Literature and Philosophy* (Glasgow, 1892), p. 80.

61. Ibid., p. 84.

62. Ibid., p. 83.

63. "Goethe displaced Byron in his poetical allegiance . . ." (Thomas Arnold, *Passages in a Wandering Life*, p. 56).

64. "Spinoza and the Bible" (1863), Super, III, 159.

65. Ibid., pp. 166–167.

66. *God and the Bible* (1875), *Works*, VIII, xiv–xv.

67. "Spinoza and the Bible" (1863), Super, III, 167.

68. "The Bishop and the Philosopher" (1863), ibid., p. 44.

69. "Spinoza and the Bible" (1863), ibid., p. 166.

70. "The Bishop and the Philosopher" (1863), ibid., pp. 43–44.

71. October 23, 1850, Lowry, p. 117. On the religious faith implicit in Arnold's mysticism see William Robbins, *The Ethical Idealism of Matthew Arnold* (Toronto, 1959), pp. 162–164.

72. James Anthony Froude, *Short Studies on Great Subjects* (4 vols.; London, 1892), I, 353.

73. Ibid.

74. Ibid., p. 393. David Masson also notes the connection. "Was there not more of what might be called Spinozism in Wordsworth than even in Coleridge, who spoke more of Spinoza?" See *Recent British Philosophy*, 3rd ed. (London, 1877), p. 15.

75. J. B. Orrick, "Matthew Arnold and Goethe," *Publications of the English Goethe Society*, n.s., IV (1928), 34. Professor Robbins seems to me right in seeing Goethe as the influence under which Arnold assimilated the various influences of Newman, Sainte-Beuve,

and Wordsworth (*The Ethical Idealism of Matthew Arnold,* pp. 56–57), and in his strictures on Orrick (p. 222).

76. See Lore Metzger, "Coleridge's Vindication of Spinoza: An Unpublished Note," *Journal of the History of Ideas,* XXI (1960), 293.

77. Caird, *Essays on Literature and Philosophy,* pp. 86–87.

78. "Spinoza and the Bible" (1863), Super, III, 168.

79. Ibid., p. 182.

80. "Over and over, in both his public writings and his private notes, Coleridge asserts the truth of his conviction that 'there is such a person alive, as God' and that, as he notes in 1817, 'will, foresight, and all other attributes of personal Intelligence' distinguish 'the living God' of Revelation from the 'Spinozistic Ground of the Universe' . . . 'for it is an "I" that is alone the Lord God— and *Him* thou shalt personally worship' " (Metzger, p. 282—see note 76 above).

81. *Literature and Dogma* (1873), *Works,* VII, 388.

82. *On the Study of Celtic Literature* (1866), Super, III, 381.

83. "Dr. Stanley's Lectures on the Jewish Church" (1863), ibid., p. 81.

84. *CA,* p. 55.

85. Ibid., p. 137.

86. Ibid., p. 136.

87. For an analysis of Arnold's rhetoric and sense of audience, see Everett Lee Hunt, "Matthew Arnold: The Critic as Rhetorician," *Quarterly Journal of Speech,* XX (1934), 483–507.

88. "Dr. Stanley's Lectures on the Jewish Church" (1863), Super, III, 80.

89. *CA,* p. 47.

90. February 28, 1849, Lowry, p. 103.

91. "Preface to *Merope*" (1857), Super, I, 59.

92. *On the Study of Celtic Literature* (1866), ibid., III, 344.

93. Ibid., p. 343.

94. *On Translating Homer* (1861), ibid., I, 102.

95. "Preface to *Merope*" (1857), ibid., pp. 58–59.

96. Ibid., p. 61.

97. *CA,* p. 147.

98. Ibid., p. 95.

99. The impulse behind Arnold's appeal to Greek art is suggested by Goethe's claim regarding the nature of the Greek sensibility: "For not yet were thought and feeling dismembered by abstraction, not yet had that scarcely remediable division been produced in the sound nature of man" (cited by Caird, *Essays on Literature and Philosophy*, p. 88).

100. *Literature and Dogma* (1873), *Works*, VII, 388.

101. *St. Paul and Protestantism* (1870), ibid., IX, 54—italics added.

102. *On the Study of Celtic Literature* (1866), Super, III, 346.

103. "Joubert" (1864), ibid., p. 183.

104. "The Literary Influence of Academies" (1864), ibid., p. 238.

105. "The Function of Criticism at the Present Time" (1864), ibid., p. 261.

106. "Wordsworth" (1879), *Works*, IV, 113.

107. *CA*, pp. 54–55.

108. Ibid., pp. 145–146.

109. Harold Höffding, *A History of Modern Philosophy*, tr. B. E. Meyer (New York, 1955), II, 133–134.

110. "The Function of Criticism at the Present Time" (1864), Super, III, 285.

111. *On the Study of Celtic Literature* (1866), ibid., pp. 368–369.

112. *God and the Bible* (1875), *Works*, VIII, 88–89.

113. "A Comment on Christmas," ibid., XI, 315.

114. "Pagan and Mediaeval Religious Sentiment" (1864), Super, III, 230.

115. "Curtius's *History of Greece* [I]" (1871), Neiman, pp. 134–135.

116. *CA*, p. 47.

117. Ibid., p. 155.

118. Ibid., p. 54.

119. Ibid., p. 149.

120. *On the Study of Celtic Literature* (1866), Super, III, 347.

121. "Maurice de Guérin" (1863), ibid., p. 30.

122. Ibid., p. 33.

123. Ibid., p. 34.

124. Ibid., p. 13.

125. Ibid., p. 33.

126. *On Translating Homer* (1861), ibid., I, 138.

127. Ibid., p. 159.

128. Ibid., p. 188.

129. Ibid., pp. 189–190.

130. Ibid.

131. "Maurice de Guérin" (1863), ibid., III, 13.

132. Arnold gives a synoptic view of the history of European literature in a letter to his brother written in 1857. See Robert Liddell Lowe, "Two Arnold Letters," *Modern Philology*, LII (1954–55), 262–264.

133. Super, III, 231.

134. *CA*, p. 38. E. K. Brown argues that the suppression of this sentence in subsequent editions was evidence of that fact that in the middle seventies Arnold's Hellenism "was at its nadir" (*Studies in the Text of Matthew Arnold's Prose Works* [Paris, 1935], pp. 31–32). Since the whole purpose of Arnold's religious criticism in the seventies was to apply to the basic documents of Christianity that "flexibility" and largeness of view which he thought of as characteristically Hellenic, I would argue that even at its "nadir" Arnold's Hellenism remains the controlling element in his attitude.

135. *Literature and Dogma* (1873), *Works*, VII, 24.

136. *Last Essays on Church and Religion* (1877), *Works*, IX, 174.

137. "Introduction to Poetry" (1880), Neiman, pp. 238–239.

138. Ibid., p. 238.

139. "Wordsworth" (1879), *Works*, IV, 94.

140. Ibid., pp. 103–104.

141. Ibid., p. 104.

142. Ibid., p. 110.

143. The power of poetry to celebrate and consecrate human life is predicated most clearly by Arnold in his late comments on the English Romantic poets, on Keats's "yearning passion for the Beautiful," on "the extraordinary power with which Wordsworth feels the joy offered to us in nature, the joy offered to us in the simple primary affections and duties," on Byron's "strong and deep sense

for what is beautiful in nature, and for what is beautiful in human action and suffering," and on Shelley as "a vision of beauty and radiance" (*Works*, IV, 84, 112, 146, 185).

144. "Wordsworth" (1879), *Works*, IV, 109.
145. "John Keats" (1880), *Works*, IV, 84–85.
146. *St. Paul and Protestantism* (1870), *Works*, IX, 234.
147. "On the Modern Element in Literature" (1857), Super, I, 28.
148. *On Translating Homer* (1861), ibid., p. 173.
149. "Spinoza and the Bible" (1863), ibid., III, 162.
150. *Literature and Dogma* (1873), *Works*, VII, 50.
151. Ibid., pp. 24–25.
152. "Spinoza and the Bible" (1863), Super, III, 164.
153. "George Sand" (1877),*Works*, X, 303.
154. This passage appears in the "popular" edition of *Literature and Dogma*, not in the original 1873 edition. See ed. London, 1924, p. 146. On the complicated history of Arnold's intentions regarding this work and of the various texts, see E. K. Brown, *Studies in the Text of Matthew Arnold's Prose Works*, Ch. VI.
155. *St. Paul and Protestantism* (1870), *Works*, IX, 53.
156. Ibid., p. 54.
157. *Literature and Dogma* (1873), ibid., VII, 144.
158. *NB*, p. 341.
159. The phrase "beautiful soul" appears in *Culture and Anarchy* in connection with Wilhelm von Humboldt (*CA*, p. 126) and in *Essays in Criticism* ("this beautiful and religious character") in connection with Eugénie de Guérin (Super, III, 85).
160. "Amiel" (1887), *Works*, IV, 239.

NOTES: CONCLUSION

1. "A Speech at the Unveiling of a Mosaic" (1884), Neiman, p. 258.
2. *Mixed Essays* (1879), *Works*, X, 94.
3. T. S. Eliot, *Selected Essays* (New York, 1950), p. 385.
4. Thomas Smart lists some 300 items dealing with Arnold in

The Bibliography of Matthew Arnold (London, 1892). This was reprinted, with addenda, in *Works. Bibliographies of Twelve Victorian Authors*, by T. G. Ehrsam, R. H. Deily, and R. N. Smith (New York, 1936), provides a comprehensive bibliography down to 1934. In a highly selective survey of this criticism, E. L. Hunt concluded that the critics' "disagreements with each other are usually more profound than their quarrels with Arnold; that Arnold, instead of being outmoded, occupies a more central position than most of his critics; and that controversies over Arnold are fundamental disagreements concerning the nature of literature and of criticism" ("Matthew Arnold and His Critics," *Sewanee Review*, XLIV [1936], 449–467). D. G. James's *Matthew Arnold and the Decline of English Romanticism* is the most cogent recent criticism of Arnold as a failed Romantic.

5. The concluding chapter of William Robbins' recent excellent study, *The Ethical Idealism of Matthew Arnold* (Toronto, 1959), defends Arnold's humanism against the background of developments in the present century.

6. Cf. E. L. Hunt's remark: "It was Arnold's role to appear to be a moralist among aesthetes and an aesthete among moralists" ("Matthew Arnold: The Critic as Rhetorician," *Quarterly Journal of Speech*, XX [1934], 505).

7. Stuart Sherman observed that Arnold's cautious public manner, at least prior to 1870, disguised the revolutionary nature of his message (*Matthew Arnold: How to Know Him*, pp. 276–277).

8. Arnold summarized his ambiguous relationship to his own class in a revealing remark: ". . . I myself am properly a Philistine,— Mr. Swinburne would add, the son of a Philistine. And . . . through circumstances which will perhaps one day be known if ever the affecting history of my conversion comes to be written, I have, for the most part, broken with the ideas and the tea-meetings of my own class" (*CA*, p. 106).

9. Albert Gerard, "On the Logic of Romanticism," *Essays in Criticism*, VII (1957), 268.

10. I. A. Richards, *Science and Poetry* (New York, 1926), pp. 44–45.

11. See W. A. Madden, "The Divided Tradition of English

Criticism," *PMLA*, LXXIII (1958), 69–80, which discusses Arnold's relation to his successors in some detail.

12. *God and the Bible* (1875), *Works*, VIII, x–xi.

13. See n. 154, Pt. II, p. 232.

14. Romano Guardini, *The Church and the Catholic, and the Spirit of the Liturgy* (New York, 1940), p. 182.

15. *St. Paul and Protestantism* (1870), *Works*, IX, 348.

16. Ibid., p. 349.

17. *God and the Bible* (1875), ibid., VIII, 116.

18. "Obermann" (1869), Neiman, pp. 159–160.

19. *The Use of Poetry and the Use of Criticism*, pp. 98–99.

20. Lowry, p. 97. On the similar tension in Goethe, see Erich Heller, *The Disinherited Mind* (New York, 1952), p. 61.

21. "George Sand" (1877), *Works*, X, 316.

22. *On Translating Homer* (1861), Super, I, 191.

23. "Maurice de Guérin" (1863), ibid., III, 36–39.

24. "Marcus Aurelius" (1863), ibid., pp. 134, 146.

25. Ibid., p. 140.

26. Ibid., I, 36.

27. Ibid., III, 157.

28. "Dr. Stanley's Lectures on the Jewish Church" (1863), ibid., p. 81.

29. Heller, *The Disinherited Mind*, pp. 31–32. Josiah Royce commented on the vagueness and unsatisfactoriness, even psychologically, of Arnold's view of sin (James Harry Cotton, *Royce on the Human Self* [Cambridge, Mass., 1954], pp. 275–276).

30. *Mixed Essays* (1879), *Works*, X, 292.

31. Heller, p. 32.

32. Super, I, 12.

33. Heller, p. 30.

34. Thomas Mann, "The Artist and Society," *The Study of Literature*, ed. S. Barnet, M. Berman, and W. Burto (Boston, 1960), p. 251.

INDEX

In the entries on Arnold (father and son), Carlyle, Clough, Goethe, and Wordsworth the indexing is topical; elsewhere the page references are listed in ascending numerical order.

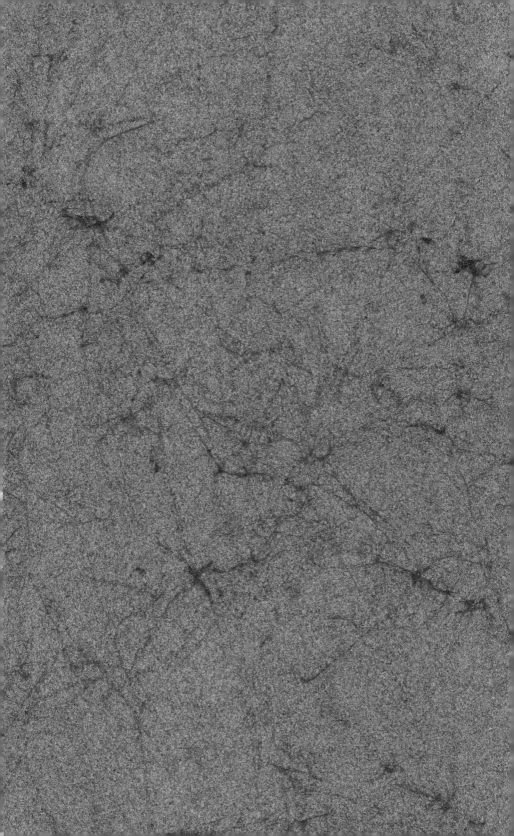